D1362703

## THE FIGHTER PILOTS

"Anyone who really wants to know what the air war was like from the point of view of the fighter pilot must read Ed Sims' wonderful book."
AIR VICE MARSHALL J. E. JOHNSON

"A serious and enthralling comparative study, a new and illuminating commentary."
THE DAILY TELEGRAPH

# Edward Sims

# The Fighter Pilots

A Comparative Study of the Royal Air
Force, the Luftwaffe and the United
States Army Air Force in Europe and
North Africa 1939–45.

CORGI BOOKS
TRANSWORLD PUBLISHERS LTD
A National General Company

# THE FIGHTER PILOTS

A CORGI BOOK 552 08356 9

Originally published in Great Britain
by Cassell & Co. Ltd.

PRINTING HISTORY
Cassell Edition published 1967
Cassell Edition reprinted 1967
Cassell Edition reprinted 1968
Corgi Edition published 1970

This book is set in 10-11½ pt. Baskerville.

Corgi Books are published by Transworld Publishers Ltd.,
Bashley Road, London, N.W.10.
Made and printed in Great Britain by
Hunt Barnard & Co., Ltd., Aylesbury, Bucks.

# CONTENTS

# LIST OF ILLUSTRATIONS

# FOREWORD

*by Group Captain D. R. S. Bader, C.B.E., D.S.O., D.F.C.*

IT IS difficult to write a foreword to a book in which one figures personally—especially when the author has described one as a decent chap! Nevertheless, I am delighted to write this.

Many books have been written by soldiers, sailors and airmen about the Second World War. In each case the author has seen war through the eyes and from the comparatively limited viewpoint of one man. This book is different. It is about 'the fighter pilots' war'. The author has selected, with the help and advice of the government authorities concerned, four pilots from the Royal Air Force, three from the Luftwaffe and one from the United States Army Air Force. He has written about them, and about the aircraft they flew and the campaigns in which they took part, and has included a detailed study of one combat sortie flown by each. The result is a unique book, fascinating alike to war veterans and others interested. The professional will recognise the accuracy of what is written, while the ordinary reader will be able to identify himself with the persons and events described.

War books are always of interest, and this is a special one. It is a book written by a fighter pilot about fighter pilots, and the author, Ted Sims, was no mean performer himself.

DOUGLAS BADER
*London* 27.6.67

*To Edward Jr. and Robert
and
the Fighter Pilots of the Second
World War*

# ACKNOWLEDGEMENTS

OF SUBSTANTIAL assistance to me in the writing of this book was the historian of the German Second World War fighter pilots' organisation (Gemeinschaft der Jagdflieger e.v.), Herr Hans Ring, of Munich. Beginning in 1962 and continuing until 1966, Herr Ring generously donated his time, provided comprehensive statistical data on the Luftwaffe and its campaigns and volunteered much advice.

General Adolf Galland, General of the Luftwaffe Fighter Arm during the war, was a valuable source of information on the German fighter effort in this period and was especially accommodating. Oberst Eduard Neumann of Munich likewise graciously helped and provided for the construction of the chapter about the late Hans-Joachim Marseille (whose commanding officer he had been in Africa) first-hand knowledge, pictures and German publications, without which the reconstruction would have been impossible. Herr Reiner Pöttgen, of Cologne, Marseille's wingman, was also of vital assistance in the creation of this chapter.

Dr Willi Messerschmitt, who provided comments on the building of the Me.262 jet fighter, and revealing information on aircraft production in wartime Germany, is deserving of thanks, as are Miss Eva Trojanowski and Dr Christa Kühner of Munich.

At the Ministry of Defence in London, the R.A.F. Director of Public Relations, Air Commodore James Wallace, was especially helpful. At his suggestion, L. A. Jackets and Stuart Gunnel were of valuable assistance, as were the staff of the R.A.F. Library at Adastral House and the historical records branch at Queen Anne's Chambers, particularly Mr

Bateman of the latter. Air Commodore Wallace arranged visits to Wattisham and Coltishall fighter stations which were of much practical benefit. At Wattisham, Station Commander Group Captain C. M. Gibbs, Squadron Leader I. R. Martin, Flight Lieutenant Allan Taylor and Flying Officer B. A. Hayward (who possesses specialist's knowledge of the Me.109) are due thanks. At Coltishall, Station Commander Group Captain R. L. Topp, Flight Lieutenant P. M. Jewell, Flight Lieutenant P. Holden-Rushworth and Chief Technician Z. Puczynski were most helpful.

In London, Mr Michael Canfield, of Harper and Row, the staff of my publishers, Cassell and Co., and Mr J. Taylor-Whitehead, of Macdonald and Co., are to be thanked. Sir Max Aitken, Mr Christopher Shores (in particular—he provided much valuable data on the R.A.F. and was to a degree the British counterpart of Ring in Germany), and Mr Jack Beaumont of Beaumont Aviation Literature were all of assistance. Miss M. M. Wilkinson, with her ability to do a difficult job well, was of material and moral value.

Colonel Ralph L. Michaelis, Air Attaché at the American Embassy in London, was most helpful.

In the United States my thanks are due to Bill Hess, one of the nation's experts on the fighter war, to Chairman Cass Canfield of the Harper and Row editorial board, to Mr M. S. Wyeth, of Harper and Row, and to Mrs Melvin Hughes.

Lastly, my thanks are due to each of the fighter aces whose most memorable exploit is herein re-created. Without their submission to hours of questioning, down to such details as what they ate for breakfast, what they wore, and so on, the missions could not, of course, have been accurately reclaimed from the past and reproduced in writing.

# INTRODUCTION

THIS BOOK began innocently enough in November of 1961, staggered through four years of intermittent labour in Europe, and reached completion in ten months of concentrated effort in England. I well remember 18 November 1961, when the first Bavarian snow of the season fell in honour of a transplanted American family moving into a small alpine house on the Starnbergersee, south of Munich. On a clear day one could see across the lake the massive peaks of the Alps, farther south, already capped with snow.

This was the country where the Second World War had been hatched, where Hitler had been spawned and the Nazi Party organized. These were the people who fell for it, lived through it, or despised it. How clearly I remember the night of 1 September 1939, when Hitler was plunging the world into war, invading Poland. Unable to believe any man could knowingly lead the world into a war which would cost millions of lives, I asked my father, a newspaper editor, if there would really be world war. I was told that it appeared inevitable, and the impression of that moment is still vivid. Two completely clear pictures remain in my memory to this day. One is of standing on the stairway landing leading upstairs on my way to bed that night, looking out through the landing window up into a clear September night sky, thinking this would be the last night of peace for much of the world, recalling the many books about the First World War which I had eagerly consumed. Would it engulf America? Would I get into it? What would it be like? That was a Friday night.

The other impression is of sitting in church on Sunday, constantly glancing at my watch. Britain and France had sent Hitler an ultimatum demanding that he withdraw from Poland. That ultimatum was about to expire, at which time England and France would be officially at war with Germany again after twenty-one years of peace. The war, of course, swept over America and I finally came to participate in it, flying a fighter from a base in England over this very German countryside. Here it all began—motivated and caused to a large extent by mistakes at Versailles. Here Hitler and Nazism gained their start, and before and during the war leading Nazis, and Mussolini after his rescue, lived for varying periods on this fashionable, beautiful lake, where I had now taken up my residence. So it was a perfect setting in which to seek out stories of the war and Germany's fighter pilots. And since I had already re-created in two books the most memorable combats of America's top fighter pilots in the war, and had flown as a fighter pilot over this very country, it was only natural that the possibility of doing the same thing on the other side exerted a strong attraction. Before much could be done that winter, deep snow and Christmas were at hand. In the time available, however, I sought out ex-Luftwaffe pilots, who flourish in and around Munich, among other knowing souls, and also the historian of the Gemeinschaft der Jagdflieger, Hans Ring, of Munich.

Things progressed and took their normal course. Interesting sessions and glider flights were enjoyed with German pilots that first summer (some in Innsbruck, one in Vienna). And one day I pointed the bonnet ring of my Mercedes 220 west along the Autobahn and then north up the Rhine, and called on General Adolf Galland, former General der Jagdflieger (General of the Fighter Arm) under Hitler and Göring. It was June of 1962. Galland agreed to help; it was a forward step. He also supplied me with a list of names of Germans he thought I should see.

From these beginnings the book began to take shape; it was quite simple at first glance—the main question being whether a creditable job could be done in the re-creation of fighter missions of Luftwaffe pilots. There was something of a language barrier, and the additional handicap that there were no Me.109s or F.W.190s left in Germany, in which one could fly or sit and study the cockpit (an Me.109 was finally located in England). But the years took care of both problems.

A commission in the diplomatic service as Consul in Munich slowed the project for two years, and then, in 1965, having done the necessary homework in Germany, I moved to England, to complete the project by seeking out R.A.F. aces, visiting R.A.F. fighter stations, and so on—including the Second World War station from which I had flown over twenty years earlier—Wattisham, near Ipswich. (A permanent R.A.F. station, before the war and now, it was little changed, which was reassuring in a world where everything is changing fast and where there's little we can cling to that might hold back the tide of time a little longer.)

If the German part of the project had at times been pleasant, with an occasional hot summer afternoon in the Augustiner Keller with an ex-Luftwaffe pilot, a litre and roasted chicken, salt and radishes and all the *'Gemütlichkeit'* of Old Munich, the English side of the project was equally so. For in London every writer is at home among the bookshops, libraries, researchers, records, and the many authors and students of the Second World War. It was, of course, a stimulating experience to seek out the R.A.F. pilots included in this volume. The selection of those to be included was made by officials in a conference at the Ministry of Defence, not by me. The choice of ex-Luftwaffe pilots was easy—the top scorer on the Russian Front, the top scorer in Africa and the General of the Fighter Arm and one of the top scorers in the West.

But then this book took on new responsibilities. The Luftwaffe and the R.A.F. fought it out for almost six years and were the first to demonstrate to the world the decisive influence of air power. There were clear-cut campaigns such as the Battle of Britain and readers would want a summary of these campaigns. They would want a look at the aircraft, the air forces themselves, and the actual losses on each side. We should examine fighter pilots of the Second World War, primarily those of Germany, the United Kingdom and the United States, and how they affected the war's outcome. We see how much more important their role was in this war than ever before—more important than it is ever likely to be again, if indeed there ever are dogfights between fighter pilots again.

We discuss the fighter campaigns in Europe, with corrected losses given for each side, and analyse the question of who won the campaigns.

Finally, we look at the air forces themselves, their fighters, their strengths and weaknesses and pre-war plans—how pre-war planning and organization affected the outcome of the air war. With this background, we move on then into the most spectacular sorties of the leading R.A.F. and Luftwaffe pilots, re-created in detail. Re-creations are based on the pilots' official combat reports which have not been released publicly, and on interviews with the pilots concerned; they were then rechecked by each pilot for errors. The reader can 'fly along' on the sortie from start to finish and see how it was for the German or British or American pilot flying one of the most exciting combat sorties of the war. He can also be assured that none of these accounts is artificially coloured. Nor is there any assumed dialogue, so popular these days. Everything included in the re-creations is what actually happened, or what was actually said, as remembered or written. The achievements of the greatest pilots of the Second World War are dramatic enough related as they occurred, without journalistic additions of colour words, flowing literary descriptions, and so forth.

Those who have read my *Greatest Fighter Missions*[1] or *American Aces*[2] will find in these accounts of Luftwaffe and R.A.F. fighter combats the same adventure and they will learn how it was done in other air forces. And the study of

[1] Harper and Row, New York, 1962.
[2] Harper and Row, New York, 1958; MacDonald, 1958.

both sides' claims and the actual losses which occurred gives us a better insight into what really took place.

What about the pilots themselves? What kind of men were they, and are they? How do they vary from country to country and what in them made them stand above the average to become the highest-scoring pilots of their air forces? There is no standard pattern into which one can fit these outstanding fighter pilots. They vary as much, in personality, appearance and behaviour, as other individuals, though they have a comradeship among themselves. All are alert: one doesn't find the dullard among them—even years after the war. The significant difference between the top-scoring 'aces' and the average pilot might have manifested itself only in the air—what they did under various circumstances, how they did it. It is probably impossible for anyone to see that today or to have seen it on the ground during the war except to a limited degree, for the fighter pilot flies alone in his aircraft. The author who writes about them must study the records, the opinions of pilots who flew with them and then observe the men themselves.

In trying to characterize the world's top fighter pilot, Erich Hartmann of Germany (Chapter 10), with 352 kills in the war, even this approach fails. In conversation with the deceptively casual and modest 'Boobie' Hartmann, one would never know this still-young, blue-eyed German shot down more aircraft than any pilot in history. Hartmann affects an easy-going, utterly relaxed personality. Is he, inside, quite that imperturbable? His record indicates that he is. For he shot down Russian aircraft regularly and steadily, in cool, businesslike fashion, for three years.

Yet of all the top aces of the war he is the greatest enigma. One suspects that somewhere beneath that surface calm, beneath that appearance of fitting into the average-pilot mould, there burns an intense, determined individual, with great self-discipline and an iron will—the man who stood before Adolf Hitler to be decorated for his singular mastery in the air.

With Adolf Galland (Chapter 13) it is different. At once one can sense the intensity and even the excitement of the fighter pilot. He fits the script with a quick smile and winning personality. He radiates charm and leadership, and it's easy to picture him the leader of a spirited fighter gaggle. Of medium height with small, dark moustache, penetrating dark eyes and devastating grin (as infectious as the late President Kennedy's), he could play the role in a film. Galland was older when the war began and soon became one of Germany's most distinguished pilots, personally decorated by Hitler, whom he advised (as well as Göring) on fighter operations, production and development over a long period. Thus he knew the war at the top and he knew Nazi leaders, having held the position of General of Fighters for three years.

I first visited Galland in connection with this book in his office—an old stone house on Koblenzerstrasse—in Bonn. At that time he was smoking fifteen or twenty black Brazils a day, holding two or three jobs and constantly on the go. Since, he has slowed his pace a bit on doctor's orders, no longer enjoys the cigars, and drinks mostly red wine. But he is still active, flies his own plane and is steady of hand and dynamic in personality.

Of the R.A.F. aces, one with something of the same pace and energy is R. R. Stanford Tuck (Chapter 4). Like D. R. S. Bader, Tuck still has the fire of the fighter pilot burning within him, and, interestingly, both were entertained by Galland during the war after being downed in France. Galland extended the invitations as Kommodore of Jagdgeschwader 26.

Tuck operates a mushroom farm in Kent these days, a successful enterprise, and often journeys to the Continent to shoot with Galland. He was and is a remarkable shot. During the war Tuck was the epitome of the glamorous fighter pilot and still exudes the traditional spirit. (But one of his sons has just chosen to enter Sandhurst!) With thin moustache and dark eyes, straight and trim, Tuck today shows all the force of personality and fun which so often figured in the lives of fighter pilots.

Douglas Bader, perhaps the most famous of all fighter pilots, is Galland's age and was on his way up the ladder of command when downed and captured. Of all the fierce and determined spirits in the war, very few indeed surpassed Bader's. He had proved his mettle when the war began for, with two artificial legs, he had already mastered dancing, golf, and normal life to a degree no other man with two artificial limbs had ever done before.

Bader was tenacious, almost without fear, positive in his views, and a dynamic leader. Like the late Graf Felix von Luckner of First World War fame, Bader is one of the most inspirational figures to emerge from the Second World War. Being human, the image may seem at times not to fit into the present world of the affairs of men, but Bader's life is story-book stuff at its very best, and meeting this freckled, blue-eyed firebrand, with all his sincerity and intensity, and charm, is an experience.

A student of First World War tactics, and before his accident one of the best stunt fliers in the R.A.F., when he put his flying skill (unhandicapped by two artificial legs), knowledge of tactics and determination into the effort in 1940 he quickly became a colourful, highly successful fighter pilot. Bader radiates power, in personality and physically (in shoulders, arms and hands). One can instantly see in him an individual in complete control of himself. (He is still a teetotaller.)

Two of the R.A.F. aces in this book remained in the flying service after the war. One was James Harry Lacey, hero of the Battle of Britain; the other was James E. Johnson. Both are retiring as this book is in preparation.

Lacey, like Hartmann, gives a deceptively modest impression which reveals little of the great talent and spirit which produced such outstanding results in the Battle of Britain. His memory for detail, however, is the best among all the aces I have questioned. Lacey undoubtedly gained keen satisfaction in achieving what he did, saying nothing or little about it and watching the unsuspecting—particularly top brass—

dumbfounded when learning of his exploits.

His was a tongue-in-cheek humour which fitted his reserve. If Tuck was the best marksman, Lacey probably had no superior at handling a fighter in the air. He was an aviation enthusiast before the war, and an instructor, and one source of his strength was his confidence in what he could do with his fighter in the air.

This no doubt explains in part why odds often failed to deter him, and why he attacked sizeable enemy formations alone. In conversation, one would not detect his aggressiveness and daring, for Lacey is soft-spoken and modest. Yet in his eyes and manner one can detect a certain resolve. But it would be a surprise to find anyone, except possibly someone whose sense of austerity might have been punctured, who disliked Lacey as a man.

The 'ace of aces' of the R.A.F., reckoning by official victories alone, was J. E. Johnson, who rose to the rank of Air Vice-Marshal after the war and became a successful author in the field of fighter strategy and tactics. Johnson's war-time and post-war record plus the charm of the fighter pilot make an altogether impressive combination. Observing him, one can immediately understand how he advanced to high rank, and why his popularity has been widespread since the war. No doubt he had the ability to learn from others, and possessed the restraint and wit of a good diplomat. Johnson began comparatively late in the war in achieving victories, and his record shows all his kills were over enemy fighters and good ones. And he shared many with less experienced pilots. To most of those who flew with him he is *the* fighter pilot of the war.

The most successful American aces? Like their British and German counterparts, each is different. Francis Gabreski, the top scorer in Europe, and an ace in the Korean War also, is an open and friendly personality, the American democratic spirit personified. Gabreski is so unaffected it is easy to underestimate him. He is a career Air Force officer.

Bob Johnson—a man of purpose—is still forceful and making his way in business years after the war. One suspects that Johnson, had he seen longer service in an operational squadron (he flew less than a year and shot down twenty-eight planes over Europe), would have pushed his score into the forties or fifties. His drive, perhaps ambition, surpasses the average by a good margin.

The top ace of the U.S.A.A.F. was Dick Bong, killed just after the war in an F.80 accident. Bong, whom I met during the war, was perhaps as modest in manner as any of the American aces. If Bob Johnson or George Preddy (and many think Preddy, shot down by his own comrades, would have been the country's highest-scoring ace had he lived) might have been the highest scorer in Europe, Bong was clearly destined to lead the field in the Pacific.

When he toured fighter bases during the war we younger pilots looked upon Bong as a remarkable marksman. He didn't agree, and spoke of himself as a poor shot—not exactly true of course. Yet he had a point, and it was that gunnery was more than fifty per cent of a successful technique in aerial dogfights—which was what Marseille learned in Africa. Someone has quoted Bong as having said that if he had been as good a marksman when he went to the Pacific as he became later he would have shot down eighty planes. He might have, too. At that time we didn't know German and Japanese aces were doing just that and more; it was considered, erroneously, out of the realm of possibility.

Bong was a good marksman, so good that he realized how far the art could be pursued, and how skilled he might get at it. Of course, few who flew in the European theatre will ever be convinced it was as difficult to shoot down a Japanese fighter as a German one.

Are there qualities all the highest-scoring pilots possess in common? Is there something about them one can detect, and point to, as being shared by all? I doubt it, unless it is a sense of fun, a certain spirit, often accompanied by a strong personality. That most of them have, plus physical coordination and agility. The training and combat experience they shared have provided a similar background, plus perhaps an attitude towards life. That may partly explain that certain affinity the fighter pilots of the last war feel for one another wherever and whenever they meet to this day. But one cannot safely generalize about them, for each is different and there is no standard type among them.

The fighter sorties re-created in this book were chosen by the aces themselves. I have related them chronologically in considerable detail. A newspaper editor for many years, I have made every effort to ensure accuracy. Because historians, reporters and photographers did not go on fighter missions (there was no place in the aircraft for them), and because fighter action was so fast, over such a considerable area, few attempts have been made to reclaim fighter sorties from the past and reproduce them in written form, in detail. It would probably be difficult for one who had not experienced fighter combat in the Second World War to appreciate all the sensations and considerations involved. It is my hope and one purpose of this book to take you along on the most eventful sorties of the war's greatest pilots and also to examine briefly some of the pilots and their fighters, and some of the fighter campaigns, of the Second World War.

EDWARD H. SIMS

*London, August* 1966

CHAPTER ONE

# THE FIGHTER PILOTS' WAR

LOOKING BACK, we can see that fighter pilots were in their heyday in the Second World War. In the First World War, with aviation in its infancy, they captured the public's imagination, and high scorers became national heroes. But in that war air power was primarily a tactical adjunct to armies. In the Second World War fighters enabled bomber fleets to carry the struggle into the enemy homeland on a devastating scale, or prevented such onslaughts from the other side. Fighters, by controlling the air, determined the fate of strategic and tactical land and sea campaigns.

This striking shift in the functioning of fighters and air power in general was demonstrated most dramatically in the Battle of Britain, when the R.A.F.'s Fighter Command, in effect, halted the march of Hitler's undefeated army and prevented an invasion of an otherwise weakly defended Britain. But the change had been obvious to careful observers before then. In the successful German seizure of Norway, in April 1940, fighters and air power in general played the decisive role. The Luftwaffe soon gained control of the seas within range of its bases and won the battle of reinforcement and supply.

In the early land campaigns, in Poland in 1939 and in France and the Low Countries during the following year, the greater capability and application of air power had been obvious to students of war. Japan was to take advantage of the new air potential to win stunning strategic and tactical victories in the Pacific during the next year, employing a highly trained naval fighter arm to gain aerial superiority.

The various nations adopted different concepts for employing their air arms. Germany and Russia emphasized that of army co-operation, while the United States and Britain, learning this technique later and applying it, also developed strategic bombing. The German *Blitzkrieg* technique of air-ground co-operation was impressive in the 1939 and 1940 land campaigns. In that concept the bomber was stressed less as a strategic than as a tactical weapon, and it co-operated with the Panzers to win lightning victories. Hitler always showed a predilection for the offensive bomber; fighters, so necessary to defence, were not of equal interest to him. Because of this stress on bombers, production in Germany at the outbreak of the war was geared to a greater output of bombers than of fighters. One of the ironies of the conflict is that, despite initial stress on bombers, the Luftwaffe never acquired an effective heavy-bomber fleet, and therefore never managed much of a strategic bombing effort[1]—while German fighter pilots, and the Luftwaffe fighter arm in general, rendered Germany outstanding service and bested the opposition in several campaigns.

The Russian concept of air power was in respects similar to the German; though the Russians built and acquired a huge air force, they never produced an effective, long-range, strategic bombing arm. The Russians always stressed air co-operation with the army.

The British and Americans, while building strong fighter arms, concentrated considerable effort and resources on heavy-bomber squadrons capable of unloading huge bomb tonnages on enemy targets at great distances. On occasion, such as in the invasion of France in June 1944, and in the breakout at St Lo in August, these 'heavies' were employed in co-ordination with tactical operation with devastating effect,[2] but primarily they were used in strategic bombing

---

[1] Adolf Galland, *The First and The Last* (Methuen, 1955), pp. 14–17 and 39–40; Wood and Dempster, *The Narrow Margin* (Hutchinson, 1961), pp. 44–5.

[2] C. Wilmot, *The Struggle For Europe* (Collins, 1965), p. 391, quotes Lt. Gen. Fritz Bayerlein, commander of the Panzer Lehr division, opposing

campaigns. The Americans and British learned how to co-ordinate tactical aircraft with advancing armour during the conflict. The British showed the way, at El Alamein, and by the time of the St Lo breakout the U.S. Army was probably receiving the most effective air co-ordination of the war.

The decisive importance of air power in the Second World War placed fighters and fighters pilots, inevitably, in a pivotal role. For it was fighters, in the final analysis, which controlled the skies. The war soon proved that a successful defence against heavy bombers was possible only if defending fighters were effective enough. In the same vein, a successful daylight bomber campaign could be carried on only if escort fighters provided bombers with adequate protection. Again it was demonstrated that tactical fighter-bombers (such as the Ju.87) could not operate successfully unless protected by fighters. Thus, in both the strategic and tactical fields, it was the fighter which in the end decided the issue in the air.

Thus overall conditions made this the fighter pilot's war. Industry and science had not yet produced an aircraft of aeronautical design and engine capability too advanced for aerial dogfights. There was still a touch of romance and colour in this kind of combat, lingering from the First World War. As a result, it was only natural that adventurous youth

---

American forces in the break-out near St Lo, on the use of heavy bombers to open up a path for attacking troops, as follows: 'The planes kept coming over, as if on a conveyor belt, and the bomb carpets unrolled in great rectangles. My flak had hardly opened its mouth when the batteries received direct hits which knocked out half the guns and silenced the rest. After an hour I had no communications with anybody, even by radio. By noon nothing was visible but dust and smoke. My front lines looked like the face of the moon and at least seventy per cent of my troops were out of action—dead, wounded, crazed or numbed. All my forward tanks were knocked out, and the road practically impassable.' In addition to this graphic description, numerous other German generals, including the German Command in Chief in the West, Field-Marshal Karl Gerd von Rundstedt, cited Allied air power as the most decisive element in the defeat of the German armies in the West. (U.S. Army interrogation of von Rundstedt.)

in all the warring countries chose to become fighter pilots. The requirements were comparatively high, physically and otherwise, and it would be no exaggeration to say that much of the cream of each nation's young generation was attracted.

Part of the appeal was the nature of the fighting. In large measure, it was individual performance—flying skill, gunnery, courage and endurance. It was probably the closest thing to the 'sporting' individual encounters of bygone centuries. And it was as impersonal as killing could be in individual combat. There came no ugly moment when one had to ram a bayonet through one's opponent's stomach and see the results at first hand. It was a nicer way of killing, done by simply pressing a button or two on the stick handle. When death resulted—the fighter pilot could always hope it didn't, and usually it didn't—one wasn't around to see it. In other words, the fighting contained at least a few of the sporting elements, and there was a small residue of the code of ethical conduct which carried over from the past. This sporting tradition existed to the extent that some of the more famous Allied fighter aces, shot down by the Germans, were entertained by their captors to dinners in their honour.[1] Likewise, air-sea-rescue services of both sides came out to pick up downed pilots in the Channel and North Sea regardless of their nationality. There were other gestures. Pilots were seldom strafed in their parachutes.[2] There was

[1] Among those so recognized by the Germans were Douglas Bader and Robert Stanford Tuck, both shot down by pilots of Jagdgeschwader 26 over France, in 1941 and 1942 respectively, and both subjects of chapters in this book.

[2] In several English-language books about the air fighting in the Second World War (including my own *American Aces*), Allied pilots have been quoted as saying that they witnessed fellow pilots being strafed as they hung below open parachutes. On the German side, General Adolf Galland alleges, in *The First and The Last*, that he witnessed Allied fighter pilots shooting at parachuting pilots of Me.262 jet fighters. Hans Ring and Galland, in conversations with me, cited examples of this practice by Allied pilots, Ring having some sixty names of German pilots who claim to have been so strafed. Generally speaking, however, this was not practised on either side (though among the Germans it is said that certain red-nosed

24

an occasional wave of congratulation if and when a dogfight ended in the mutual exhaustion of ammunition. Bombers, fatally damaged but still flying, were often escorted down to a landing in Germany by Luftwaffe fighters if they signalled their intention to land. And admiration for a splendid demonstration of flying skill by one's opponent was forthcoming from pilots on both sides. It was, then, one of the cleanest and most sporting ways to fight the war, though a dangerous one. And it seems almost certain that, with the end of the war, this singularly colourful form of individual aerial combat also ended for all time. Modern-day fighters and intercepters are much too fast for the twisting-turning dogfights of the two World Wars. Nor does it seem likely that the combatants next time—if there is to be a next time—will feel the same instincts and traditions. It is far more likely to be a business of automatic electronic firing devices, applying largely to missiles, and one can't easily envisage any sportmanlike waves across the sky to a gallant foe. It seems highly likely that that day is past, as are many of the customs and ethics of Old Europe as we have known them. This is one of the several high costs of progress to the nuclear age.

In this book we are only interested in the war as it was fought by fighter pilots in the skies over Europe and Africa. The three major air powers in that conflict were Great Britain, Germany and the United States. Russia might be considered a fourth, though her fighters were not up to the standard of the best in these countries, and her fighter arm lacked all-round capacity. Generally speaking, Russian fighters were not equipped with oxygen, for example, and were thus precluded from combat at higher altitudes. They played, largely, a tactical, army co-operation role in the war. Italy possessed a significant fighter force, but most of her aircraft were obsolete by the standards of the three major Western Nations. France's fighter force was likewise practic-

---

and red-tailed Mustangs were notorious for it) and it is likely that many mistook the actions of opposing pilots when actually the target was something other than a descending airman.

ally obsolete by the best British and German standards at the onset of the war.

In Great Britain, Germany and the United States the training of fighter pilots was a long and demanding process in which a considerable percentage of trainees was killed. Another large percentage, especially in the United States, was washed out during the course of training. Those who won their wings (in the R.A.F. and in the Luftwaffe both non-commissioned and commissioned officers) had survived rigid entrance examinations, mental and physical, and had mastered various aircraft at different flying schools.

At the beginning of the war German pilots had the edge in experience, for they had profited by lessons learned in the Spanish Civil War. They gained more combat experience in the comparatively easy campaign against Poland in September of 1939. Additional experience and victories were gained in the fighting which opened in the West on 10 May 1940.

They also possessed the best equipment. Against the Allied fighters, the Me.109E (then the standard German fighter) had a distinct advantage. It was, all things considered, superior to the Hurricane, which was used by the R.A.F. and some of the squadrons of the Low Countries on the Continent, and to French fighters. The only fighter at that time which could take on the 109 as an approximate equal, the R.A.F. Spitfire, was not sent to the Continent. It first appeared in force (flying from British bases) over Dunkirk and in the Battle of Britain. The achievement of the British air industry prior to the war was that it managed to have the Hurricane and Spitfire operational in some strength for the crucial test in 1940. The achievement during that year was the winning of the fighter production race with Germany in the Battle of Britain, all-important to its outcome.

R.A.F. pilots were well trained and flew good fighters (many thought highly of the Hurricane because it climbed faster than the Spit, was tougher and carried more machine-guns in some early models), but they lacked combat experience. This was reflected in the R.A.F.'s choice of tactical formations and attack patterns, which were, in the first part of the war, obsolete.[1]

American fighter forces, which began arriving in Europe in 1942, profited from lessons learned the hard way in the R.A.F., but until the arrival of later-model P.47s and P.51s more than a year later, these pilots, well-trained in the States, found themselves overmatched against the Me109F and the F.W.190. The tide turned by 1944, during which year P.51s in considerable numbers began to penetrate deep into Germany. They were capable of holding their own, or better, with all Luftwaffe fighters—with the exception of the Me.262 jet which appeared late in 1944, in small numbers. By that time also later-model Spitfires and other British single-engined aircraft were in operation—many (including the Mustang) using the Rolls-Merlin engine which played such a vital role in gaining for Allied fighters superiority and finally supremacy.

German fighter pilots won numbers honours for kills in the Second World War. Flying against the R.A.F. and U.S.A.A.F., eight Luftwaffe pilots scored over 100 kills! The highest-scoring German pilot flying against the Allies in the West was Heinz Bär with 124. The top Allied fighter pilot against the Germans was the R.A.F.'s J. E. Johnson, with 38 confirmed kills. The top American in Europe was Francis Gabreski, with 31 (aerial) victories.[2] German pilots flying against other opponents compiled even more staggering totals, two Luftwaffe aces achieving more than

[1] J. E. Johnson, *Full Circle* (Chatto and Windus, 1964), p. 94 and pp. 106–7; Also, from conversations of the author with Johnson, Tuck, Bader and Galland. Other references to this R.A.F. handicap in the early part of the war are to be found in many of the biographies of the leading R.A.F. fighter pilots.

[2] The U.S. Eighth Air Force, based in England, awarded kills on a different basis from the system used in the R.A.F., the Luftwaffe and most other U.S. air forces, confirming destruction of enemy aircraft on the ground by strafing. In this book, since the R.A.F. and the Luftwaffe did not award confirmations for such kills, Eighth Air Force awards for strafing are subtracted from totals.

300 kills on the Eastern front. The highest-scoring German, Erich Hartmann, as already noted, was credited with 352 kills. The top American ace, against all opponents, was Major Richard Bong of the U.S.A.A.F. with 40 kills (against the Japanese) and the top R.A.F. ace is generally considered to be Johnson with his 38 kills, though a recent volume on R.A.F. fighter pilots[1] credits M. T. St John Pattle with 41. The top Russian fighter pilot of the war is supposedly Major General Ivan N. Kozhedub, who had 62 victories. (German pilots say, however, that one Russian not on the list had over 80 kills.) The top Japanese ace, C. W. O. Hiroyashi Nishizawa, was credited with 104. The leading ace of the French Air Force, who served much of his time with the R.A.F., was Lt. Pierre Clostermann, with 33 kills. The top Italian ace, Major Adriano Visconti, scored 26 victories. There were other high-scoring pilots, some who flew within the R.A.F. representing their occupied countries (like Clostermann) and others such as Hans H. Wind, of the Finnish Air Force, with 75 kills. Prince Constantino Cantacuzino, of Rumania, was credited with 60.[2]

The fighter forces of the three powers treated in this book (the R.A.F., Luftwaffe and U.S.A.A.F.) were employed in slightly different ways. Basically, the R.A.F. and the Luftwaffe concentrated primarily on fighters best suited to defence, while American fighters, especially in the last two years of the war, were primarily offensive, capable of flying great distances and many hours. Neither R.A.F. nor Luftwaffe fighters could approach their performance. This was a logical outcome of the geographical situation. The R.A.F. won the Battle of Britain with fighters designed to defend the country. The Luftwaffe, its basic fighters designed in the

---

[1] C. Shore, *Aces High* (Spearman, 1966), p. 242. E. C. R. Baker in *Pattle: Supreme Fighter in the Air* (Kimber, 1965), credits Pattle with 42–3 kills. It is believed that Pattle, who was the greatest ace of the Greek campaign in 1940 and 1941, had at least 40 probables, in addition to his confirmed kills. He was a South African.

[2] Lists of the top Luftwaffe, R.A.F., and U.S.A.A.F. fighter aces are to be found in the appendixes.

same period, likewise fought the Battle of Germany with short-range fighters, suited to defensive purposes. U.S. Army fighters in Europe, on the other hand, were sent for the express purpose of carrying the attack deep into Germany, by escorting bombers engaged in the daylight strategic bombing offensive, and were designed later than the Me.109 or the Spitfire. Heavy losses suffered by the Eighth Air Force when its bombers attacked well inside Germany by day without fighter escort[1] made it necessary for fighters to accompany them all the way. Because of their experiences in the early years of the war, both the R.A.F. and the Luftwaffe discontinued daylight bombing of targets well inside the enemy homeland. The successful staging of this daylight bombing campaign over Germany, made possible by long-distance fighter protection, was the outstanding achievement of American air power in Europe.[2]

As for the pilots of the three air forces, it is difficult to make generalizations. It would probably be accurate and reasonable, however, to say that because the Luftwaffe's pilots were kept in the 'meat-grinder' for six years, taking on superior numbers while defending Germany in the biggest air battle of the war, the pilots of the Reichsverteidigung (home defence), flew the greatest number of missions, had

[1] Galland, pp. 228–9, citing official German and U.S. losses, says that for the first time U.S. heavy bomber losses reached nineteen per cent of the actual bomber force (60 Flying Fortresses shot down out of 315 which reached the target) in the first Schweinfurt-Regensburg raid in August 1943. Another 100 were damaged. The cost to the Germans: 25 fighters (not 228 as originally claimed by Fortress gunners). These and heavy losses on other raids when the heavies were not escorted by fighters all the way to the target finally convinced U.S.A.A.F. commanders of the necessity for long-range fighters such as the P.51, which Göring believed to be a technical impossibility.

[2] Full Circle, p. 226. Describing the final success of the U.S. effort to build a fighter which could roam the length and breadth of Germany, Johnson calls this one of the 'finest extant examples of selecting an aim and sticking to it'. He notes that the original aim of the R.A.F. was daylight bombing, as was that of the Luftwaffe, both abandoning the effort because of heavy losses. Thereafter, the Air Staffs of both air forces thought long-range daylight bombing technically impossible.

the greatest number of opportunities for kills and therefore the most experience, and were among the best in the world. A brief look at the number of missions flown by top Luftwaffe aces, whose missions reached not into the hundreds but into the thousands, shows they had more experience than fighter pilots of any other country. This was especially true of night fighters, whose skill was perfected to a high degree in Germany because of the R.A.F.'s long bombing offensive. Because Germany was outnumbered in the air, surrounded, and fighting for survival under a ruthless dictatorship, demands were made upon Luftwaffe fighter pilots for continuous duty which were not made on British and American pilots, who, in fact, were rotated after a period of sustained operations. And Luftwaffe pilots usually had the advantage of flying over Germany (especially in the last two years of the war, when the air battles involved far greater numbers than earlier), which allowed many who were shot down to return to their units and continue on operations.

It would therefore seem a reasonable assumption that British or American pilots, put through the same desperate trials, with the nation's survival hanging in the balance, would emerge with similar scores. On the other hand, a good case can be built on behalf of the natural inclination of the German for military duty and combat of any kind. And it is true that, despite the R.A.F. victory in the Battle of Britain, the three top German fighter pilots to emerge from that battle (Helmut Wick, Werner Mölders and Adolf Galland) had scores in the neighbourhood of fifty victories apiece, or about twice those of the highest defending R.A.F. pilot.[1]

[1] At the end of 1940, the three top-scoring German aces were: Adolf Galland, 57 kills; Helmut Wick, 56 (he had been killed 28 November); and Werner Mölders, 55. A tentative and unofficial list of the top R.A.F. scorers in the Battle of Britain, provided for me by the historical branch of the Ministry of Defence, at my request, shows the top three scorers to have been Flight Lieutenant E. S. Lock, D.S.O., D.F.C. and Bar (deceased), 20 kills, Squadron Leader A. A. McKellar, D.S.O., D.F.C. and Bar (deceased), 20, and Sergeant J. Frantisek, D.F.M. (deceased), 17—plus 11 prior to the Battle of Britain.

It has been of more than passing interest to me, in the twelve years spent in the preparation of three books on fighter battles and pilots in the Second World War, to meet and talk to the highest scorers of each country. The reader might be interested in a few general comments about them as a group, for it is unlikely that many writers have interviewed the top surviving pilots of the three countries, having themselves been fighter pilots in Europe in the Second World War, and thereafter having lived in both England and Germany and conversed at length with ex-Lutwaffe flyers in their native tongue.

In general, of the surviving aces of the Second World War, none appeared to me to be suffering from shattered nerves, the jitters, jerks, or any other personal abnormality as a result of wartime service. On the contrary, they all seemed reasonably well-adjusted, alert, and in good spirits. It is probable that this is a better post-war average than would be found among the ordinary soldiers or sailors who saw extensive combat. This would, of course, contradict a popular conception, frequently nursed by some sophisticates it would seem, that fighter pilots were more often than not aggressive, rowdy types, even misfits, whose goal in war was glory and fame and who were basically juvenile delinquents licensed to kill; that they were usually reckless, irrepressible types who would not be able to adjust satisfactorily to civilian life when the war was over. The reverse seems nearer the truth. Not only have the great pilots I have seen adjusted satisfactorily to civilian life, but most of them have achieved a degree of success and have emerged as leaders in society and business. And this analysis applies to the pilots of the three countries with which I am concernd.

An oversupply of youthful enthusiasm or exuberance infected some of them to a degree: those who perhaps believed what they saw in films or read—in freely-flowing books—about dashing, romantic fighter aces of both World Wars. Writers and admirers who bracketed the aces with Robin Hood, Wyatt Earp or the Pied Piper added to the process. One part of this phenomenon is the tendency of some people to rate everyone by scores and to make a case for the proposition that five victories in the air entitled a fighter pilot to unofficial status as an 'ace', supposedly something special. Such over-simplification, and the immature tone of much written about fighter pilots, have tended to cloud the fundamental and often decisive value of their accomplishments during the war.

In Germany, in any event, five kills by a fighter pilot were never considered a landmark of accomplishment. German fighter pilots rated their comrades by performance judged over a long period and spoke of a pilot whose flying was above average as an *'Experte'* regardless of the number of his kills. German pilots with ten, fifteen or twenty kills were often not considered *Experten*.

There need be no apology, however, for recording the exploits of the war's top pilots, for patriotic men of that generation felt in their duty to fight for their country and its survival as has been the honourable course for centuries. In this volume no effort is made to glorify war, which so many of us have seen at first hand. Nevertheless, impressive performances in battle and in the line of duty, individual achievements which reflect bravery, courage and skill, can be applauded by the fair-minded on both sides. It has been said, and in part rightly so, that accounts of fighter missions such as appear in this book tend to overlook the horror of war. The same could be said of most of history's stories of heroes in battle. It should be kept in mind that such accounts stress the exceptional achievements in a world-wide carnage, a tragedy of immeasurable proportions. The fact is that the human race has experienced wars throughout the centuries, and that in each there have been outstanding examples of men who fought bravely and inspired others by their devotion to duty and courage in combat. Without such men freedom would have been lost long ago, and might have been lost in the Second World War.

It can be argued that both sides could not have been fighting for democracy, and that is true. On the other hand, pilots, like soldiers and sailors generally, fight primarily for their country. The great majority of the millions engaged in the two World Wars felt that they were fighting for their country's cause. Home-country propaganda, coloured news and the utterances of politicians (or in the case of Nazi Germany a controlled press and radio) are enough to convince the average citizen, who is rarely sufficiently perceptive to see through a coloured presentation. Thus wars are not fought by millions of citizens dedicated to a right and just cause as impartially proclaimed by their governments, but by millions of citizens fighting for their country, and trusting and hoping that their government is right, and that what they read and hear is accurate. It is demanding too much to expect each private citizen to gleam the truth from the world-wide picture through individual investigation, knowledge and insight. The leaders who control the helm of state, and those who manipulate press and airwaves, bear that responsibility, and often pay the price of their deeds. The average man, or youngster, merely fights for his country when the nation goes to war, as his duty, or because he is called to the colours by the legal authority of the state.

Therefore the episodes re-created in detail in this book are not intended to constitute a glorification of war or mortal combat, but should be considered in the light of the preceding remarks.

Though more information will be found in the appendixes of this volume, the following were the top fighter pilots of the Second World War (to the nearest half-aircraft):

## GERMANY

| _Western Front_[1] | | _Eastern Front_ | |
|---|---|---|---|
| Hans-Joachim Marseille | 158 | Erich Hartmann | 352 |
| Heinrich Bär | 124 | Gerhard Barkhorn | 301 |
| Kurt Buehligen | 112 | Gunther Rall | 275 |
| Adolf Galland | 104 | Otto Kittel* | 267 |

[1] Includes Africa. In the totals for Western Front, Heinrich Bär's 96

# GREAT BRITAIN

| European Theatre[1] | | Overseas Theatres | |
|---|---|---|---|
| James E. Johnson | 38 | M. T. St J. Pattle* | 41 |
| Adolph G. Malan* | 35 | George F. Beurling* | 31 |
| Pierre H. Clostermann | 33 | Neville F. Duke | 29 |
| Brendan E. Finucane* | 32 | Clive R. Caldwell | 28½ |

# UNITED STATES

| European Theatre[2] | | Far East Theatre[3] | |
|---|---|---|---|
| Francis S. Gabreski | 31 | Richard L. Bong* | 40 |
| Robert Johnson | 28 | Thomas B. McGuire* | 38 |
| George E. Preddy* | 26 | David McCampbell | 34 |
| John C. Meyer | 24 | Charles H. MacDonald | 27 |

*Deceased

In scanning the above lists it should be remembered that
there are no official lists of 'aces', a designation not recognized

---

victories in other theatres are not included. If these were added his total
for the war would be 220. Totals listed under Eastern Front include five
kills by Hartmann against fighters of the Western democracies and three
by Rall.

[1] Of the eight R.A.F. aces in these two lists, only two are Englishmen.
Pattle and Malan were South Africans, Clostermann is French. Beurling
was Canadian. Finucane was Irish and Caldwell is Australian. The top six
English aces, in addition to Johnson and Duke, above, were: Robert R. S.
Tuck (29), John R. D. Braham (night fighter, 29), James H. Lacey (28),
Frank R. Carey (28), Eric S. Lock (26), and Billy Drake (24½). Of the four
overseas R.A.F. pilots listed above, Beurling's total includes 5 victories
scored in Europe and Duke's total 2 in Europe. Eight of Caldwell's
victories in the above total were against Japanese over Australia, the re-
mainder against Axis aircraft in Africa.

[2] This list does not include the name of Lance C. Wade, one of the
R.A.F.'s great pilots with 25 victories, a Texan who volunteered for flying
duty with the R.A.F. in 1940 and went on to become one of the highest-
scoring Americans in the war. He was an R.A.F. Wing Commander at the
time of his death in a flying accident in Italy in 1944.

[3] This list includes only victories scored by American pilots while serving in the regular armed services. Gregory Boyington is credited with 6
victories as a 'volunteer' flying for Chiang Kai-shek's forces and scored 22
as a Marine Corps pilot. David McCampbell, U.S. Navy, was the high-
scoring ace among Navy and Marine pilots in the Second World War.

in Germany. The semi-official lists are constantly undergoing revision, as students and statisticians check and study the records of the war. But the totals above are the scores generally accepted by official military historical offices in the three countries, and by those writing about the fighter pilots of the Second World War.

It will be noted that more than half the top scorers in the above lists survived the war and, in fact, an even better survival rate is found if one extends the length of the U.S. and R.A.F. lists a bit, though among the top 104 Germans the rate of survival was only fifty per cent. The top-scoring pilots shot down a far greater percentage of the enemy's total losses than many realize. The top ten Germans reportedly accounted for 2,588 Allied aircraft[1] and Luftwaffe historian Hans Ring estimates that 300 German pilots shot down almost 30,000 Russian aircraft. Considering the fact that total Russian losses to the Luftwaffe were about 44,000 planes, one can readily appreciate the contribution made by the best pilots and understand why so many commanders preferred one excellent pilot to a number of inexperienced ones. Inadequately trained pilots (especially in the Luftwaffe in the last desperate years of the war when petrol was scarce and other difficulties prevented adequate flying training) were often those who fell first.

Thus the greatest fighter pilots of the Second World War, the first war in which air power played such a decisive role, exerted a major influence on the war's outcome, from the Battle of Britain until the German surrender on 8 May 1945. Reclaiming some of their most memorable missions is not only exciting reading but is important to the understanding of what was probably the last war in which dogfighting was possible, and in which the fighter pilot played such a decisive role.


[1] R. Toliver and T. Constable, *Fighter Aces* (Macmillan, New York, 1965), p. 235.

# CHAPTER TWO

# THE BATTLE OF BRITAIN

A LOOK at the aerial campaigns of the Second World War, based on revised estimates of losses, shows that not all of them turned out as the public was led to believe during the war, and has largely accepted since. Although the veil of secrecy to some extent continues to plague the researcher investigating Allied losses, this is not the sole reason more candid efforts have not been forthcoming. There is always a natural tendency to proceed slowly in developing conclusions which debunk or seem to minimize what have been accepted as victories. This involves a degree of emotional inertia in direct proportion to the number of years which have passed. And so it no longer requires a thick skin, more than twenty years after VE-Day, to assess objectively the major aerial campaigns of the Second World War—even if that must depreciate some earlier conceptions.

A good example is that of the Battle of Britain. Was it really like the public's conception of it? And the fighter war in the two succeeding years, 1941 and 1942—who won, as far as losses are concerned? Who won the fighter war in Africa (1940-3)? How and when did fighters decide the Battle of Germany? These are interesting questions, and a brief look at the answers provides the reader with a reasonably accurate general picture of the fighter war—before we move on to detailed re-creations of the most interesting flights of some of the top pilots on each side.

To evaluate these aerial campaigns properly it is helpful to keep in mind the goals of each side and the technical performance of aircraft engaged, as one proceeds to the vital information of accurate statistics on losses.

Obtaining accurate loss figures as distinct from original or inaccurate ones is still not always simple. German records, which were captured are readily accessible. But certain Allied records, totalized or period losses, are still not officially available. In some cases this is because of laws forbidding release for a specific number of years. Sometimes it is simply because of the staggering amount of work involved in compiling them (although I always feel that *someone* must have required such totals in wartime). And it is alleged, in some cases, that they are not readily released because of an element of national pride involved, since publication would perhaps change the prevailing image of an air battle or campaign. German sources sometimes suggest this latter consideration as a reason for a lack of full information; it is also argued, in this connection, that officials who compiled campaign figures for accepted and 'official' works have an interest in preserving their reputation for accuracy.

Be that as it may, most of us would certainly agree today—over twenty years after the end of the war—that it is time that we faced figures as accurately as they can be assembled, whatever the picture, and regardless of any myths or illusions which might be shaken or dispelled by them. German loss records having been captured and fully publicized, it is only reasonable to seek complete and accurate totals on Allied losses so that the aerial campaigns of the war can be more fully comprehended and accurately appraised.

It is possible to put together a fair approximation of the outcome of many of the campaigns, utilizing books and articles on the subject, German records, squadron books, individual research, and an impartial approach. This chapter follows that guide-line, and also takes into account the conclusions of several researchers now compiling Allied loss totals for selected campaigns, which should make interesting reading in a few years. From this process there evolves certain interesting conclusions.

In speaking of losses, it should be remembered that there have been at least three sets of figures for air losses in the last war. First, there were the newspaper and radio claims, which came immediately after an air action. These were in the form of news releases, and were based on the claims of returning pilots, before final confirmation. They were highly inaccurate. Examples of exaggeration are plentiful. Two will serve to illustrate the process. On a mission over the Continent American bomber gunners claimed 102 German fighters shot down or damaged; the actual loss proved to be one destroyed, none damaged.[1] A more famous example is the R.A.F. claim on 15 September 1940—the day since selected as Battle of Britain Day, and observed as such each year. English claims were 185 aircraft destroyed. Actual German losses were 60.[2] There were similar examples almost daily throughout the war.

On the German side Dr Josef Goebbels's Propaganda Ministry consistently turned out distorted figures, exaggerated number of victories and understated losses. That is generally known, since the German press and radio were controlled and manipulated. The Allied press and radio were not so manipulated, but by releasing claims before confirmations had been made, they often achieved about the same result.

Eliminating newspaper stories in the war days, and their claims, as a source of accurate information, we come to the confirmations. On each side, confirmation totals were the result of decisions by official bodies charged with the responsibility of allotting the right number of victories to the right claimants. Official confirmations, on both sides, came only some time after the claims were made and after investigation of the facts. On the Allied side, confirmation usually required visual corroboration by a fellow pilot, or wing camera pictures. On the German side the drill was, for all practical purposes, the same. The Abschusskommission, notwithstanding the pronouncements of Goebbels's propa-

[1] Johnson, *Wing Leader* (Chatto and Windus, 1956), Chapter 10, refers to this mission, to Lille, commenting that if all the claims of Fortress gunners had been correct the Luftwaffe would soon have ceased to exist.

[2] Wood, p. 353. Hans Ring says the correct figure is 49. Other sources put it at 56.

ganda organization, took considerable time in the study and processing of claims and sometimes confirmations required months, even as long as a year. When there was a definite kill and it was not agreed which pilot was responsible, neither was given the confirmation, though the unit was allowed to add it to its total. The Kommission's confirmations during the war, of course, totalled far fewer aircraft than the total of claims which appeared in the German press.

Then there has been a third, and more accurate, tabulation of losses. This takes into account official loss records. In this way one can correct for errors in confirmation totals, the unintentional mistakes of bodies on both sides. This tabulation gives the most accurate picture available of the outcome of various fighter actions and campaigns. However, it is not always complete on the Allied side. It has sometimes been arrived at by researchers and students checking and probing data to fill the gaps. While this chapter may not contain absolutely final figures on actions and campaigns discussed, it does contain up-to-date estimates where official figures are not available—figures which I believe will prove reasonable ones.

Such tabulations always show some 'victories' to have been defeats and that the total of official, individual confirmations is higher than the enemy's losses. Yet these individual scores are seldom, if ever, corrected downwards. On the contrary, a constant process is underway in the three countries, concerning these scores, and they are still being adjusted upwards—more than two decades after the end of the war.

One of the traditional and human inclinations of man in combat is to overestimate the strength of the adversary. In wartime this is better than underestimating it. Nevertheless, it would seem that we were certainly prone to follow human nature in this respect during the Second World War. It stood to reason, especially in the last few years of the war in Europe, that Germany, fighting practically all the world, would be up against numerically superior Allied forces. There was Russia on one side; America with her vast production, operating aircraft from English bases, and Great

Britain, who possessed an impressive aircraft industry and large air forces, were on the other. Since German aircraft production did not become impressive until 1944, the last full year of the war,[1] it would have been impossible for Germany to have enjoyed numerical superiority, except at selected points on the periphery at which a special effort was made. There was a time, at the beginning of the war, when the Luftwaffe did enjoy numerical superiority—but not as great as we have been led to believe. With these considerations in mind, let us look for a moment at the Battle of Britain, one of the least-known and most intriguing examples of the misinterpretation of numbers and losses.

We all know that Fighter Command's victory in 1940 was one of the decisive strategic triumphs in modern history, and the first in which air power (fighters) determined the fate of so many—to paraphrase Churchill. In the United States and Great Britain, during that fateful struggle, the officially approved news was that heavily outnumbered R.A.F. fighter squadrons, in battle with greatly superior enemy numbers, were bringing down German aircraft in a two-to-one or three-to-one ratio to their own losses. Since the war, this impression has not been altogether modified, at least in the public mind, and it requires a careful reading and some original thinking and computing for the average reader to obtain an accurate mental picture of conditions, and of strengths and losses. What were the numbers of fighters engaged, the numbers of bombers, and what were the losses and fighter production on each side?

Using the date preferred by the Germans, 13 August, as the opening of the battle, a fair estimate is that the Luftwaffe had arrayed against England 805 single-engined fighters to

[1] Galland, p. 246, reveals that Germany in 1944 produced 38,000 aircraft of all types. Lord Tedder, *With Prejudice* (Cassell, 1966), p. 246, quoted German production chief Albert Speer as saying that one reason this sharply increased German production was not felt more was because Allied air attacks on Germany 'destroyed the aircraft as soon as they were made'.

the R.A.F.'s 749 available for operations.[1] Probably the main reason so many people have confused ideas as to the numbers engaged in the Battle of Britain is the tendency of writers to list opposing strengths by giving the number of German fighters and bombers combined, while giving only the number of R.A.F. fighters.[2] There is, of course, justification for this, because the intercepting R.A.F. fighters took on both the German bombers and fighters, while R.A.F. bombers were assaulting enemy concentrations and invasion ports across the Channel in different actions at different times. But to list opposing strengths in this way is nevertheless misleading. German records show that Luftwaffe strength available for operations against England was over 2,600 aircraft of all kinds, in the two Luftflotten in France and one in Norway (which took little part in the battle), including 316 practically useless Stukas.[3]

Of the approximately 2,500 German aircraft in France,

[1] Luftwaffe totals from official German records; R.A.F. totals from various sources. Wood, p. 416, lists 749 operational fighters for Fighter Command as of 10 August 1940. Several sources give figures between 600 and 700 for R.A.F. strength. J. F. C. Fuller, *The Second World War* (Eyre and Spottiswoode, 1948), p. 88, lists R.A.F. fighter strength at 59 squadrons. Gleave, in a good article on the Battle of Britain in *Flight International* (16/9/65) gives R.A.F. strength at the beginning of the battle as 57 squadrons. Since the flying strength of a squadron was normally 12 aircraft, one would arrive at a figure—not counting spares—of 684. This figure does not include squadrons forming or reforming but does include 2 of Blenheims and 3 of Defiants. It does not include 6½ night-fighter squadrons, nor the Fleet Air Arm's fighters. Gleave puts German fighter strength at 809. Capt. B. H. Liddell Hart, *The Other Side of the Hill* (Cassell, 1948), p. 156, says that these 57 squadrons, with reserves, added up to 1,000 aircraft. Galland, p. 17, says R.A.F. fighter strength was 'numerically stronger' than that of the Luftwaffe.

[2] Most of the accounts of the battle published during or immediately after the war listed combined German fighter-bomber strength at close to 2,700 and R.A.F. fighter strength at approximately 600, which gave the impression that the opposing air forces were in that proportionate strength.

[3] Gleave says that the strength of the two Luftwaffe air fleets (Luftflotten 2 and 3) assembled in France for the battle was 2,502 aircraft. Wood, p. 229, estimates Luftwaffe strength, in serviceable aircraft, deployed against England on 10 August as 2,550. These figures are from official German records.

which for all practical purposes carried out the assault, there were 1,131 bombers, more than 800 fighters, 316 Stukas (which were soon withdrawn) and 246 twin-engined Me.110 long-range fighters. After the Ju.87s were withdrawn, the Luftwaffe had just under 2,200 aircraft of all kinds in France for the battle.

A comparable figure for the R.A.F. must obviously include bombers. Bomber Command numbered, at the beginning of 1940, some fifty-three squadrons, plus six or seven which were in France attached to the A.A.E.F. The R.A.F. also contained a number of Coastal Command Squadrons.[1] Estimating operational strength (at the beginning of 1940) at ten bombers per squadron, we have a figure of about 600 bombers for Bomber Command, not including various types of aircraft of Coastal Command or the Fleet Air Arm. German Intelligence estimated Bomber Command's strength at about 1,100[2], which was excessive.

In summary, while R.A.F. bomber strength was apparently less than that of the Luftwaffe by several hundreds, the overall difference in strength between the two forces committed, counting fighters and bombers of all commands, was not boundless.[3] R.A.F. bombers were certainly an active force in the battle, and one reliable source reports losses among aircrews of Bomber Command attacking the build-up of invasion forces in France as 'at least as great' as those suffered by Fighter Command.[4] Of course, R.A.F. bombers

[1] Sir Charles Webster and Noble Frankland, *The Official History of the Second World War* (H.M.S.O., 1961), Vol. 4 (The Strategic Air Offensive Against Germany), list Bomber Command strength at the beginning of 1940 at 15 Battle squadrons, 10 Blenheim, 10 Wellington, 10 Hampden and 8 Whitley.

[2] Wood, p. 106

[3] Webster, Vol. 1, p. 410, gives the total strength of the two air forces, as of August 1940, as (approximately): Luftwaffe, 4,500 aircraft; R.A.F., 3,000.

[4] Gleave, p. 502. Macmillan, *The R.A.F. in the World War* (Harrap, 1942–50), appendix, lists R.A.F. bomber losses in 1940 as 752, Coastal Command losses 269, for a combined total of 1,021, which does not include Fighter Command losses, Fleet Air Arm losses, and so on. Sir

were not in *the* battle in the public eye, which was generally considered to be the aerial clashes over Kent and Sussex. Certainly R.A.F. bombers would not be sent up to meet these invading enemy formations and therefore, because of the defensive role of the R.A.F., its fighters were constantly engaging more numerous combined enemy formations (a situation defending fighters, on both sides, usually found themselves in throughout the war), creating an impression of vastly superior German numbers and a battle in which the R.A.F.'s bombers were inactive, an incomplete one.

In addition, Fighter Command employed limited commitment tactics in fighting the battle, and never was more than a part of the R.A.F.'s total operational fighter strength stationed in the south, on Eleven Group base. This, of course, meant that small R.A.F. numbers were often pitted against very large enemy forces.

If we assume, then, that fighter strengths were about equal[1] at the beginning of the battle and that two bomber efforts were being made simultaneously, an interesting next step is to determine the advantages possessed by each side. The greatest advantage in the battle was that of the defensive. This lay with the R.A.F. Fighter Command, pilots forced to bail out or crash-land were not lost (and at this time pilots were scarcer than fighter aircraft in the R.A.F.), but German pilots who parachuted became prisoners of war and were lost to the Luftwaffe. Being able to land immediately after an engagement also proved a tactical advantage to R.A.F. pilots flying over their homeland, and being unable to do so

---

Arthur Harris, *Bomber Offensive* (Macmillan, New York, 1947), p. 42, notes the bomber effort: 'The influence of the bomber force has been much underrated . . . all the credit for preventing invasion . . . has been given to Fighter Command, and the significance of Bomber Command's share . . . has been largely overlooked. . . . In point of fact, Fighter Command's losses were very low as compared with the normal casualty rate for our bomber operations.'

[1] A special edition of *The Royal Air Force News* of September 1965 contains an estimate of 1,200 as the number of R.A.F. fighters available in 1940.

was a major handicap for Luftwaffe fighter pilots, who had only about thirty minutes' flying time over England. This extra combat time of defending R.A.F. fighters, comparatively, gave them many more operational hours in the air. German pilots, according to Galland and others, suffered acute psychological strain because of the necessity of re-crossing the Channel to return to bases and the ever-present anxiety that their fuel supply would not be adequate to get them back. This lack of fuel capacity greatly limited the radius of action of the Me.109s over England.

The R.A.F. benefited from the excellent radar warning and control organization of Fighter Command—certainly at that time the best in the world. Not only were enemy formations accurately plotted as they flew in to the attack, but intercepting R.A.F. fighters were accurately guided to the bomber boxes by ground controllers. Thus the normal offensive advantage, that of being able to choose the place of battle, and of concentration in that area, was offset by radar, and by the limited range of the Me.109. German fighters, in addition, were handicapped to some extent by having to fly close protective patterns with the slower bombers,[1] which were themselves under-armed and almost at the mercy of R.A.F. fighters when without protection.[2] So uneven was the fight between Stukas (Ju.87s) and R.A.F. fighters that the Stukas had to be withdrawn from the battle in its opening phases. The Me.110s were also a disappointment to the Luftwaffe, and single-engined fighters had to be assigned to fly with them as protection. Thus the single-engined fighters of the Luftwaffe were certainly assigned numerous tasks and responsibilities, and flew against certain handicaps. Considering all that was asked of them, it is not surprising that they were unable to accomplish it all; yet their achievement, as we shall see when we come to look into losses, was not insignificant.

[1] *Wing Leader*, Chapter 4.
[2] Harris, p. 42, describes the shooting down of unescorted German bombers by R.A.F. fighters as 'very similar to shooting cows in a field'.

The German fighters also enjoyed several advantages. On the credit side for Luftwaffe pilots was, first of all, an advantage in equipment. They flew the best fighter. If one ranks the Spitfire I and II equal with the Me.109E (and some might challenge this)[1] it is nevertheless true that the R.A.F. possessed only 19 squadrons of those available for the battle in August. Most of the others were equipped with Hurricanes (27) and Defiants and Blenheims (5). All Luftwaffe single-engined squadrons were equipped with the Me.109, which could outdive—and, above 20,000 feet, outclimb—all R.A.F. types, possessed more effective guns (20 mm. cannon), was superior at high altitude and enjoyed the advantage of automatic fuel injection. And the 109 was faster than all but the Spitfire, with which it was about on a par[2] (probably a bit slower than the Mark II, with which squadrons began to be equipped in June 1940). The Spits and Hurricanes could out-turn the 109, an advantage in itself, but when one considers all performance features of the 109 versus those of the combined R.A.F. types, the German fighter pilot enjoyed, on the average, the advantage of the best fighter.

Another advantage enjoyed by Luftwaffe fighter pilots was their greater experience. Some of the top German pilots had had much operational flying in Spain. Many had flown in Poland in 1939 and against France and the Low Countries in May and June of 1940. This experience proved especially valuable in perfecting their tactical formations, which were in general, superior to the line-astern and other vics employed widely by the R.A.F. In fact, the German pilots referred to the obsolete line astern formations of the R.A.F. at that time

[1] There were various models of the Spitfire and the Me.109 introduced throughout the war. The Me.109E was pitted against the Spitfire I and II in the Battle of Britain. From time to time various performance figures of one (such as speed) surpassed that of the other.
[2] *Wing Leader*, p. 49; Johnson says the Spitfire had a slight speed margin in the Battle of Britain. Galland, p. 21, says the Me.109 was faster by 15 to 20 m.p.h. Wood, Appendix 1, quotes performance figures which indicate the Spitfire I was about equal in speed, the Spitfire II slightly faster (than the Me.109E).

as the *Idiotenreihe* (idiots' row[1]). Thus we see that the two sides were not too unevenly matched as far as fighter strength was concerned, the Germans having an edge in equipment and a few more single-engined fighters, but facing disadvantages because of the circumstances under which they were forced to fight.

Before discussing losses, let us look very briefly at the production (replacement) picture for that summer. In the end, the side which could replace its losses would inevitably win a prolonged battle. The reader may not be aware of comparative production. It was not even close[2]. British industry, spurred on by the energy of Lord Beaverbrook, outdid the Germans all summer and for the year as a whole. Beginning with June, the following are monthly fighter production figures in the two countries for five months:

|           | England | Germany |
|-----------|---------|---------|
| June      | 446     | 164     |
| July      | 496     | 220     |
| August    | 476     | 173     |
| September | 467     | 218     |
| October   | 469     | 200     |
|           | 2,354   | 975     |

In pilot replacements, there are conflicting accounts. Germany had ample man-power, counting Me.110 pilots. But her training programme was still in low gear. The R.A.F., while below its establishment, recruited pilots from the Fleet Air Arm and from Bomber Command. It also received an influx of pilots from occupied countries on the Continent, some American pilots, and other useful allies. In the end,

[1] Statement made to the author by General Galland, confirmed by other Luftwaffe pilots in other conversations.

[2] *The Royal Air Force, 1939–45* (H.M.S.O., 1953) and Wood list British fighter production for 1940 at 4,283. German fighter production for the year totalled 2,424, according to the files of the Ministry of Armaments and War Production (Wilmot, p. 54). Monthly figures on German fighter production are from official German Quartermaster reports.

the supply of pilots did not prove to be decisive on either side, though the proportion of German fighter pilots to aircraft lost was higher than that of the R.A.F. (largely because many German pilots were captured after parachuting, or went down in the Channel).

And so one comes to perhaps the most interesting question of the battle. Who won, as far as losses are concerned? In Germany today some researchers say aircraft losses were roughly equal. A recent estimate placed R.A.F. fighter losses at approximately 1,200 (the number usually listed in British accounts, such as Churchill's *The Second World War*, is 915). In addition, it is estimated, the R.A.F. lost about 300 bombers over Germany during the period, plus an additional number of aircraft assaulting French ports and suspected build-up areas for the planned invasion. If this estimate is accurate, R.A.F. losses for the period would have totalled over 1,500 aircraft of all types. If the 915 figure for fighters is accepted, a figure between 1,215 and 1,500 can be arrived at. Concerning R.A.F. losses, contradictory claims and confusing figures make acceptance of a final figure somewhat difficult. There is much published information on the subject but few simple, easily followed loss totals. Where there are such totals, they are often complicated by certain qualifications or terminology.

A widely accepted and respected English volume on the battle[1] lists battle casualties of R.A.F. fighters for the period June-October (the same period for which German losses will be considered) of 1,305. The same source reports an additional 745 fighters having been damaged, which makes a grand total, for fighters, of over 2,000. How many of these were aerial combat casualties? Another reliable English source[2] lists 515 R.A.F. pilots (and crewmen) killed between 10 July and the end of October, plus another 500 or so wounded, and certainly many pilots were shot down who were not even wounded. It would be gratifying to see com-

[1] Wood, p. 471.
[2] Gleave, p. 501.

plete records on all aircraft losses for this period in simple form, but until such an official report is available one must accept either the German estimate or the lesser one. Taking the lower, we have the 915 figure for fighters lost, another figure for fighters damaged in the air (many of which were no doubt claimed by Luftwaffe pilots) and another for bomber losses. In addition, a number were strafed and bombed on the ground—which must be considered in arriving at total fighter losses.[1]

German losses are widely known, and while slighly varying figures are given in various accounts, practically all place the number at over 1,700.

The number of German losses cited in this book is 1,789, slightly higher than the number given by most British sources, such as the 1,733 cited by Johnson in *Full Circle*. However, the figure comes from a reliable German source, having been compiled recently. Broken down into types, the Luftwaffe's losses apparently were: combat losses, 1,385; other causes, 404. Of the combat losses, 502 were Me.109s (600 lost from all causes), 224 Me.110 long-range fighters, 488 bombers (Do.17s, Me.111s and Ju.88s) and 59 Stukas. Keeping in mind that some of the R.A.F. losses cited were also non-combat losses, the difference in both combat and grand total losses for the battle would not appear to have been very great. And, of course, R.A.F. fighter losses (the great majority of its losses in England) were considerably higher than Luftwaffe's, perhaps by a ratio of as much as two to one. Thus one cannot judge the efforts of German fighter pilots in the Battle of Britain harshly. They suffered some of their losses as a result of anti-aircraft fire, while the R.A.F. suffered losses from ground strafing and bombing. In the dog-fighting the Me.109 apparently acquitted itself, all things considered, very well. It would not be illogical, to conclude that, all in all, total losses on each side were not too far apart.

[1] The roll of honour at Biggin Hill contains the names of 1,494 fatalities —448 from Fighter Command, 718 from Bomber Command, 280 from Costal Command, 34 from the Fleet Air Arm, and 14 others.

Of course, whatever the losses, the Battle of Britain constituted a major victory for the R.A.F., with far-reaching consequences for all the free world, because the Luftwaffe failed in what it attempted to do (some of the blame for which can be attributed to mistakes by the Luftwaffe Command). What the figures cited demonstrate—and this is all they do demonstrate—is that the battle was not as one-sided as has been believed. R.A.F. fighters were shooting down more aircraft in most of the air battles over England, but since the Germans were sending over large numbers of bombers, always at a disadvantage against fighters, this was inevitable —as the R.A.F. and U.S.A.A.F. were to find out in the last years of the war when heavy bomber losses, plus escort fighter losses, were so often far greater than those of defending Luftwaffe fighters. And R.A.F. bombers were also being lost during the battle, as were aircraft on the ground, which is not generally taken into consideration.

If one appreciates the magnificence of the British victory, one must also acknowledge the tremendous effort of German pilots and crews in the battle, who did not enjoy the benefit of such outstanding leadership and organization. Luftwaffe bomber crews (in Do.17s, He.111s and Ju.88s—the 88s being the best of the three) flew to their targets with a growing realization that their bombers were underarmed, and both bomber crewmen and fighter pilots faced a trip back home over water. Their losses were heavy from the beginning and great demands were made on them.[1] They were faced—in the latter stages of the struggle—with the grim fact that the number of R.A.F. fighters was increasing. The Luftwaffe's greatest effort in the battle came on 15 August, not 15 September as some believe, and actually the ratio of losses was improved somewhat in September.

[1] A. McKee, *Strike from The Sky* (Souvenir Press, 1960), in the chapter, 'The Crisis of Fighter Command', discusses the strain in the Battle of Britain on both British and German pilots, noting that the Germans, unlike the British, were not taken out of the line for rest or refitting, but were kept on operations throughout the battle.

# CHAPTER THREE

# THE R.A.F.

IF THE SECOND WORLD WAR was the fighter pilot's war, how were fighter pilots produced and how much emphasis did the pre-war air forces place on fighters? The outcome of the war was to hinge, to some degree at least, on plans and concepts for fighter forces. The R.A.F. in particular was suddenly to need its fighters to save the country from invasion; pre-war preparations then paid decisive dividends.

The fighter war in Europe was fought largely with aircraft originally designed before the war and improved during the war years, and pre-war production plans largely determined the outcome of the production battle in the opening campaigns. Many critical mistakes were made in planning, production and tactics. And some proved fatal in decisive campaigns.

As the Great War had demonstrated, England was vulnerable to German air attack, and a war plan had been drawn up as early as 1923 which envisaged an attack approximately on the lines of that which materialized in 1940. Although major expansion of the R.A.F. began only in 1936 (barely in time), in plans and overall organization they had begun to prepare for the war in 1919, when the father of the modern British air service, Air Chief Marshal Sir Hugh Trenchard, composed a memorandum which Winston Churchill presented in Parliament as a White Paper.[1] This was the basic organizational plan of the R.A.F. in the interval between the wars and during the war, and it proved a remarkably farsighted document. Expansion programmes were often

[1] Wood, p. 66.

initially approved in the interval between the wars, but until well into the thirties they were always postponed or negated by Government economies. Trenchard had seen the finest air force in the world, in 1918, cut to the bone in the demobilization which followed the German surrender. From a force of 188 operational squadrons and 199 training units with 675 bases, the service had shrunk to 12 squadrons by 1919. (Only seven months before the end of the First World War, after a study by General Jan Christian Smuts, the various air forces had been combined into a third military service on the strength of his recommendation.) The basic elements of the Trenchard organization were a small, highly trained professional force, which could be expanded rapidly in time of need, and concentration on research to provide the best training methods, weapons and organization. Under the plan, a Cadet College at Cranwell was established, as were a Central Flying School where instructors were trained, and a training system which guaranteed that every future R.A.F. officer would have a working knowledge of the service and flying.

The Trenchard plan looked to the future, when quick expansion would be needed, by creating the Auxiliary Air Force (for the part-time training of civilian enthusiasts), university squadrons and short-service (five-year) commissions. All these, and the Volunteer Reserve established in 1936, were effectively utilized to expand the R.A.F. in the crisis of 1939–40. Fighter Command was formed in 1936.

During this time the guiding concept of the R.A.F. (and the Luftwaffe) was the primary importance of the bomber. Both Britain and Germany, who would see the critical battle of 1940 decided by their fighter forces, generally accepted the theories of the Italian General Giulio Douhet. The British (including Trenchard) saw in the bomber their first line of defence, a weapon which would destroy the enemy's aircraft industry and its aircraft on the ground. A major factor in this extreme 'bomber-consciousness' was undoubtedly the memory of the raids on London in 1917—18. The Germans also saw in the bomber that potential, but stressed to a greater degree the bomber's usefulness for tactical co-operation with an advancing army.

The R.A.F. emphasized development of a heavy bomber arm as the spearhead of its strategic weapon, while the Luftwaffe, in a planning error, never developed a heavy-bomber arm and relied on smaller bombers.

In 1934, shortly after Hitler came to power in Germany, Britain embarked upon an expansion programme, designed to increase the first-line strength of the R.A.F. to more than a thousand aircraft by the spring of 1939. In the same year, to facilitate training expansion, elementary flying training was farmed out to civilian schools (a method later copied in the United States). The expansion and auxiliary training programmes were carried forward until 1939 (implemented by further, more urgent measures), by which time R.A.F. manpower stood at 118,000, with a trained additional reservoir of more than half that figure. By the time of the Battle of Britain, Fighter Command possessed $57\frac{1}{2}$ fighter squadrons, several others forming or reforming, $6\frac{1}{2}$ night-fighter squadrons and 5 or 6 Coastal Command fighter squadrons, and could call upon the more or less obsolete squadrons of the Fleet Air Arm. It also operated the best radar defence organization in the world.

The pilot-training programme had been expanded in the thirties to include the Dominions, first proposals having been made in 1935, and a glance at the list of top R.A.F. fighter pilots will demonstrate the contribution of South Africa, Australia, Canada and New Zealand.[1] Prime Minister Mackenzie King of Canada, convinced that to join in the R.A.F. training programme would commit Canada to war, in large measure refused to go along with it until after the outbreak of war. Australia, New Zealand and South Africa responded, South Africa providing two of the three highest scoring R.A.F. pilots of the war in M. T. St John Pattle and Adolph G. Malan.

[1] See Appendix I, p. 295.

The first commander-in-chief of the newly-formed Fighter Command, in 1936, was Air Marshal Sir Hugh Dowding, who prepared for and directed the fighter effort in 1940. He then believed that at least 45 fighter squadrons would be needed to defend Britain against an air attack over the North Sea. What was not envisaged was that for the crucial air test of the war the Luftwaffe would be assembled in strength across the English Channel, only twenty miles distant. Dowding's contribution in building Fighter Command into the effective organization it was, from 1936 until the outbreak of war, was one of the foundations of success in 1940.

It was in the field of radar, so crucial to victory in the Battle of Britain and to the defeat of the U-boat campaign, that the R.A.F. thoroughly bested its adversary. The first steps toward perfection were taken in 1934 when A. P. Rowe, in a memorandum to his chief, H. E. Wimperis, Director of Scientific Research at the Air Ministry, gave warning of the prospect of defeat unless science found a new way to assist the defence.[1] Wimperis proposed to the Secretary of State for Air that a committee be formed to look into this, and suggested a well-known physicist, H. L. Tizard, to head it. The committee also included as members Wimperis, Rowe, Dr A. V. Hill and Professor P. M. S. Blackett. Wimperis later consulted Superintendent Robert Watson-Watt, of the National Physical Laboratory's Radio Research Station, on the subject, and the latter had certain calculations made. One of his staff, A. F. Wilkins, prepared figures which showed the possibility of using radio beams for detection and direction finding. From this beginning the committee proceeded. A first demonstration was staged in the winter of 1935, with Dowding attending. It proved successful and shortly afterwards £10,000 was allocated for work on the project, camouflaged under the name of 'radio direction finding'. The first detection station in what was to become a chain was completed in May 1937, and three were functioning when air exercises were held later that year. Results were promising,

[1] Wood, p. 127.

53

and the Air Ministry drew up specifications for a twenty-station chain. The treasury approved the plan in August.

Also contributing to the R.A.F. defence capability was the work of the Royal Observer Corps, an organization of civilians dedicated to detecting, by sound and vision, aircraft passing above. In the last year of the First World War General E. B. Ashmore, commanding London's defences, had organized a system whereby spotters reported to a central operations table at his headquarters. When, in 1924, air defence was again being studied, Ashmore's experience was put to good use, and he organized the first observation exercises with civilians performing spotting duties. A network, connected by telephone, was built up, and by 1939 had grown to 32 centres, more than 1,000 observer posts and some 30,000 observers using instruments to detect height and course. With the help of aircraft recognition clubs, the pioneer club being that headed by H. J. Lowings of Guildford, the Corps managed to provide a massive number of rapid sighting reports to Fighter Command throughout the war.

Private-enterprise industry developed, and managed to have ready for the Battle of Britain, two modern fighters, the Hurricane and the Spitfire. The Hurricane constituted most of the first-line fighter strength of the R.A.F. in 1939 and 1940, having been built and integrated into Fighter Command prior to the beginning of the war. It was followed by the Spitfire I slightly later. First deliveries of the Spitfire II to operational squadrons began only a short time before the opening of the Battle of Britain, at which time there were twenty-seven Hurricane and nineteen Spitfire squadrons.

The Hurricane, while not really the equal of the Me.109, was nevertheless not so outclassed that it entered into battle with no prospect of success. It was only about 30 m.p.h. slower and if an altitude advantage was enjoyed it even had the advantage. It was adequately armed—not as well as the 109, but better armoured and more ruggedly constructed, and able to take more punishment (see the comments of

James Lacey in Chapter 5). Battle of Britain Hurricanes had a top speed of about 320. They carried eight .303 Browning machine-guns. The Hurricane could out-turn the Me.109, a defensive advantage which was undoubtedly the salvation of many R.A.F. pilots, and considering the fact that the first one flew in 1937, a year before Munich, one can appreciate the accomplishment of private industry in developing such a fighter at this early date.

The Spitfire, which came a bit later, was about 45 m.p.h. faster, and was thought to be a bit faster even than the Me. 109E, though many still argue this point. It too could out-turn the 109, and usually carried the same engine and guns as the Hurricane. While not as sturdily constructed, perhaps, as the Hurricane, it was nevertheless rugged, and could probably take more punishment than the 109. The top speed of the models which flew in the Battle of Britain was over 360 m.p.h. Improved models of Hurricanes and Spitfires were introduced as the war progressed, and both were used until the end.

But the Hurricane and Spitfire were not the only R.A.F. fighters of the war by any means. At the end the R.A.F. possessed a number of newer models, including many squadrons of the best American fighter, the P.51, work on which was first begun in the United States as a result of an R.A.F. order (before America was at war). Hawker's turned out several excellent fighters after the war began, including the low-level Tempest, said to have been influenced by the F.W.190, and the Typhoon fighter-bomber. It was the Typhoon which took the measure of the fast F.W.190s which had been sneaking up on English radar defences low over the water, hitting targets quickly and dashing back to their French bases. These later British models were fast and well armed and, though lacking the range of the P.51, they were outstanding fighters. R.A.F. P.51 squadrons and others took part in the Battle of Germany, and flew all the way to Berlin and back as escorts, as well as to other targets even deeper inside Germany.

The De Havilland Mosquito was also outstanding. Though not classed as a fighter (it was an all-wooden, twin-engined aircraft) it was as fast as many fighters and its reconnaissance and photography work over Germany proved invaluable.

The R.A.F. also produced a number of light, medium and heavy bombers. Although this work is concerned with fighters, it would be in order to point out that the 'heavies' of the R.A.F., such as the Lancaster, the Halifax and the Wellington, dropped a greater weight of bombs on Germany than those of the United States. This was not only true in the first years of the war, but continued to be so throughout.

One of the few weaknesses of Fighter Command at the outbreak of war was its tactical formations. Fighter Command's senior officers clung to the set and orderly patterns of formation flying and firing passes. The basic flying unit was the three-plane 'vic', two of which made up a flight. A squadron was twelve aircraft (two flights of six), and several squadrons formed a Wing. The squadron 'V' and line-astern formations were inferior to the formations flown by German fighter pilots (a lesson from Spain), and as things go in the services, change came hard. Squadron commanders had long practised their men in set-pattern firing passes, in which each man lined up in a certain pre-arranged spot, then—by order—delivered an attack according to the book. However, in battle it didn't work out that way, and as one of the R.A.F.'s best fighter pilots remonstrated after the war, the last words of many a gallant R.A.F. fighter pilot in the early years were, 'Red Two commencing firing pass B . . .', as others watched and waited their turn. If the fighter war was a gentleman's war, to any degree, it was not this much of a gentleman's war, and the enemy did not properly respect these orderly and dignified approaches to battle, which is regrettable but understandable.

The greatest testimonials to R.A.F. training methods were the morale and fighting spirit of its fighter pilots once the war began. At no time was this more evident than in the Battle of Britain, when those pilots who bore the brunt of the German onslaught were called upon to fly several missions a day, and to remain all day on readiness. Despite such demands, and despite the fact that they were encountering determined and capable opponents in good aircraft, pilots responded spiritedly time after time. It was this spirit, the radar warning network, adequate training and equipment and the leadership and organization of Fighter Command which were unbeatable in 1940.

Like the Luftwaffe, the R.A.F. awarded wings to commissioned and non-commissioned officers. Many flying sergeant pilots served with distinction and achieved high scores, and in recognition were quite often granted commissions. Commissioned flying ranks in the R.A.F., beginning at the bottom, were as follows:

Pilot Officer
Flying Officer
Flight Lieutenant
Squadron Leader
Wing Commander
Group Captain
Air Commodore
Air Vice-Marshal
Air Marshal
Air Chief Marshal
Marshal of the Royal Air Force

A word is in order on one of the unpublicized assets of Fighter Command. Perhaps more than those of the Luftwaffe, and certainly more than those of the U.S.A.A.F., the permanent stations of Fighter Command were comfortable and carefully planned to provide a home for pilots. The central point of a typical permanent fighter station was a brick building surrounded by lawns and tennis courts in which were located pilots' bedrooms (batmen in attendance), laundry service, central heating, restaurant, bar and a quiet reading-room, where loud talk and ordinary behaviour were not in order and not in evidence.

Pilots of Fighter Command, living in comfort and dignity, enjoying the mutual adventure and danger of flying, a degree of informality in military life and the R.A.F. tradition of fun when off duty, developed a bond which added greatly to morale and thereby to strength. It was no wonder so many of the nation's élite were attracted to such a life. The attractiveness of pilot life was not an unimportant contribution to the building of the *esprit de corps* so vital to victory.

# CHAPTER FOUR

# CRISIS AT DUNKIRK

*23 May 1940—Flight Lieutenant R. R. Stanford Tuck, R.A.F.*

THE MAN who was perhaps the best marksman in the R.A.F. in the Second World War was a handsome, elegant epitome of the fighter pilot, Roland Robert Stanford Tuck. His father, Captain Stanley Lewis Tuck, who had served in the Queen's Royal West Surrey Regiment in the Great War, was a firearms expert, and saw to it that Robert and his brother became proficient in the use of arms at an early age. Robert developed into an exceptional rifle- and pistol-shot— a skill which augured no good for the pilots who would engage him in fighter battles in later years.

He attended St Dunstan's and then, in search of adventure, went to sea as a cadet in the Merchant Navy. He had not excelled in his studies at St Dunstan's, though he exhibited a talent for foreign languages, possibly due to the influence of his Russian governess, who taught him her language, one sentence a day, for years. (It was to be a vital asset to him several years later.) But he had done well as a gymnast, fencer, swimmer, boxer, on the playing field and especially on the rifle range, where he had been the school's best shot. Two and a half years on the seas broadened and toughened him and perfected his shooting still further—he learned to kill sharks neatly with one shot from a rifle, a difficult feat.

But the stimulation of seeing the world on ships began to fade—ships seemed to take a long time to get from place to place. While he was spending a few days' leave at his father's home in Catford, in 1935, Tuck's eye was caught by an advertisement which stirred his imagination: '*Fly With The R.A.F.!*' Whatever the insertion cost the R.A.F. was well spent. It attracted into the service one of its greatest fighter pilots.

Tuck conveyed his desire to sit the R.A.F. examinations to his father, who reluctantly agreed. He underwent a written examination, a thorough medical and finally an oral by a board of five regular officers. After two weeks of suspense, he received a letter from the Air Ministry informing him that he had been accepted. He had done well in the first two examinations, and the oral examining board must have liked the answers and the looks of the tanned, lean, well-dressed candidate, for only a small percentage of those who competed were given the cherished rank of Acting Pilot Officer (on probation). Tuck was ordered to be at Uxbridge R.A.F. Station by noon on 16 September. On that morning in 1935 thirty-three young men arrived at Uxbridge (six or eight are still alive) to begin two weeks of drills, lectures and various aptitude tests.

From there Tuck was sent to Grantham Flying Training School in Lincolnshire, and for the first time in his life stood next to an aeroplane, an Avro Tutor. As his biographer, Larry Forrester, describes it in *Fly For Your Life*,[1] he was shocked. It looked so fragile—in comparison with the ships on which he had been sailing. However, he soon became accustomed to the flimsiness of 1935 aircraft.

And now Tuck's over-eagerness almost brought him failure. Fortunately, he had a sensitive and understanding instructor, Flying Officer A. P. S. Wills. Wills noticed from the beginning that Tuck, full of enthusiasm, couldn't get the hang of it no matter how hard he tried. As others chalked up their solos, he continued to fly unimpressively and was unable to relax. His failing was in over-correcting with a heavy hand instead of manœuvring stick and rudder lightly and smoothly. As the normal time for a solo flight came and passed, and two other trainees were 'bowler-hatted', worry and nervous tension added to Tuck's difficulties and to the rigidity of his flying. Wills tried everything to ease him unob-

[1] Muller, 1956.

trusively out of his tenseness. He was careful to be casual and friendly in correcting flying technique. He would chat informally about the scenery below to break tension. Tuck's flying comrades were sympathetic and joked to cheer him up, to help him relax. Still he was tense. He had flown thirteen hours, and could no longer continue without a test flight with the deputy flight commander, Flight Lieutenant Tatnall. Unless he showed promise or improvement on that ride, Tatnall would have to fail him.

Tuck secretly knew in his own mind that it was hopeless, and became more or less resigned to his fate. On the morning of what could have been his final flight the strain and resignation combined to make his hands and feet almost useless. When Tatnall ordered him to take off, he responded as if half numb. Yet he made a good take-off, climbed straight and turned . . . smoothly. He flew as if it no longer mattered too much, and the vital lesson suddenly came to him—as it never had before. It was easy if one didn't try too hard. How little effort it took! He continued to fly smoothly; hope came back. After fifteen minutes of vastly improved flying, Tatnall instructed him to land. When he had touched down properly and the aircraft had come to a stop, the deputy flight commander climbed out of the cockpit and said casually, 'Off you go.' It was one of the most dramatic moments of Tuck's life. Instead of being failed, he was being given a chance to go solo. Tatnall walked away, betraying no lingering doubts. Tuck gunned the engine and began his take-off. He lifted nicely off the field, circled carefully and came in for his first solo landing. He concentrated on his newly-found light touch with stick and pedals and eased the biplane down smoothly, touched lightly and rolled straight.

Wills, Tatnall and other instructors were anxiously watching from the side of the field. Someone coming up from behind spoke: 'Now *there's* a promising lad.' They turned to see who it was and saluted Flying Instructor W.A.B. ('Jimmy') Savile, a twinkle in his eye; he too had been aware of the struggle they were having with Tuck.

From this critical stage, Tuck progressed steadily and was soon justifying the extra effort instructors had made to help him. In course after course he was rated exceptional and before long confidence overwhelmed him. He even became looked upon by senior pilots as being too reckless or cocky at times. During the next two years there was often justification for such opinion. Quick at the controls, he sometimes took questionable chances. There were several close brushes with death. Finally, in 1938, he was abruptly sobered up, perhaps just in time.

He was flying in a tight formation when it suddenly hit bumpy air. The pilot in front abruptly pulled up. Tuck couldn't avoid him. They collided, and Tuck's prop struck and killed the pilot. Because of extensive damage to his own falling fighter, Tuck couldn't force the canopy open. He was plummeting to sure death when the crumpled wings broke loose, freeing his canopy. He barely managed to get out in the time remaining—having already clawed his hands bloody in seeking a way out of the cockpit. As he struggled free a piece of sharp metal cut the side of his face, permanently scarring him and causing considerable loss of blood. Though he was flying again nine days later, the experience was a grim one.

In April he was involved in another mid-air collision and barely managed a safe landing as his wings were rapidly working loose from the fuselage, though again he was not to blame. 'Tuck's luck,' ground staff said it was. He had experienced luck on several other occasions. Once he was dismissed from the service for a traffic offence—which had cost him only ten shillings in a civilian court. Only his excellent flying record and gunnery grades, when reviewed by the Air Ministry, brought about the cancellation of his dismissal orders.

After successfully completing flight training, Tuck had been posted to 65 (East India) Squadron at Hornchurch, where after two years he was promoted to Flying Officer. (It was at Hornchurch that he experienced his two near-fatal crashes.) Shortly afterwards, a slightly more mature Tuck was selected from 65 Squadron to be tried out in the new Supermarine Spitfire. Only one pilot from each of the future Spitfire Squadrons was selected; it was a significant semi-official acknowledgment.

Tuck reported to Duxford R.A.F. Station at the end of the year. There the Chief Test Pilot for Vickers (Supermarine) Works, Jeffrey Quill (a former R.A.F. pilot), tested him in the Spit. Like all those who had never seen the sleek new fighter, he was overwhelmed. He spent an hour in the cockpit with Quill learning controls and procedure before his first take-off. As he manœuvred the new fighter around the sky he became more enthusiastic over it than over any he had flown. He returned to Hornchurch in January of the fateful year 1939 with glowing words of praise, words eagerly drunk in by fellow pilots of 65 Squadron. At that time—just seven months and three weeks before the war began—Tuck was one of very few pilots to have flown the Spitfire. It was not too early, for next year he would be flying one in his first combat over the beaches of Dunkirk, as Spitfires were committed in numbers by Fighter Command for the first time.

Tuck saw no combat, however, in the opening months of the war, to his bitter frustration. He was a relatively experienced veteran with 700 hours in his logbook. Yet other squadrons and young and inexperienced pilots were seeing action while 65 was held back. (Generally speaking, Fighter Command withheld its Spitfires and relied on Hurricanes until Dunkirk and the Battle of Britain.)

On 1 May 1940 he was posted from 65 to 92, based at Croydon. There he was promoted to Flight Lieutenant, which meant leading the second flight of six in squadron formation. It was with 92 Squadron, commanded by a South African who had become a well-known London barrister, Roger Bushell, that Tuck met the enemy for the first time. It is to this day that we now turn our attention.

On 10 May 1940 the German Army and Air Force struck at France and the Low Countries, and began the push to the coast and Paris which would knock Holland, Belgium and France out of the war in fifty days. R.A.F. Hurricane squadrons in France (at first there were six, then the number was doubled), handicapped by poor facilities and conditions, did what they could to stem the tide in vain. The rout became worse and worse on the ground, and the British Army was separated from the main French armies, its back to the sea. Fighter squadrons moved from one field to another, just ahead of the advancing German Army, and were finally recalled to England. Some 200 Hurricanes had been lost in the fighting and chaos, some having been burned on French fields as they were hastily evacuated.

These were serious losses for Fighter Command, which had at its disposal at the onset of the German offensive only about 800 operational fighters. The trapped British Army converged on Dunkirk by the hundreds of thousands, as did various French, Belgian and Dutch units. It soon became apparent that if the troops were to be brought back from the Continent, Dunkirk would have to be the point of evacuation. For this desperate operation Fighter Command would have to do everything possible to prevent the Luftwaffe from controlling the air over the evacuation beaches. Thus Fighter Command, though feeling acutely the losses in France, was compelled to make a major effort (which included the new Spitfire squadrons as well as Hurricanes) to protect the embarking army at Dunkirk. The Luftwaffe was given the assignment of destroying the retreating British, and thus the two air forces met, for the first time, in a major fighter confrontation relatively close to R.A.F. fighter bases. The struggle was sharp, and losses on both sides were heavy. The R.A.F. effort enabled thousands to be brought home who would not otherwise have made it. Yet some R.A.F. squadrons thrown into the fight lost almost half their strength in two or three days. One of these was Tuck's squadron, which also gave as good as it got. With Tuck flying as a flight leader, it went into action for the first time on 23 May. For Tuck it was a memorable day.

In one of the bedrooms of a two-storey brick officers' mess building at Northolt R.A.F. Station Batman Thomson, a mug of hot tea in his hand, shook Flight Lieutenant R. R. Stanford Tuck awake in the darkness before dawn on 23 May 1940. This spring morning 92 Squadron was to fly to Hornchurch, from where it would fly patrols over a port soon to be famous—Dunkirk. Pilots were eager, having seen no combat since the war began nine months earlier. Tuck greeted Thomson with the standard question: 'What's that bloody awful stuff you've got there?' Thomson gave him the standard reply: 'It's tea, sir.' Tuck drank it as he climbed out of bed, shaved and dressed—in blue trousers and tunic plus a red silk scarf, heavy white socks and black boots with sheepskin linings. Since he was to make a test flight to observe weather conditions, he wouldn't eat breakfast. After a cup of coffee with Squadron Leader Roger Bushell, they drove in a Humber to a little black dispersal hut on the edge of the perimeter. After a check with operations, Tuck walked out to his aircraft . . . a Spitfire I, fifty yards from the hut. His crew had warmed the engine and soon he was strapped in the cockpit, propeller turning. Since no one else was involved, there was no co-ordinating procedure to fuss with and Tuck gunned the engine and taxied out. Mist hung over the field but was lifting. Soon he was roaring across the grass, then into and through it, out and up into blue sky. Weather above—ideal After a few minutes he descended and with throttle back and flaps down found his way through the mist and fog patches and glided in for a landing. Taxi-ing to the hut, he hopped out and gave his assessment to operations by telephone: 'Okay to get the squadron off.' He then drove back to the officers' mess and enjoyed a robust breakfast of bacon and eggs. Shortly afterwards the pilots drove out to the dispersal hut to prepare for take-off.

Bushell led the squadron off east by south-east, and the twelve brownish-green Spitfires landed at Tuck's old home station of Hornchurch twenty minutes later. Here the twelve Spits of 92 Squadron would join three other squadrons (54,

Take-off at 10.45 a.m. and landing at 12.45 p.m.

Hornchurch
Dunkirk
Calais
Boulogne

## FIGHTER

SPITFIRE

Alone, Tuck recrosses Channel, lands undamaged at Hornchurch at 12.45 That afternoon Tuck again patrols Dunkirk, shooting down two more German aircraft

## FIGHTER SQUADRON

92 SQUADRON

## FIGHTER STATION

HORNCHURCH

**MISSION FLOWN BY:**

uck takes off as Flight
ommander (of six) in
fighter squadron
rmation for Dunkirk

HORNCHURCH

Reaches Dunkirk
and patrols above
evacuation, over
Dunkirk-Calais-
Boulogne

DUNKIRK

CALAIS

BOULOGNE

Squadron jumped from
above by gaggle of
Me. 109s, dogfight
developing

Tuck dives inland
after 109 leader,
catching him at bottom
of dive, opening fire

Shoots off aileron
and right wing,
109 plunges into
ground at low
altitude

R.A.F. FLIGHT LIEUTENANT R.R. STANFORD TUCK
23 MAY 1940

65 and 74) for the day's effort over Dunkirk. And it was here that pilots got final confirmation and details of the day's operations, at a briefing held by Group Captain (later Air Chief Marshal) Cecil ('Boy') Bouchier, who told senior pilots: 'For the first time, you'll be glad to know, we see action today . . . there's oil at Dunkirk in flames . . . an evacuation is underway . . . go in and attack any aircraft attacking our troops or ships.' Pilots were told they could expect to meet German fighter gaggles of up to forty aircraft. There were questions from squadron commanders about flying heights, weather and intelligence reports, and then all departed for their dispersal areas. Back at 92's hut, Bushell and Tuck discussed formation, heights and other data with tense pilots.

It was 10.30 when the phone in the hut rang and it was soon empty. Tuck had pulled on tan chammy gloves (over white silk ones) and, helmet-in-hand, was hurrying out to his Spit. He greeted the crew, jumped up on the port wing and lowered himself into the cockpit . . . where he immediately went to work. It was fast and disciplined: brakes set, trim—white lines together for take-off, flaps up, mags off, petrol full, undercarriage down and locked, radiator flaps open for maximum engine cooling. Satisfied, with oxygen connected and straps fastened, Tuck called 'All clear', and primed the engine. Being connected to the starter trolley, he pushed two buttons on the right of the panel (the fitter pressed a button connecting the trolley to his power supply) engaging the prop. It jerked once or twice, then faster, white and dark smoke puffs shooting back from the exhausts. The 1,175 horsepower Rolls-Merlin caught up, and the wind swept back over the open cockpit. The battery trolley was disconnected and the fitter jumped down off the wing. Tuck looked towards Bushell's fighter; the Squadron Leader was taxi-ing into take-off position. He signalled to his flight, released the brakes, and pushed the throttle forward. The Spitfire engine roared louder, fitter and rigger waved good luck, and he began to roll.

Five Spits follow in position . . . 92 will take off in two flights of six aircraft, each broken down further into two vics of three. Over the earphones comes the squadron commander's voice: 'Taking off.' Bushell is roaring across the field with the first three. Shortly afterwards three others follow. Tuck brakes to a stop, watches them lift into a clearing sky, and pushes the throttle almost to the limit. The first three fighters of his flight gather speed and grow lighter and lighter. Tuck pulls gently back on the stick, the Spit responds, leaving the grass rushing by below. Changing hands from throttle to stick and from stick to gear lever, he retracts the landing gear. Now he eases the throttle, closes the canopy, locking the butterfly switch overhead. A glance behind . . . flight off in order. He scans the sky for Bushell's six, sees them banking left ahead, and begins to close on the Squadron Leader. Tuck and 92 Squadron are off . . . on the way to their first dogfight. It is 10.50. (And though Tuck doesn't know it, it's his last day as flight commander.)

Tuck's six Spits rapidly cut off and form up with Bushell, and the squadron sets a south-easterly course for Dunkirk. The expert marksman switches on the gunsight; electricity throws an orange-red light ring and two horizontal bars on the glass in front of his eyes. (He can set the distance between bars with the knob at the bottom for enemy wing-spans.) It is working perfectly. He has scratched a nick in the windscreen with which he can aim if the gunsight fails and rehearses exactly where his head should be in sighting on the nick. His guns are specially loaded, with more than the usual percentage of De Wildes, combined armour-piercing and incendiary shells which leave tracers. The heavier loading of De Wildes fouls the barrels, but Tuck lets his armourers worry about that. He considers the De Wilde far more effective than normal ball ammunition. He turns his stick firing button from safety to fire. The squadron, reaching upwards, crosses out over the English coast at 5,000 feet.

The twelve Spits cut higher into the blue towards the morning sun . . . 6,000, 7,000, 8,000 feet. There's radio silence; nothing can be heard but the steady drone of the engines. Down below ships and boats leave their wakes as they move back and forth. A pall of smoke, rising up over the coast . . . far ahead . . . Dunkirk! One can see it a long way off. The formation, spread only slightly now, continues on course toward the evacuation port. Tuck sees several Hurricanes below, going home after an earlier patrol. Above there's a layer of stratus, but the squadron levels off well below it. Gradually the airspeed needle spirals upwards above 200 towards crusing speed; the climb is over. Pilots twist in their seats and scan both sky and beaches ahead, intensely interested in the drama beneath them. As the fighters approach the port, Bushell banks sharply left and leads the squadron up the coast. No enemy in sight but every pilot is searching . . . expecting. Staying at 8,000 feet, Bushell flies up the coast and banks to come back down—carrying out what orders describe as an 'offensive sortie'. But there are no enemy planes against which to take offensive action, at the moment. The squadron continues to patrol.

A black puff a short distance away—flak! A few more . . . far off course. The Germans are shooting from some distance; the squadron is in no immediate danger; Tuck has time to catch glimpses of movement below. He sees bomb explosions near ships off the beach. Where are the bombers? He scans the sky and doesn't find them. But he can't watch for long periods at a time since he must constantly maintain his formation and check his tail. He doesn't like the tight formation R.A.F. squadrons are trained to hold in close proximity to the enemy. It makes radical or quick movement dangerous, as he knows well, and shortens the time pilots have to observe the sky around them. The squadron hits a patch of bumpy air; the formation wavers, and quickly reforms. Tuck feels uneasy. On each reversal of course Bushell gives the order over the radio; now he orders: 'Turning right—go,' and the twelve fighters' left wings rise as they bank starboard in a 180-degree arc. They're over Dunkirk, and Tuck looks at the men nearest him on both sides. For some reason he waves to them, and they reply by holding up their fingers in a V-sign.

A shout over the earphones—Tuck can't make it out—an excited one. He turns his head quickly. Something happening . . . back left, coming down out of the cloud from above, fast . . . diving . . . fighters! Me.109s! They're almost on the Spits . . . coming straight for them. Tuck hits his throttle just as a Spitfire erupts into flames. It's happening fast. Radio silence is broken. Several pilots shout warnings. Bushell shouts a command. Chaos . . . Spit pilots act instinctively, and the squadron breaks up! Tuck banks off sharply and out of the line of fire, then back. The leading enemy 109, perhaps the pilot who exploded the Spit, flies right through the formation and on out ahead. Since he dived from perhaps 5,000 feet up, the German fighter has the all-important speed advantage which he can use to regain altitude and get out of range of the Spits and their eight .303 Brownings. Tuck watches the enemy leader, out in front to the right, checking his own tail as he keeps an eye on him. Could he get to him? In a split-second decision he decides he'll give it a try. Other fighters, Spits and Me.109s, are mixing in every direction. Tuck rams the throttle knob the rest of the way forward. The Rolls-Merlin bellows and Tuck eases forward slightly on the stick to gain airspeed. The enemy fighter is ahead, to his right, and he keeps his eyes locked on him . . . as he banks into a slight turn to the left, beginning to pull out of his long diving pass. Now Tuck has his chance. As the enemy fighter turns, he can turn inside him from behind and cut him off. He pushes the stick sharply left and keeps his nose down. The enemy pilot apparently hasn't seen him. The Spit closes in the sharper turn. Now the enemy is banking harder left. Tuck eases forward on the stick, holding it left, and begins to feel the excitement as the 109's silhouette appears in the centre of his gunsight glass.

He manoeuvres his pedals and stick to get in position for firing. He banks more sharply left to move the sighting circle in front of the smaller Me.109's pointed nose. The 109 is obviously making good speed, but in the cut-off turn Tuck stays on him and is coming into range. All his training, all his preparation in the pre-war years, has been for this moment, his first combat in the Second World War. As one of the best gunners in the service, he *should* be able to do to the low-wing German fighter ahead of him what he has done to so many towed targets in firing practice through the years. But he has never fired at a human being in another fighter . . . until now. In range! Checking again to see if the banking fighter is properly compensated for in the sight—it is—Tuck presses his thumb down. Eight ·303 Brownings roar, and the Spit vibrates. He has heard the sound many times and seen the towed sleeve ripple in the wind as shells passed through it. But never has he seen the effects of eight guns on another aircraft. And so as the roar of the guns adds to the engine's roar he tensely watches the enemy fighter ahead.

The first signs of accuracy are vapours from the tracers . . . they lead straight and true into the top of the 109, still banking left and pulling up sharply from its dive. Now Tuck can see his shells striking the right wing. The enemy has given him a big target . . . he's pulling up in front of the Spit roaring down from behind and showing a large wing-area. Tuck's shells continue to penetrate the right wing and he sees pieces fly off backwards. The 109 continues pulling up, Tuck easing back slightly on the stick to follow. Now its right aileron tears away from the right wing, flies backwards, tumbling and turning down. Tuck keeps the 109 squarely in his sight and shells pour into the damaged right wing.

The wing being one of the 109's weakest points (German pilots have been known to pull them off in dives), Tuck's accurate fire is fatal. The Messerschmitt seems to dip and begin to level off; then Tuck is startled. The whole right wing separates from the fuselage, falling slowly downwards as the heavier fuselage and left wing go into a faster plunge. Tuck, no longer firing, watches fascinated as his first victim of the war spirals toward the coast below. Checking behind to be sure he has no visitors, he banks back and forth just long enough to see the fuselage and left wing strike the ground.

The right wing is still tumbling, falling more slowly. And now he looks back, up and around. He is alone. Having chased the enemy inland, he has become separated from his squadron. Like all lone fighters over enemy territory he is vulnerable. Quickly he swings the nose of the Spit around into the north-west . . . toward England and Hornchurch. He is back on cruising throttle now, and will have ample fuel provided he doesn't encounter another enemy gaggle.

The coast of Dunkirk is just below and he approaches the water, wondering how many of the squadron were hit, how many Spits went down and how many of the enemy the squadron accounted for. A glance at his watch shows that it's exactly 12.10—he has been airborne about an hour and a half. Over the Channel now, he regularly looks back. But no enemy aircraft are to be seen and gradually he begins to relax and thinks in snatches of his first victory over the fastest and best of the enemy's aircraft—a good start. The minutes tick by with Tuck reflecting, feeling more secure and somewhat flushed with the excitement of this first success. In another minute or two the coast of England is in view . . . faintly, stretching like a low line on the horizon ahead. It's friendly land and a welcome sight.

Off to one side, below, he sees a shadow racing across the tops of the waves, to the north-west. He looks above and sees what's making it . . . another fighter. He looks closely at the shape of the wings . . . Spitfire! He does have company, though the other Spit is a few thousand feet below. Now he presses the mike button and tries to reach 'Cornflower', the code name for Hornchurch. No response. He calls again. Cornflower comes in. Tuck reports his position, estimating that he will be over the field in ten minutes. Now at least they know Bushell's flight leader is not a victim. He crosses in and sets course for the field, just to the east of London. The green of the countryside flashes beneath his wings faster and faster as he loses altitude. In a few minutes he picks out the open space ahead which is Hornchurch, and calls for permission to land, which is immediately granted. He turns into the circular pattern after dropping his wheels, and lowers flaps. He comes back on the throttle to cut the Spit's speed, and rolls out of the bank just 300 feet above the ground on the final approach. His speed drops as he holds the nose up and settles in . . . 130, 120, 110. The ground is rushing up. Over the boundary. Hold her off. Thump! Stick back. Keep her rolling straight by juggling pedals.

The Spit slows to turning speed and Tuck taxies straight to his parking area, canopy back, looking ahead at his waiting crewmen. He pulls up, wheels the Spit around and breaks into a smile as he cuts the throttle and the engine dies. 12.45. Fitter and rigger scamper up to greet him. He tells them of victory number one and as they offer congratulation he's suddenly aware of intense activity all around him. Crewmen are readying other Spits near by. Some pilots are already by their planes. He is one of the last back. Crewmen say there might be another patrol!

He hurries to the hut, where he fires questions at other pilots as they fire away at him. Several have victories. Most of the squadron got back safely. But Pat Learmond is missing. Bushell is depressed over the loss, as is Tuck. But what's the form—the talk of another patrol? The squadron is on standby for another scramble, another patrol over Dunkirk! He describes his victory to the Intelligence Officer (and a few comrades) and learns that the total for the squadron, in the wild fight that morning, was five victories claimed for the loss of one. Everyone is happy about the ratio. Tuck eats lunch after congratulations from all around and then returns to the dispersal hut. But no new orders arrive and time passes slowly. Hours go by. It is 3, 4, then 5 p.m.

Then—a call from operations. Take off! Once again he is hurrying out of the door and out to the Spit. For the second time Bushell leads six fighters off, Tuck following with six more. It is 5.20. Course setting the same, 92 Squadron heads back for the Dunkirk beaches. The morning's victories have whetted their appetites, and thoroughly stimulated everyone. The twelve Spits—a replacement pilot is flying in

Learmond's place—cross out over the Channel. Once more Tuck turns on and checks his gunsight, switches on the guns. No combat for nine months, now two patrols in one day!

Formation is again too tight, in Tuck's opinion, but the style is still holy writ in the R.A.F. The neatly formed squadron gains altitude as it aims straight for Dunkirk. In minutes the heavy smoke pall is in sight ahead. And in another few minutes Dunkirk is in sight. At Bushell's command, the squadron, now at 10,000 feet, banks into a turn to begin patrol. It's 5.45 and the sun is sinking in the west. Tuck keeps formation and scans the sky, especially above since the squadron is low, to protect troops and ships. That leaves a lot of sky and sun in the west and more than one pilot thinks of the First War slogan of Allied fighter pilots— *Beware of the Hun in the sun.* It's a clear afternoon and the intense activity of troops, vehicles and ships below is easily observed.

Over the earphones . . . shouts! Tuck makes out one of the voices—enemy aircraft diving from above. (Several pilots see the enemy at the same time.) He jerks his head up, looks above. Bushell orders a left turn, into a sort of Lufberry, a defensive circling manœuvre. Tension building, pilots follow . . . keep their eyes on the sky above. Tuck sees little dark forms coming down steeply . . . they're bigger than single-engined fighters. He sees two-engined nacelles in front . . . but they're not bombers, not attacking Spits in dives. Me.110s! Twin-engined German fighters! It's the first time he has seen them. They're armed with cannon and machine-guns forward, a rear gunner and swivel gun directly behind the pilot.

Tuck watches them come on, as Bushell leads the twelve Spits round in a tight circle. The enemy gaggle is large . . . twenty or thirty. Tuck has little time to worry about the odds. The leading 110 comes on . . . headed straight for the Spitfires. Now the light flashes from his guns and tracers spew out toward the circling Spits. At this moment 92 Squadron pilots begin manœuvring for themselves. Other 110s are just behind the leader, streaking in to the attack. Each pilot looks out for his own tail and tries to escape the line of fire and get in position to go after one of the enemy attackers. Tuck banks sharply to evade the path of enemy fire. Spits in position to give them head-on bursts open fire. Tuck looks for a shot, a victim. He must bank vertically to avoid one zooming 110 and then another . . . he notices the 110s are banking too, to mix with the Spitfires. They're not going through the formation and down and out to escape. Dogfights are therefore developing in every direction.

Suddenly a dark form lifts from below his nose, almost directly ahead . . . a twin-engined form . . . a 110! Tuck's left hand rams the throttle forward. The 110 is banking slightly; the rear gunner, startled, sees the Spit just behind him. He whirls his machine-gun and opens fire. Tuck sees tracers stream back towards him as he frantically pushes his rudder pedals and depresses the stick slightly to bring his guns to bear on the enemy fighter. Too late. Thump! Thump! He hears the hits . . . sees the tracers come straight at him. He instinctively ducks for a second . . . smells cordite . . . he is hit. He must do something fast . . . a quick glance through the gunsight glass. The 110's wings in range . . . his thumb presses the firing button. Meanwhile, shells ricochet off his heavy windscreen and several penetrate the bottom of the cockpit . . . where the cordite smell is coming from. But his heavier fire (eight guns against one) turns the tide . . . the De Wilde loading shatters the lightly-constructed Me.110, armour-piercing and incendiary shells rip straight through the glass into the rear gunner's compartment, who is no longer firing. The black-helmeted face is looking at him no longer, gun stilled.

By now Tuck is very close. The 110 makes the slightest turn . . . Tuck presses his thumb down again. This time the stream of tracer leads to the port engine. At such close distance the shells smash the wing and engine nacelle (his guns pour out ·303 shells at a rate of more than a hundred per second). It's too much for the enemy fighter, which now emits a thin stream of dark smoke from the left engine. The 110 begins to yaw . . . one way and then the other. The pilot is losing control or dead. The Messerschmitt is rolling over.

Tuck stops firing, watches . . . he is almost on the enemy's tail. Over it goes on its back . . . the nose starts down and the stricken Messerschmitt dives for the beaches below. A column of smoke from the port engine marks its descent. Victory number two!

All around the dogfight is still raging. Tuck is not alone as he was in the morning after his victory over the 109. To the right and left he can see fighters, diving and turning . . . and over the earphones hears shouts and warnings about too much radio chatter. He shouts a command into the mike for pilots to quiet down but the calls continue. He steps on the rudder and banks into the centre of activity . . . just then a Spit passes near by, on the tail of a fleeing 110. He recognizes Tony Bartley . . . almost eating up the enemy's tail with his propeller as the 110 is taking hits. To the side there's a sight not so encouraging. A Spit plunges downwards in flames. Tuck thinks it's Sergeant Klipsch; he sees no one get out and the heavy thought is on his mind when . . . thump, thump, thump! Hit again! Tuck snaps his head . . . there, ahead, coming straight on, light blinks on the leading edge of the wing—Me.110!

He lines up the oncoming silhouette, using his rudder and stick, and presses his thumb. The 110 comes on . . . he thinks he sees hits, but from head-on one can see little and the enemy aircraft offers a slim target, only engines and the leading edges of the wings. The two fighters close at nearly 600 miles an hour and Tuck has only seconds to zero in . . . the ·303s are scoring . . . but he's almost on the enlarging, oncoming silhouette. He's headed straight for the enemy machine . . . neither pilot changes course, both keep firing. Neither wishes to present the other with an enlarged target by pulling up. It is, in a sense, a question of nerve. Tuck ducks his head, knowing the two fighters will crash. They converge, there's a zoom. The enemy fighter went over or under . . .

77

Tuck's not sure which.

He looks behind . . . there! The 110 is banking east, inland, turning away . . . not coming back. Tuck has fired a lot of ammunition, but may have enough left . . . if he can catch him. He stands on the starboard wing and dips stick. The enemy is diving earthwards. He's more than a mile away and Tuck cuts off some distance in the turn. The Spit is once more at full throttle. The 110 is not as fast as the 109 and Tuck, diving at full power, gains steadily. The enemy spots him now, sticks his nose down steeper. Tuck follows, closing fast. He will catch him and soon. The 110 is near the deck, obviously heading for home. Tuck can see the rear gunner sitting facing him, waiting, his gun trained backwards. He is quickly coming within range. The 110 is hugging the tops of trees now as the Spit roars up from the rear—500 yards, 400 yards. Tuck looks through his gunsight and steadies his aircraft. The enemy pilot attempts to throw his aim off, jinking and skidding. But Tuck waits and eases up on him . . . closer, closer, making slight corrections . . . now . . . in range. Fire! Tracers streak toward the 110; the rear gunner fires back. What look like white roman-candle balls reach back, arching slightly in the wind. Whump! Tuck feels a hit. He sees another on his windscreen. The enemy gunner is good.

They're so close to tree tops and roofs that one mistake would be the last. He sees hits on the 110. But the enemy pilot turns and banks. Tuck fires again, a short burst. The enemy pilot dips. Just ahead . . . high tension cables. The German goes under them. Tuck hesitates, pulls up at the last minute. As he does his belly is exposed. The rear gunner fires immediately and Tuck hears the thumping below. He's taking hits. He must get the gunner before the Spit is fatally hit over enemy-occupied territory. Nose down, now after him. The enemy pilot still takes evasive action, but this time Tuck hangs on him with fierce determination . . . in sight . . . in range . . . flying straight and level. Fire! Tuck doesn't know how much more ammunition he has but he must get the gunner first. The Spit is almost on him. Hits register on the back of the enemy's canopy. The gunner drops limp, the long barrel dips over the side and swings loosely. He has him!

The pilot ahead knows it. He banks sharply. Tuck follows. The Me.110 is at his mercy. It streaks towards an open field ahead. Tuck is levelling out behind, about ready to press his thumb, but the 110 is lower, lower . . . slowing. He's over-running him; he banks away. The 110 is going down. He watches as the twin-engined machine skims the field, touches . . . ploughs a furrow amid a cloud of dirt and dust. Tuck banks again, flying round the crash, and sees the pilot jump clear. He stands by the aircraft, looking up at the low-flying Spit. A good pilot . . . but the Spit was too fast for him. Tuck passes over, flaps down . . . he slides the canopy back and waves at his beaten foe. A hole appears in the side of his canopy; a little thump, and there it is. He looks back. The enemy pilot stands with something in his hand. Did he shoot? Tuck's blood comes to a boil. He stands the Spit on a wing and streaks back down, pointing his nose at the crashed 110 and the pilot nearby. Before the enemy pilot has time to move, or know what he is in for, the Spit is on him, a few feet over the ground. Tuck presses the button. There is still ammunition. The guns spit a line of shells, the dirt ahead kicks up and the 110 is ripped open and blazes. Tuck doesn't see what happens to the enemy pilot—but this time no bullets strike the Spitfire. He pulls up and heads for the coast.

Now he feels the effect of the battle and the long day. He is alone and low and deep over enemy territory. He must get home without being bounced. He keeps the Spit's nose pointing west and continues to climb, constantly checking the sky behind. Mercifully, it's clear. He has little time to think of his two victories . . . three for the day! His thoughts are on navigation, fuel and the enemy. As he gains altitude he sees the coast ahead, Dunkirk off to his side. He banks into the north-west and soon flashes across the beaches . . . towards England.

After a few minutes he feels more secure, though still looking back. Off to the side, another aircraft . . . same course . . .

Spit. He edges over. The Spit slides in toward him: 92 Squadron. Tony Bartley! He looks closer at Bartley's aircraft, sees many holes. Bartley radios him, remarks that Tuck's Spit is badly holed! They stick together and make for Hornchurch. The English coast is visible ahead and soon they are crossing in . . . both engines still running. But Tuck's engine gauges are creeping up into the red. His coolant has all leaked out. The Merlin continues to turn but is beginning to sound rough. And the temperature goes higher and higher.

The field appears ahead! Bartley is beside him; Tuck tells him he's in trouble. Tony tells him to land first, that he can wait. Tuck dips his nose and eases back on the throttle to come down. At that moment his engine begins to clank, and to miss badly. He looks at the needles—all the way in the red, at the stop. He must sit her down, no pattern—straight in. He lowers the landing gear and watches the airspeed drop steadily, pushes the stick forward and glides in. He won't make the normal landing area . . . he's short. The engine clanks to a dead stop. No power. Tuck must put it down. He just makes it to a grass strip by the control tower. Stick, back, rudder pedals . . . a bump, bump . . . she's rolling along, propeller frozen in position. She tries to veer to the right. Tuck has to use heavy left brake and left rudder to keep her straight. Obviously the right tyre is flat. He manages to avoid a ground loop and finally the battered fighter rolls to a stop. Tuck slowly raises himself and unhooks straps and wires, steps out on the left wing. Now he can see the holes up and down the fuselage and in the wings. The first man to drive up is Bouchier, the field commander, who is agitated. He shouts to Tuck immediately that he'll have to move the aircraft. Obviously ruffled, he suggests Tuck knows quite well he can't park there. Bouchier is worried about other aircraft landing, colliding with Tuck's Spitfire. As he briskly strides up, still shouting instructions to move the fighter, Tuck looks him in the eye with a curious expression. Bouchier walks closer, takes a look at the Spit, stops talking. He looks at the flat tyre, the holes, the damage up and down. Then he realizes the absurdity of it all, and suddenly bursts out in self-conscious laughter. He laughs so loudly and in such good humour that Tuck begins to laugh with him.

From that first day of combat, Tuck waged a fierce war against the Luftwaffe for almost eighteen months. On many other occasions in that period he charged in close to the enemy, risking and taking hits to destroy his adversary.

At the end of its first day in combat, 92 Squadron had lost five pilots including Bushell (almost half a squadron). These were exceptionally heavy losses for one day and at that rate of attrition the squadron would be wiped out in three days. However, the next day losses were not so bad, though fighting was again heavy. On that day Tuck led the squadron successfully, intercepting a formation of Do.17 bombers sent to bomb Dunkirk. In the attack which broke up the enemy formation and chased the bombers away Tuck shot down one and then climbed back into the formation and got another. But he was again hit by return fire from the formation and brought back a heavily damaged Spitfire. 'Tuck's luck', however, saved him again, though this time he had a bullet in his hip. He continued to lead 92 with distinction, adding steadily to his victories. He soon became one of the R.A.F.'s most publicized and admired squadron leaders, and one of his country's highest-scoring fighter pilots. But 92 Squadron was pulled out of close proximity to the enemy before the start of the Battle of Britain, and did not engage in many of the July, August and early September battles. Nevertheless, Tuck managed to find Ju.88 bombers which were often over Wales, and he shot down a number, twice being badly hit by their cannon fire and once baling out at 500 feet after particularly heavy damage. By the middle of September he had given up command of 92 and taken over 257 Squadron (Hurricanes). He led this squadron into the raging Battle of Britain on 15 September, when he shot down an Me.110, and moulded it into one of the R.A.F.'s outstanding fighter squadrons. He had eighteen victories by the end of 1940.

In July 1941 he was promoted to command of the Duxford wing and was back in Spitfires. He led the wing with much success until, late in the year, he was sent to the United States to advise on combat and training techniques. He enjoyed this American interlude, during which he engaged in (and won) a pistol match with General H. H. ('Hap') Arnold, Commanding General of the U.S. Army Air Corps. He was given a warm welcome everywhere; in New York, Rita Hayworth, then one of Hollywood's brightest stars, escorted him. (But Tuck had already met the girl who was to be his wife while leading the Burma Squadron—Joyce Ackerman. He had met her one night in Norwich at a dance. He found in Joyce a refuge and the stabilizing influence he so badly needed. After knowing her a few months he never wavered in his goal of marriage, even throughout three years in a prison camp—where she wrote to him regularly. Asked recently what the colour of her dress was on the night they met, she replied unhesitatingly: 'Blue.' Asked what her first impression of Tuck had been, she smiled and said: 'I thought he was smashing.')

Returning to England from the United States near the end of 1941, Tuck was given command of the Biggin Hill wing. Leading this wing in January 1942, he was shot down by anti-aircraft fire while strafing ground targets near Boulogne. By that time he had twenty-nine confirmed victories. He was captured by German soldiers but only after he had turned on the gun crew that had hit him and destroyed them and their vehicle. Shortly afterwards occurred a remarkable conversation with a German fighter pilot then leading Luftwaffe fighters against the R.A.F., Oberstleutnant Adolf Galland. Galland knew of Tuck, for the last time they had met in the air he had almost caught Tuck from behind. He sent him an invitation to dine with Jagdgeschwader 26 on the first night after his capture. As he greeted Tuck he remarked that he had almost killed him in their last meeting. Tuck reflected a moment and recalled the mission. He had been leading the wing on a fighter sweep, and had been bounced by 109s from above. The two leading 109s passed through the rear of the Spit formation, coming straight on for the leader—Tuck. At the last second Tuck desperately banked away, but the Messerschmitt behind him had shot down his wingman. Tuck had, in turn, shot down Galland's wingman. 'So that was you,' Tuck said. 'I got your number two as he passed in front.' Galland replied: 'And I got yours, which makes us—how do you say it—even stevens?'

Tuck was sent to a prison camp (Stalag Luft III), where he was to meet Bushell, Douglas Bader and many others. He escaped death only through good luck on several occasions. Once, when due to take part in what has since become known as 'the Great Escape' (the book of that title, by Paul Brickhill, gives the story in detail), he was suddenly transferred to another camp for two weeks. The escape went off as planned, and seventy-six prisoners tunnelled out. But all but three were recaptured and fifty, including Roger Bushell, were shot by the Gestapo.

After repeated attempts, he succeeded in escaping from a camp in Poland in the bitter January of 1945. For weeks he moved with a fellow escapee at night, eastwards, towards advancing Russian armies. Several times he was almost trapped by German soldiers. Frost-bitten and half-starved, he finally met the Russians, who almost shot him before accepting his story. He couldn't prevail upon them to send him to Russia, and was forced to fight the Germans for two weeks, retracing his escape route to the west. Finally, he escaped from the Russians and made his way from Poland to Russia, where he managed to telephone the British Embassy in Moscow. The Embassy advised him to catch the next train to Moscow, which he did.

From Moscow he was sent to Odessa, where he boarded a ship for England and within a week after his return he and Joyce were married.

Tuck's total of victories is remarkable in that at the end of the war he was still the eighth-ranking pilot in the R.A.F., though he had been a prisoner-of-war for three years! In post-war years he has been recognized as one of the greatest fliers of the war, both by former foes like Adolf Galland and by his comrades. He was awarded the D.S.O., the D.F.C. and 2 bars and the American D.F.C. The boy who almost failed at flying training school and who had been the object of a special effort by his instructors had proved worth that effort.

# CHAPTER FIVE

# BADER INTERCEPTS EAST OF LONDON

*30 August 1940—Squadron Leader D. R. S. Bader, R.A.F.*

AMONG ALL the stories about Allied fighter pilots in the Second World War, perhaps the most inspiring is that of Group Captain Douglas Bader. Many readers will be familiar with this story which has been told in Paul Brickhill's *Reach for the Sky*[1] and in the film of the same title. Nevertheless, a brief summary is here in order.

Douglas Robert Steuart Bader was the younger son of Frederick and Jessie Bader, and was born in London in 1910. In 1914 his father went to war, dying after the Armistice while still in France from the lingering effects of a shrapnel wound. Douglas had hardly known him.

Though his mother was eventually married again—to a Yorkshire clergyman—Bader's father's death had made it necessary that he win a scholarship if he were eventually to attend a public school. Finances had become a primary family consideration. Aware of his limited circumstances, Bader studied conscientiously and won a scholarship; at thirteen and a half he was off to St Edward's, Oxford, where he excelled at studies and sports. As his next goal he elected to sit the competitive examination to Cranwell—the Royal Air Force College—in an effort to win one of only six prized cadetships. He studied long hours for months, was placed fifth in the competitive examination and thus was admitted to the Royal Air Force's élite cadet school as a result of his own efforts.

At Cranwell he excelled in all sports—he had captained the rugger team at St Edward's—and discovered his ability

[1] Collins, 1954.

and liking for boxing, at which he became a knock-out expert. He also began to take a somewhat light-hearted view of studies. This and frequent breaking of minor regulations led to a stern warning that no more of his exuberance would be tolerated. Threatened with dismissal, Bader buckled down almost overnight becoming once again a serious student. He graduated in 1930.

His first post was with 23 Squadron at Kenley, where he flew Gloster Gamecock fighters and became well known throughout the Royal Air Force in athletics and in acrobatic flying. So good was he at rugger that he was selected to play for the R.A.F. team. So good was his flying that he was also chosen to perform at the annual R.A.F. display at Hendon before 175,000 people. *The Times* described his performance and that of his Flight Commander, Harry Day, as the most impressive air exhibition ever witnessed in England. Bader was on top of the world, a member of the Combined Services XV, a recognized leader of men, favourably publicized, sought after by the opposite sex.

At that time 23 Squadron was re-equipped with the heavier Bulldog fighter, faster but less manœuvrable than the Gamecock. It was in a Bulldog that Bader suffered an experience which was, in the course of time, to make him a legend. On a December morning in 1931 he was flying a routine training mission with two fellow pilots. The three officers landed at an auxiliary strip and after take-off Bader did a roll over the field at low altitude. Having fractionally misjudged height or speed or the heavier Bulldog's performance, his wing caught the ground as he was coming out and he crashed.

He was rushed to the nearest hospital in critical condition, and their his life hung by a very thin thread. He was so weak that surgeons would not immediately amputate his right leg, which was necessary, but waited until he recovered just a bit from shock, an hour or so later. He then barely survived post-operative shock. Some days later the left leg also had to be amputated. It was another stern test for his constitution but he survived. The famous pilot and athlete, with such recent promise as a flyer and sportsman, was a legless man.

Now began a story which was to capture the imagination of a nation and later of the world. Bader was determined not to let the loss of his legs halt his flying career. Yet there was no precedent for a legless man accomplishing what Bader set out to accomplish now. Though friends and attendants humoured him few believed he would ever fly again or even continue in the service. The majority seemed right many times. Bader suffered heart-breaking disappointments. Perhaps the most bitter came after he had mastered (through much effort) two artificial legs, had learned to walk and to drive a car and had been tested at the Central Flying School —where he passed. Instructors had found his flying ability unimpaired. Thinking the battle largely won at last—and it had been a long, hard one—he reported to the Medical Board which alone could give him final clearance to fly solo again. Since the Medical Board (perhaps convinced he would fail at flying school) had sent him off to be flight tested, Bader assumed he would be cleared. Instead, the senior medical officer, somewhat embarrassed, told him the Board could not approve his clearance because there was 'nothing in regulations' to cover his case!

After he had shown in flight tests that he could meet requirements in the air, it was a shattering blow. Bader was assigned to the Transport section at Duxford fighter station. Here he soon received an equally staggering blow. He was called in by the acting station commander, an old friend, who confessed he was doing the hardest thing he had ever been asked to do in the Royal Air Force. He handed Bader a letter from the Air Ministry. It was brief and to the point, noting: (1), that in view of the final finding of the Medical Board, Bader could no longer serve in the General Duties Branch of the Royal Air Force; (2), suggested, therefore, that Bader retire on the grounds of ill health; and (3), stated that a further communication would be sent proposing a date, disability pension and retirement pay. The Royal Air Force had been and was Bader's life and home; thus the effect of this letter can be imagined.

Perhaps the development which saved him from utter despair was his growing fondness for a girl he had met while convalescing after his accident—Thelma Edwards. To her he turned for comfort and companionship in times of disappointment and by now they were close. Yet he had little to offer a prospective wife—a legless ex-flyer with a total pension and disability pay of £200.

He visited an employment agency in search of a job. After an interview he was hired by the Asiatic Petroleum Company at a salary of £200 a year. Not long afterwards he and Thelma were secretly married. But because they were still unable to afford a home she continued to live with her family and they announced only that they were engaged. It was October 1933. At Christmas-time he won a fifty-pound-a-year rise but it was still not enough to enable them to have a home of their own. Not until 1937, four years after they were secretly married, had they saved enough to rent a flat in West Kensington and buy furniture. Then they were married in a church ceremony. By that time Bader had won the admiration of many by mastering the game of golf—he now went round in the low eighties. (As far as anyone knew, no legless man had ever managed that.) Bader also played tennis, though more handicapped because of its demands for quick movement.

By the time of the Munich crisis, September 1938, Bader knew war was inevitable; he wrote to the Air Ministry requesting a refresher course in flying. The Ministry responded negatively, saying he was considered a permanent accident risk, but inquiring whether he would be interested in an administrative job. Bader turned it down. He still had his heart set on flying. Six months later he tried again. In the spring of 1939 he wrote to the new head of personnel in the Air Ministry, with whom a close friend had spoken on his behalf. Air Marshal Sir Charles Portal responded in what appeared at first to be another negative reply but close examination of the letter revealed the change in tone. Portal wrote that in peacetime Bader would not be permitted to join the flying reserve, but added that in the event of war he could rest assured that the Air Ministry would 'almost certainly' welcome his services in a flying capacity, if the doctors agreed. He had opened the door a bit.

Hitler invaded Poland in September and war came to Europe for the second time in twenty-five years. Bader began bombarding friends and officials with requests for recall. Finally, in October, he was ordered to report for a medical. It had been six years since his chances to continue flying had been dashed by just such a medical. When he entered the room to begin the examination and introduced himself, he found everyone assumed he was seeking a ground job. When an officer questioning him asked what kind of job he preferred, he was somewhat shaken and replied in certain terms that he was only interested in flying. The officer (Air Vice-Marshal Halahan) had been his commandant at Cranwell and told him he was only dealing with ground jobs. Bader's hopes sank, but he expressed his determination once more. After a pause, Halahan wrote out a note, told him to take it across to the medical people and wished him good luck.

Medical personnel—not encouragingly—remarked casually that he could never be classified A.1.B. But Bader countered with optimism. He finished the examination and came to the final interview—across the desk from a medical officer, where he had been disappointed six years earlier. The officer began by saying that aside from his legs he was completely fit. Then he showed him Halahan's note—the highest recommendation. Then he paused. Bader, recalling the moment years later, felt the officer did not want to face him. There was a silence with Bader looking straight into his eyes and finally the medical officer said he agreed with Halahan—and gave him A.1.B.! It was an unforgettable moment. He was back in the R.A.F., A.1.B., after six years of struggle and separation. When he returned home to Thelma and broke the news it was with some emotion on both their parts.

He was ordered to report to the Central Flying School at Upavon on 18 October 1939, for his first test flight. Luckily, a former cadet classmate at Cranwell, Squadron Leader Rupert Leigh, was to give him his test and that eased the tension; he passed easily. It had been the first time he had flown in seven years. He was accepted for a full refresher course, and on 27 November 1939 the moment at last came when his instructor stepped out of the cockpit and told him to take off, alone. He taxied the Tudor out and took off, flew twenty-five solo minutes, and landed. It had been a long road back.

He completed the refresher course in February 1940, and was posted to 19 Squadron as a Flying Officer. He won promotion to flight commander (rank of Flight Lieutenant) in April—with 222 Squadron. And it was with 222 at the end of May that he saw his first combat. The unit was one of those Spitfire squadrons which had been held back for just such an emergency. Posted far to the north (Kirton-in-Lindsay), it was ordered to Martlesham near the Suffolk coast one day at dawn. Bader and other pilots knew little of what was happening on the other side of the water, where the beaten British Army and remnants of others were converging on Dunkirk. For several days 222 patrolled the beaches at Dunkirk and saw the situation at first hand and then on the morning of the 31st, as the Spits were chasing off a formation of Me.110s, they were bounced by a gaggle of Me.109s. In a fierce dogfight Bader coolly shot down one of the German fighters, becoming separated from the rest of the squadron in the process, and flew home alone. That afternoon he flew another patrol and sent an He.111 bomber down in flames, another Spit joining him in the final seconds after he had killed the rear gunner and set fire to the bomber. The 'legless wonder', as E. C. R. Baker calls Bader and as he was to be known later, had passed the test of combat against the enemy's best fighter. He was definitely A.1.B.

In June 1940 Bader was promoted to Acting Squadron Leader (which meant he had caught up with most of his

Cranwell class in rank) and given command of 242 (Hurricane) Squadron. Leading the squadron was quite a challenge and Air Officer Commanding 12 Group, Air Vice-Marshal Trafford Leigh-Mallory, who knew Bader well, chose him especially for the job. The squadron was composed primarily of Canadians and had served in France amid the confusion and demoralization of the Allied rout and evacuation. With inadequate facilities, co-ordination and control it had suffered fifty per cent casualties. Pilots were either bitter or disgusted, leadership was lacking, and a dynamic leader was needed to restore morale. It was into this situation, at Coltishall near Norwich, that Bader arrived as the new, and legless, squadron leader. When some of the Canadian pilots heard the news about his incapacity, they assumed he would do little flying and prove to be a somewhat inactive leader. It was one of the worst guesses of the war.

Bader lost little time in rejuvenating 242. Replacing two flight commanders immediately, stressing neat appearance and discipline, setting an energetic (and precision flying) example, he infused a new spirit into the squadron. When he encountered inefficiency in supply and maintenance of spare parts and tools he raised such a storm of protest the bitterness reached all the way to the Commander-in-Chief of Fighter Command—who called Bader in to report. The result was that a supply officer at Coltishall and a higher ranking one at Fighter Command were removed from their jobs within twenty-four hours. The spare parts and tools for Bader's Hurricanes then arrived immediately. In short, he was a doer; he got things done and his pilots were soon infected with the spirit.

As the Battle of Britain opened in July and continued into August, 242 was still not ordered south into the fray and Bader was beside himself with impatience. He was so keen to get at the enemy, so eager to have a go, that when 242 was finally allowed to take part every pilot in the squadron was psychologically ready. The squadron did not participate in the battle until 30 August, weeks after the heaviest Luftwaffe assaults had begun. Since 242 was a 12 Group squadron, based near Norwich, considerably north of the battle area, it was too far removed to engage the enemy unless flown to a more southerly field in the early morning and scrambled there once the enemy's course had been charted on radar. Bader repeatedly and even impatiently requested that his squadron be used in this way. Finally, he was given his chance. It is to this day, 30 August, and 242's first interception of the Luftwaffe during the Battle of Britain, that we now turn.

The 29th of August—in that exceptionally fine summer of 1940—had been rainy but the 30th dawned fair over the Channel to the south and over Norfolk. North of Norwich lay Coltishall Fighter Station, on which Hurricanes of 242 Squadron, dispersed about the grass, were being warmed up as the clear sky brightened in the east.

Bader's batman, Stokoe, walked down the hall of the two-storey brick officers' mess, opened a bedroom door and found the Squadron Leader awake. Bader was a light sleeper and Stokoe seldom caught him asleep. He bade the Squadron Leader a respectful good morning, left a cup of tea by his bed, near a pair of artificial legs, and departed. It was 6 a.m. Bader was out of bed in an instant, made his way, on his hands, to the adjoining bathroom and into the tub for a bath and a shave with a Gillette safety razor. He was out of the tub and back in the bedroom in fifteen minutes, and put on his legs—as quickly as other pilots put on their shoes. He dressed in blue uniform, black tie, and wrapped a blue scarf with white dots around his neck. At 6.25 he was in the mess, sitting at a long table and talking to 66 Squadron Leader Rupert Leigh (66 was also stationed at Coltishall) and other pilots.

He ate a light breakfast of toast, butter and marmalade, his thoughts all the while turning to the day's flying. He was eager to get out to the dispersal hut and his hopes were, of course, to fly south to take part in the interception of the Luftwaffe. He and his pilots had been waiting for the chance for weeks. Thus, after only a few minutes at the breakfast table, he was walking out of the mess with that special gait, the only visual betrayal of artificial legs. He plopped into a Standard four-seater waiting outside and drove off to the dispersal area where he and other 242 pilots were soon fetching Mae Wests, checking flying equipment, drinking tea and waiting. During recent weeks of heavy fighting the pilots of 242 had sat it out in the hut and this morning began no differently. But in a few minutes the telephone rang.

Bader answered. It was Operations and what he heard produced visible enthusiasm. Other pilots began to take an interest. Bader put down the receiver and shouted triumphantly: 'All right chaps. we'll start out!' A ripple of excitement ran through the hut as pilots scurried out toward their planes. Bader's fighter was just outside—a short walk—and he was already standing by the brownish-green Hurricane as the others departed in a van to be dropped off at other aircraft. The crew had already started the Hurricane and the wind swept backwards over the grass. His parachute always remained in the cockpit, contrary to normal practice, and after greeting fitter and rigger he put his left hand on the rigger's left shoulder and stepped up on the port wing. He swung his right leg into the cockpit first, with his hands, and then, holding on to the side of the cockpit, swung in the other and lowered his body into the seat. The fitter, standing on the right wing, helped him with his waist- and shoulder-straps and oxygen.

Bader checked instruments and controls and was soon starting the engine. Near by the propellers of the other aircraft began to turn and soon twelve Hurricanes were taxi-ing out to take off. Laycock Red Leader (Bader) braked to a stop, checked the aircraft behind and the sky ahead, cockpit open, and pushed the black throttle knob on the left all the way forward. His vic of three fighters began to roll; behind it three more waited momentarily, then followed. Soon all four sections were strung out behind and to the side, roaring

Take-off at 4.50 p.m. and landing approximately 5.50 p.m.

Setting course to intercept from west, 242 climbs at "buster"

Squadron sights large gaggle, of Do. 17s and Me. 110s to south-east

Bader detaches three fighters to investigate bigie below

FIGHTER

HURRICANE

FIGHTER SQUADRON

242 SQUADRON

FIGHTER STATION

DUXFORD

MISSION FLOWN BY:

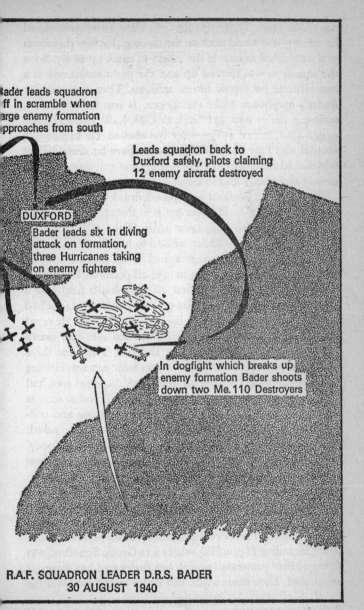

Bader leads squadron off in scramble when large enemy formation approaches from south

Leads squadron back to Duxford safely, pilots claiming 12 enemy aircraft destroyed

DUXFORD

Bader leads six in diving attack on formation, three Hurricanes taking on enemy fighters

In dogfight which breaks up enemy formation Bader shoots down two Me.110 Destroyers

R.A.F. SQUADRON LEADER D.R.S. BADER
30 AUGUST 1940

across the grass. Bader was first off, lifted his wheels, closed his canopy and eased back on the throttle. He flew due south at a slow speed to enable the others to catch up easily. Soon the squadron was formed up and the flight continued at a low altitude for ten or fifteen minutes. Then a voice over Bader's earphones broke the silence. It was the controller, ordering Bader and 242 back to Coltishall! Bader, highly aggravated, fumed at the order but obeyed. He turned 242 around and flew back to Coltishall, where he immediately telephoned and spiritedly asked what was going on. He was calmly and firmly told to await orders.

Disappointed pilots sat and waited, drank tea or coffee and wondered if they would ever get into the air war. An hour later the telephone rang once again. Take off (again) for Duxford! Once more Bader walked to his Hurricane as the others drove and was soon strapped in the cockpit, starting the engine and then taxi-ing to take-off position. The twelve hump-backed Hurricanes lifted off Coltishall's field into a clear southern sky slightly after 9 a.m.—not late—but it had already seemed a long day for Bader and 242 pilots. He eased back on the throttle, the squadron closed into line astern formation and course was set for Duxford. This time there was no recall and twenty-five minutes later 242 was circling Duxford's field and peeling off to land. A dispersal area had been prepared similar to the hut at Coltishall and as soon as Bader had taxied up and parked, he went inside and tele-phoned operations. 'Woody, what's the form?' he asked. 'Nothing at the moment,' replied Wing Commander 'Woody' Woodall, a friend of Bader's. Woodall explained that 242 was on stand-by, to be used if needed.

At that moment Germain aircraft were actually crossing the Channel to the south, a force of about 100, but a number of 11 Group squadrons were being scrambled to meet them. So 242 waited. The German invaders raided several R.A.F. fields, including Biggin Hill, where a 12 Group Squadron was flying airfield protection patrol, but Bader and 242 were not scrambled. Then came a lull. But Bader would not leave the hut area and the pilots lounged around parked Hurricanes in the sun, ate sandwiches for lunch . . . and waited.

Bader was sitting by the telephone in the hut much of the time but no call came. At 1.30 p.m. three Luftwaffe gaggles were picked up by radar in the south and crossed in south of Dover. The enemy was attacking 11 Group fighter fields at Biggin Hill, Tangmere, Shoreham and Kenley. Eight 11 Group squadrons were scrambled to intercept them. But there was no call for 242, and the sun began to lower in the west. Having waited so long to get into the war and having been sent back to Coltishall once, Bader found the waiting and inaction at Duxford deeply frustrating. It was now 4 p.m., and some had concluded that the day was to be a dry run for 242.

Minutes tick by. 4.15, 4.30, 4.45. German aircraft in the last attack are back at bases in France. However, unknown to Bader, other gaggles are on their way. They cross the Channel and from radar screens it becomes apparent there are many waves headed for various targets. Operations, busy watching plots and planning interceptions, decides what squadrons to scramble. When a Luftwaffe wave heads toward North Weald, a fighter station on the north-eastern outskirts of London and south of Duxford, it's decided to scramble 242. The telephone jangles. Bader picks it up. Woodall's voice: 'Scramble, there's trade approaching!' Bader slams the receiver down, shouts 'Scramble!' Everyone is in motion.

The crew has the fighter roaring as he hurries up, clambers in and fits straps, guns the throttle and begins to roll away. All over the area 242's aircraft are already started. Pilots leap in and gun throttles to follow. Bader taxies a short distance over the green grass and then gives the engine full throttle and is accelerating fast and bumping over the grass. Yellow, Green and Blue sections follow in order, each of three aircraft, Eric Ball leading Yellow, George Christie Green, and Georgie Powell-Shedden Blue.

The Hurricane roars at maximum thrust. Bader eases

back on the stick; she lifts nicely off the field. Heading: due south. The fighter climbs rapidly (she outclimbs the Spitfire) and as soon as he has wheels up, flaps up, shutters and canopy closed, Bader calls Woodhall on the R/T: 'Laycock Red Leader calling Steersman. Airborne. What height?' 'Angels fifteen,' comes the response. Woody adds: 'Trade approaching North Weald. Vector one-nine-zero. Buster.' The squadron complies and goes to full power, fire now constantly jetting out of the three stacks on each side of the Merlin. The sun is in the west and the tactic of the enemy in recent raids has been to take advantage of that—to come in out of the sun. Bader decides to vector a bit more right—west, get in position to do the same to the enemy. It's the same game as in the First World War. His three sections check in over the radio. 'Yellow Leader—in position . . . Green Leader—in position . . . Blue Leader—in position.' Bader switches on gunsight, carefully turns the firing button to 'Fire'. He glances at the gunsight glass, where a yellow light circle in the centre and yellow lines to each side are visible. With the little knob at the bottom he adjusts the yellow lines for a wing-span of forty feet. The Me.109's is about thirty but the 'trade' probably includes bombers with wider wing-spans.

The four vics, stacked down, climb on a heading of 220 degrees at 140 m.p.h. into the south-western afternoon sun. They are over Hertford, ten minutes from North Weald. In the distance the Thames Estuary is visible, and the great mass of London. Suddenly a voice cracks over the earphones: 'Blue Leader to Laycock Leader, three bogies, three o'clock low.' Bader looks and spots the dots ahead, below, tells Powell-Shedden to take his section and investigate. Blue section's left wings flip up and Powell-Shedden banks three of Bader's twelve fighters off and away starboard; 242 is down to nine aircraft.

Bader reaches back to the left and turns on oxygen—full blast. Altitude increases . . . 12,000, 13,000, 14,000 feet. The constant speed props, at full throttle, pull hard; the brownish-green pointed noses of the Hurricanes slant higher and higher into the sky. Steersman continues to give plots. The last course ordered was a change to 'two-four-zero' which should put the squadron on an interception course. Bader criss-crosses the sky ahead, and above, sees nothing. The roar of engines fills each cockpit, otherwise all is silent; pilots constantly turn their heads first to one side and then the other, then behind. It is 5 p.m.

Altitude 15,000, 16,000 feet. To the east the reservoir at Enfield is in clear view though a slight haze reaches up to 7,000 feet. He calls Steersman. Woody replies: 'North Weald being attacked.' Can he see them? Tingling with excitement, Bader scans the sky in the direction of North Weald, ahead left, sees nothing. He sees North Weald . . . but no bandits! Where can they be? Ahead, puffs over the air-field . . . Flak! The enemy must be there. The radio crackles: 'Red Two here, bandits left front.' It's Willie McKnight, his wingman, who spots the gaggle. Bader focuses his eyes on the area ahead left . . . now he sees them . . . dots, many dots, coming on. He presses the mike button: 'I've got 'em.'

Each of the nine pilots feels the tension of anticipation as the enemy gaggle comes on about level, to the left. Each can see its size. There are two big boxes each with thirty or more aircraft. They get bigger and bigger and blacker and blacker. And then above the bombers Bader sees more, smaller dots . . . fighters! They're slightly higher than 242. They have to be dealt with. Bader has nine Hurricanes. Three can attack the top box. He presses the mike button: 'Green section, take on the top lot.' Christie acknowledges, his three aircraft peel off to the right, climbing; 242 is down to six aircraft! Bader stays on course, climbing straight ahead. The bombers are mostly two-engined, greyish Dornier 17s, the 'Flying Pencil'. They're formed in rows of four or more and Me.110s are interspaced among them, heading north-east. Bader's six Mark Is move toward them on a south-by-south-east course, slightly above. With the bombers already over North Weald he hasn't time to follow the action of Green Section, above. He steps into left rudder, moves the stick left, and the six fighters stand on their port wings, curving into an arc which will bring them out of the south-western sun down into the enemy boxes. This is it.

Bader presses the button of the helmet mike. 'Line astern, we'll go down in sections.' Three thousand feet above the boxes he dips the nose. The Hurricanes gather speed in the dive out of the sun. Bader doesn't take his eyes off the twin-engined bombers; he wants to break up the formation first and will go right through them. The air-speed needle steadily winds. The roar of the engine and the wind increase. Enemy bomber silhouettes grow bigger and bigger through the glass. Bader is coming down fast now; he won't be able to go through the first line or the second. He'll pass through the third.

Leading the three brownish-green Hurricanes straight in he opens fire and is suddenly among the bombers, then streaking down, having dived between two rows. As he rockets through the formation and down and out shocked enemy pilots of Dorniers and 110s turn in all directions. The second section flashes through the scattering bombers, also firing; Bader is in the bottom of an arc below, pointing his nose back up—where he will deal with separated aircraft. His opening burst was scattered among them. As he pulls back up, with McKnight behind on his left, and Crowley-Milling behind on his right, he sees above and ahead three Me.110s turning right. He focuses his eyes on the last in the formation and points the nose of his Hurricane toward the trailing twin-engined fighter. After a 3,000-foot dive and at full throttle he is making good speed. Bader watches the 110's 53-foot wing-span broaden rapidly in his sight. The enemy pilot climbs and banks more sharply right. Bader turns with him. The wing-span widens in the glass. He rapidly closes ... closer ... closer. He's on him ... in range.

His thumb presses down, unleashes the eight ·303 Brownings with a roar. The Hurricane shakes with the vibration. So close is Bader that a full, concentrated pattern of shells smashes into the stricken 110 instantly. Pieces fly backwards. Fire appears at the starboard wing root. Bader, almost eating up the enemy's tail with his propeller, lifts his thumb. The twin-engined Messerschmitt falls out of its turn, down and right, a stream of smoke marking the path of its fall. Bader can't watch. He looks right, left and behind . . . other Dorniers and 110s are scattering. In the action he has lost the other two Hurricanes, now after victims of their own. Again he checks his tail and turns. All clear. He flies alone, realizing he has scored his first victory in the Battle of Britain!

He has, however, little time to think about it. Below . . . off to the right . . . another 110. Stick right, nose down, Bader feels the sharp drop in his stomach as he dives after him. The Messerschmitt has just come out of a sharp turn or a stall. Bader manœuvres the rudder pedals and stick to line up the wing-span in the yellow light lines on the sighting glass. But now the enemy pilot pulls up . . . begins a climb. Bader pulls the stick back and follows. The 110's nose dips and it dives. Bader pushes the stick forwards, stays behind, still closing. It's a strange tactic; he can't imagine what the enemy pilot thinks he's doing. The 110 pulls up sharply again . . . and Bader follows, steadily getting closer as the enemy fighter continues up and down. Now he's diving again and Bader is close enough to fire. Down after him! Then up he goes. Bader pulls back on the stick. The wing-span fills the distance between the yellow lines. He can easily see black crosses on the wings. In range! Almost on him, Bader pushes thumb down and the eight Brownings spurt a stream of ·303 shells into the starboard wing. The pattern, visible from the ammunition's vapour trails in the air, concentrates there.

The weight of fire at such close range is too much. The wing is holed, pieces fly backwards. Bader is so close he can't miss. Then a streak of light runs down the wing. Fire! The twin-engined fighter's nose drops, the port wing goes up and it plunges downward. Bader, no longer firing, watches. The enemy is falling, smoking, wings turning, straight down. He clears his rear, then has another moment to watch. The

Me.110 grows smaller and smaller below. No 'chutes emerge. And only now does it come to him—he hasn't even noticed the rear gunner in either 110! Did they fire at him? He will never know!

He looks back again. Just in time. A black shape behind . . . twin-engined fighter, Me.110! Instantly Bader hits right rudder and pushes the stick right, racking the Hurricane into its steepest bank. The enemy was almost in firing range . . . another second or two and it might have been too late. The 110 can't turn with the Hurricane; Bader is cutting inside his arc. The enemy pilot sees what's happening, decides not to wait for Bader to come round on his tail . . . dives almost straight down. Bader plunges the stick forwards, rolling out into a near vertical descent behind him. But the enemy's initial dive velocity has opened a gap between them and the 110 must have its throttles open wide. The invader and the pursuing fighter, gradually flattening out, plunge downwards, and Bader keeps him in view through the glass. He's not gaining. The 110 dropped away too far in its dive before he spotted the manœuvre and could follow. The Hurricane is flat out, still not gaining. The enemy will get away. At least he didn't succeed, though he came close, in downing the squadron leader of the intercepting and defending fighters. Bader banks away and climbs back into the general area of the battle. He steadily gains altitude and looks around the sky.

No aircraft anywhere! Where are all those who were—minutes ago—all around him? He can enjoy the satisfaction of having sent two twin-engined enemy fighters down. He S-turns and presses the mike button: 'Laycock Red Leader here chaps . . . going home.' He banks into a northerly heading still watching for friend and foe—behind and on both sides. He sees a solitary fighter in the distance, closing, making for him. Bader banks towards him, doesn't take his eyes off the silhouette. He makes out the shape . . . low wing, single engine. A Spit, Hurricane, or Me.109. He watches it come on. Closer, closer . . . he identifies it: Hurricane! The friendly fighter curves in behind and pulls into formation. McKnight! His wing man is back in formation. Bader holds up two fingers with a grin—two kills. Willie grins . . . holds up three! That's five between them. Bader wonders about the rest of the squadron, flies on northwards. How many were lost! Did North Weald get it? Another Hurricane banks into position, another 242 aircraft. Now there are three headed home. Then a fourth 242 pilot finds them, curves into the formation. Bader calls Woody: 'On my way back.' A few minutes from Duxford and a fifth 242 pilot finds the squadron; thus five Hurricanes roar over Duxford and circle the field for a landing.

Duxford has not been attacked and soon the Hurricanes are peeling off to land. Bader comes in first. He eases the throttle back and loses speed, drops the landing gear, flips the red hydraulic flap handle on the right as he banks into the approach. Airspeed drops to 90, 85, 80 . . . he's skimming the grass . . . thumps down. As soon as he's slowed sufficiently, he turns toward the dispersal hut, roars up and switches off, shouting the good news with a grin. A group quickly gathers around the Hurricane, having noticed its open gun ports and as soon as Bader is out ply him with questions. As other pilots pull up and park they come over to the Squadron Leader's aircraft. Shortly most of the squadron, including the Intelligence Officer, is gathered on the grass, and every detail of the action is discussed.

Bader questions the jubilant pilots and totals the score. His twelve shot down twelve of the enemy. No losses—every pilot is back. It's a perfect victory in their first interception of the enemy in the Battle of Britain. Bader is elated. His two victories are his fourth and fifth. He writes out an account of the action for the Intelligence Office, describing every detail of the bounce and everything he can remember. Then it's time for the squadron to fly back to Coltishall. It's late, but the long summer day keeps the sky lighted until nine. Bader and 242, for the fourth time that day, gun the 'Rolls-Merlins' and lift off the grass—this time headed north.

The success of 242 Squadron in its first interception of the enemy on 30 August convinced Bader that the greatest hope for maximum scores against the enemy lay in the assembling of larger attacking forces of fighters. Though satisfied with his one-sided victory he couldn't avoid speculating what his score would have been if he had led three or more fighter squadrons. He was certain he would have scored very heavily and so convinced of his strategic ideas was he that, from this point onwards, he pressed them at every opportunity with comrades and higher-ranking officers. Thus began a hotly contested debate within the service which has not been fully stilled to this day, over twenty-five years after the battle. Because of Bader's role in this sometimes bitter controversy, a brief summary of it is appropriate.

After landing at Coltishall Bader discussed his strategic ideas with fellow pilots. The A.O.C. 12 Group, Air Vice-Marshal Leigh-Mallory, called to congratulate him and the squadron on its 12–0 victory and asked for Bader's ideas on future interceptions. Bader told him if he had led thirty-six fighters instead of twelve he could have shot down 'three times as many'. He elaborated on his view that larger formations were the best tactic against the enemy, formations scrambled early enough to gain the necessary height—as he had almost gained that afternoon.

Bader believed in the doctrine of First World War pilots: that three absolutely basic principles for fighter success were height advantage, sun advantage and close-in shooting. He proposed that 12 Group squadrons should be scrambled early and these interception tactics employed. If this were done, he felt certain enemy losses would increase and R.A.F. losses decrease. Air Vice Marshal K. R. Park was largely directing the Battle of Britain, tactically, as A.O.C. 11 Fighter Group (Southern England). Park was often sending fighters up in small units as soon as radar reported the strength and course of large enemy formations. R.A.F. fighters were, therefore, often bounced at low altitudes by Me.109s as they climbed to intercept the bombers. But with only twenty fighter squadrons, and seeking to avoid being drawn into battles between massed formations of fighters, Park did not feel the situation allowed 11 Group to place primary emphasis on the assembling of large forces, which took time. And he was often succeeding in breaking up bomber formations before they reached their targets or dropped their bombs. He was also inflicting heavier losses on the enemy than he was sustaining.

Leigh-Mallory, to the north, where there was more time to assemble wings, was impressed with Bader's reasoning and promised Bader he would be given three squadrons, a really strong interception force, to test his theory. Bader used the three squadrons to achieve an impressive score a short time later. This convinced some, especially in 12 Group, that the strategy had merit. On the other hand, Park and his supporters felt that conditions were different in the exposed southern (11 Group) area, and that the advantages of smaller interceptions outweighed the disadvantages, though Park did issue orders favouring larger interceptions if circumstances permitted. In a meeting on strategy at the Air Ministry, Air Marshal Sir Hugh Dowding, Commander-in-Chief of Fighter Command, largely supported Park, who was allowed to conduct the battle according to his own judgement. A few months later Park and Dowding were rotated to other posts, some thought unappreciatively, and Leigh-Mallory given command of 11 Group. Air Marshal W. Sholto Douglas, a supporter of Bader's theory, was named new Commander-in-Chief of Fighter Command.

In post-war years analysts and historians treating the battle have not been unkind to Park. He, after all, won the crucial air battle so important to England and the free world. That does not imply that Bader's ideas, which to a large degree were based on proven principles outlined by the great pilots of the 1914–18 war, were without merit. Possibilities in 12 Group and 11 Group were different and slightly different tactics were appropriate to each, for geographical reasons. Many English writers and pilots agree that better co-ordination between 11 and 12 Groups was desirable or, failing that, tighter control from Fighter Command. However, in the end, all these arguments face the incontrovertible fact that Park and Dowding, with the help of rotated fighter squadrons and squadrons in 12 Group (the Duxford wing), won the battle. They were, of course, helped by errors in strategy and tactics on the German side and by certain advantages enjoyed by the defence. Whether they could have fought the battle even more effectively and economically is a good question (as it is after every engagement) and employing hindsight it seems probable they might have, to a degree. That would have been the perfect battle which has not yet been fought, nor could critics have fought it without their own mistakes. The fact which does emerge as an outstanding feature of the controversy concerning Bader is that a lowly squadron leader presented and demonstrated his strategic ideas so effectively that they became a major influence and topic in high command deliberations. It is doubtful if any other squadron commander could have exerted more influence.

Not long after his success of 30 August, Bader led larger groups of fighters against the enemy, and again did well. On 7 September, with one squadron, his pilots claimed eleven victories. On the 9th, this time with three squadrons (242, 310 and 19), the wing claimed twenty. With five squadrons on the 15th (242, 310, 19, 302 and 611) the wing claimed 52 victories! Bader was proud of these one-sided scores and believed that his numerically low losses reflected the soundness of the tactics employed. In recognition of his efforts, he received his first decoration—the D.S.O.

He continued to lead the Duxford wing until the end of the Battle of Britain, at which time he had a total of twelve victories. When the R.A.F. went on the offensive in 1941 Bader was put in command of the Tangmere wing with three squadrons of Spitfires (145, 610 and 616). He contributed an aggressiveness unsurpassed in the R.A.F. and had soon flown more sweeps over France than any other pilot. He was advised to take a rest as he flew almost daily in the good weather of mid-summer 1941, but rejected the advice. (At this time he ranked fifth among the highest-scoring R.A.F. pilots.)

On 9 August he flew his last sortie. Near Le Touquet he led the wing in an attack on a formation of Me.109s. He shot down two before another rammed him, severing his Spitfire's tail section, and sending him plummeting earthward. Bader had a life and death struggle to get out of the cockpit, until the leather belt holding his trapped right leg broke, and he fell free. His parachute opened but he landed hard and was inevitably soon captured.

German fighter pilots knew almost immediately who he was and he was treated with respect. Oberst Adolf Galland sent a car to the hospital where he was confined to take him on a visit to the pilots of Jagdgeschwader 26.

The 'legless wonder' was still full of spirit and a few nights later, with the help of a French nurse inside the hospital, managed to escape! He tied together sheets from several beds, lowered himself out of the window and managed to get out of the yard and through the night to a peasant farmer's house. He missed being spirited away by the underground by a day—betrayed by another hospital nurse and captured just before being picked up by an underground member. Meanwhile, the Luftwaffe had sent a message to the R.A.F. that Bader's legs had been shattered and offered to give an English plane safe passage to drop a spare set. The R.A.F. refused the safe conduct but made the drop, and the Luftwaffe duly delivered them to Bader.

On several later occasions Bader again attempted to escape but his nature and spirit were now recognized and he was sent to the special security camp, Kolditz. He remained a prisoner until April 1945, and after being freed and taking two months' leave was made a Group Captain in the R.A.F. But he resigned his peace-time commission and took a job with his old employer (now known as Shell) in 1946, where he is today.

Bader was awarded the D.S.O. and Bar, the D.F.C. and Bar, the Legion d'Honneur and the Croix de Guerre. He was unquestionably an expert on tactics, exceptional at the controls of a fighter, a natural leader, and endowed with almost unlimited courage. He had scored $22\frac{1}{2}$ victories when his fighter was rammed and he baled out over France. Had it not been for this, it is hard to estimate how many enemy aircraft he would have shot down. It is also difficult to estimate the value, to his country and the R.A.F., of a man who would not accept physical handicap or defeat and who possessed such determination. His example—and legend—was an inspiration to war-time fighter pilots, to those who followed later and to millions all over the world in various walks of life.

# CHAPTER SIX

# ONE OF THE *FEW*

*15 September 1940—Sergeant Pilot James H. Lacey, R.A.F.*

THE TOP-SCORING surviving British fighter pilot of the
Battle of Britain is a soft-spoken redhead from Yorkshire,
James Harry ('Ginger') Lacey. Lacey was one of the im-
mortal 'few', who in the summer of 1940 flew and fought their
way to victory over the Luftwaffe and captured the heart of
the free world. Millions watched the critical test of strength in
skies over Sussex and Kent and Ginger Lacey's name was
soon on every Englishman's lips. That was more than
twenty-five years ago and in that span of years the young
fighter pilot hero of 1940 has slipped, to a degree, into
anonymity. Where is he today and how has fate treated him
in the post-war years?

To get the answer, and to obtain details of his most interesting sortie in the Battle of Britain, I boarded the 'White Rose'
at King's Cross on a dull winter day in 1966. Three hours
north (to the early industrial terrace houses of Leeds), a
change of trains and an hour travelling east, and we were
approaching Hull. Students boarded at suburban stops,
probably little different from their counterparts of the
thirties. Did they know much about the air struggle that
saved their country in 1940, or that the top surviving pilot of
that struggle lived among them as a fellow Yorkshireman?
One wondered, watching their good humour, their carefree
laughter. No threat of imminent war or invasion clouded
their thoughts or future . . . a different time and a different
world! But were they vastly different from another young
man from the same county who thirty years before, intrigued
by flying and internal combustion, joined the Volunteer

Reserve of the R.A.F.? Was there one among them capable of doing what that other youngster did—the self-made pilot who shot down sixteen aircraft in two months in the crucial air test of the war for his country? Who can say?

As a sergeant pilot in the reserve, Lacey had been called to active service at the outbreak of war, sent to France on the day the German offensive in the West began, 10 May, and had shot down five German aircraft (three over the pivotal Sedan front) in the short time British forces remained on the Continent. Brought back to England, he then served south of London in the forefront of the Battle of Britain from beginning to end.

After that start, in 1940, air activity slowed a bit, but Lacey remained on flying duty near the Channel until July 1941, adding additional victims to his total. From then until the end of the war he served in Training Command, in headquarters posts or in the Far East—and had little opportunity to shoot down more of the enemy. Even so, at the end of the war his 28 victories ranked him among the R.A.F.'s top scorers.

Lacey, the son of a Yorkshire cattle-dealer, learned to fly before he was twenty. His imagination was stirred for the first time when an R.A.F. team won the Schneider Trophy for Great Britain, but his parents gently dissuaded him from flying. His father died in 1933, at the low ebb of the Depression, at which time he was an apprentice chemist with two more years to serve. They were slow years—1934 and 1935— partly because Lacey wasn't working in chemistry, which he had hoped to be doing, but was—for the most part—wrapping packages and selling perfume! Completing the three-year apprenticeship in 1936 he was at last free to join the R.A.F.V.R. He asked his mother's permission to take the physical; she agreed, though she didn't think he would pass. Lacey was then nineteen and the war was three years away.

Because there was a chance he would fail, he told no one he was taking flying training. Somewhat reserved in the English tradition, he knew he would have less explaining to do if he failed. But from the day he began, with twenty-nine others at Scone, Scotland, there was little danger of his failing. Instructor Nick Lawson rated him above average from the beginning; he was the first in his class to solo.

After six weeks and sixty-five hours of flying he had successfully completed the course and was a qualified pilot. (The class was the first group of sergeant pilot trainees in the Volunteer Reserve programme.) Under the R.A.F. training plan of that day he returned home to continue reserve training at week-ends. Only now did he and his mother reveal that he had successfully completed the flying course and was a licensed pilot.

Though there was time during the week for other interests or work, Lacey seldom strayed far from the local airfield at Brough. His heart was one hundred per cent in flying and he enjoyed the comradeship he had formed with other pilots, the bond of adventure and danger they shared. Having soloed in a Tiger Moth, he now began to fly (at week-ends) the Blackburn B.2S.

Then the Hawker Hart arrived at Brough. The Hart flew at almost 200 m.p.h., could climb to 21,000 feet (Lacey had never been above 10,000) and was twice as heavy as the B.2S. Lacey was one of the first two reserve pilots allowed to solo it and flew it as much as he could thereafter. He often flew eight hours a day, though not all in the Hart. Flying almost constantly, obviously a naturally gifted pilot, he was soon good enough to take the instructor's course at nearby Grimsby. Successfully completing the course, he applied for the instructor's job at the Yorkshire Aeroplane Club, and was accepted.

It was 1938, and only a year remained before the war. During that year Lacey flew as instructor, for hire and privately—as much as he could. The R.A.F. at that time invited reserve pilots who accumulated 250 hours to serve six weeks with a regular R.A.F. squadron. Lacey received an invitation late in the year. His reply was demanding and yet his terms were accepted by the Air Ministry. He had accepted on condition that he be posted to a single-engined squadron on the south coast, preferably No. 1 Squadron at Tangmere. He was posted to Tangmere, reporting in January 1939. There he flew the Hawker Fury, which had a top speed of 240 m.p.h., for the first time. And after a few weeks a new fighter landed at Tangmere which attracted unusual interest —the Hawker Hurricane. As Lacey approached it, twice as heavy as the Fury, longer and ten feet wider from wing-tip to wing-tip, he was inwardly convinced that he could never learn to fly it—a thought which passed through the minds of so many trainee fighter pilots in similar circumstances during the war. But those who had mastered it encouraged him and built up his confidence. After a short time he had learnt the instrumental panel and cockpit drill. And then, at last, he soloed. So enthusiastic was he over the Hurricane that he was sorry to leave Tangmere at the expiration of his six weeks' training, when he said good-bye to the pilots of No. 1 Squadron and the Hurricane and returned to Yorkshire.

On 2 September 1939, the day before Britain declared war on Germany and the day after German troops invaded Poland, Lacey and other reserve pilots in Yorkshire were ordered to report to the Town Centre in Hull. There he was told that he was posted to 501 Squadron (County of Glouces-ter), stationed at Filton near Bristol. The best part of it was that 501 was equipped with Hurricanes. Reporting to 501, however, Lacey found flying at Filton uninspiring. It con-sisted primarily of practice and submarine patrol over the Bristol Channel.

Three months later 501 was posted to Tangmere. Here too things were surprisingly quiet though Lacey flew several night scrambles to protect shipping. A few months went by and then in May 1940 he and 501 were caught up in the sweep of fast-moving events.

The R.A.F. had six fighter squadrons in France on the day Germany began to attack in the West. The six were divided into two groups, two in the Advanced Air Striking Force, four attached to the British Expeditionary Force. On 10 May six additional squadrons were dispatched. Three went to the Expeditionary Force and three to the Advanced Striking Force. Lacey and 501 joined the Advanced Striking Force and by late afternoon on 11 May 501 was established at Betheniville near Rheims—to remain only briefly. The rapid German advance disrupted all Allied plans and kept squadrons on the move. Yet Lacey flew with distinction. Among dispirited allies, defeat and chaos on all sides and constantly on the move, he engaged in numerous combats, and shot down five enemy aircraft, including one of the vaunted Me.109 fighters. He was himself almost killed on one occasion when his damaged fighter flipped on its back and trapped him in the cockpit as it sank into a swamp in which he had attempted to land near Le Mans. Finally, in late June, 501 returned to England with other R.A.F. units and the more than 300,000 evacuees from Dunkirk. France had been crushed, and had surrendered, in less than fifty days.

Lacey was stationed briefly at Croydon and at Middle Wallop in Hampshire. Then 501 was posted to Gravesend as the Battle of Britain began. On 2 July Channel ports and convoys were heavily attacked by large numbers of aircraft and these attacks continued regularly, while at night cities in every part of the British Isles were raided. On 8 August the pressure increased further and major attacks were delivered on the 11th and 12th. But it was on the 13th (the first day of the battle, according to German accounts) that the Luftwaffe loosed its full strength, flying 1,485 sorties in coordinated attacks. On the 15th the Luftwaffe flew an even greater number of sorties. In addition to aircraft from Luftflotten 2 and 3, across the Channel, bombers flew to the attack from Luftflotte 5 bases in Scandinavia. R.A.F. fighters inflicted heavy losses on the Germans (75 on 15 August) during the opening days of the Battle. Luftwaffe tactics then changed. Greater gaggles of fighters protected the bombers more closely and became more successful. Formations were breaking through British defences, even though a price was still being paid. The attrition of the battle was beginning to tell on both sides.

Then German tactics were switched once again. London became the chief target—in retrospect one of the mistakes made by the German High Command during the battle. While the raids on London were spectacular and caused damage, they were not damaging to Fighter Command installations and communications—which were given a respite. The most devastating daylight raid on London, and the first, came on 7 September. Every Luftwaffe bomber and fighter available participated. Bad weather intervened and it was not until the 15th that the Germans mounted another all-out attack. This day—15 September—has been selected as Battle of Britain Day because of the gallant defence thrown up by the R.A.F. German losses were heavy and it was this day as much as any other which convinced Luftwaffe chiefs that an invasion of England would not be feasible for a long time, that the R.A.F. was going to be a very difficult foe to subdue if indeed the Luftwaffe could subdue it. On the 15th the Luftwaffe lost 56 aircraft and many others were damaged. Two days later Hitler postponed Operation Sealion—the invasion of Britain. On 15 September, as we shall now see, Ginger Lacey did more than his share.

A clear summer-night sky arched over a bomb-pocked field at the R.A.F. fighter station of Kenley, thirteen miles south of London, on Saturday, 14 September 1940. Though invisible in the darkness, the holes were evidence of the military importance of Kenley and the accuracy of the Luftwaffe. Around the pitted field stretched barbed wire—which also enclosed several commandeered private houses. One at the south end of the big rectangular grass field was a two-storey weathered brick building covered with scarlet virginia creeper. On the second floor, in a rear bedroom, Sergeant Pilot James H. Lacey of 501 (Volunteer Reserve) Squadron slept soundly in a black iron bed.

He had gone to bed at ten. The all-out German aerial assault had been underway for a month and R.A.F. fighter pilots, often flying several times a day, were always tired at the end of the day. There was another reason: Lacey had been shot down the day before—Friday—and had suffered painful burns on both legs before managing to bale out of his burning fighter. But he refused to remain in a hospital and, in fact, concealed his burns, drew a new uniform and flying kit and reported fit for duty. He had therefore been scheduled to fly next day—Sunday, 15 September.

In almost constant scrambles and dogfights since the battle opened Lacey had engaged in more than a score of major air actions and on eleven occasions had shot down his opponent. He had also been hit in some of these battles and had baled out of fatally damaged fighters on several occasions. The narrow escape he had experienced the day before made headlines, for he had pursued and caught the lone He.111 bomber which enraged public opinion by bombing Buckingham Palace. The weather was so bad that a volunteer was asked to go up. Chances were very much against the bomber being found in such weather but Lacey volunteered, raced to his aircraft, took off and located it in the thick greyness. As he closed behind the 111 he fired a burst and killed the startled rear gunner. As he prepared to finish off his adversary he himself was startled, another crewman suddenly manning the rear gun turret and opening fire on him. He was hit but refused to break off the attack, opening fire on the second gunner, killing him, and setting the 111 afire. Only then did he turn away.

His aircraft was burning and he had to get out immediately. His chute opened and he dropped through clouds during much of his fall, then broke out underneath. He saw members of the Home Guard rushing about, and they saw the He.111 crash near by, as did Lacey. About 500 feet directly below was an armed guard and Lacey shouted to him. He looked in all directions, but not above. Lacey again shouted: 'Right above you!' The guard caught sight of Lacey, lifted his double-barrelled shotgun and took aim, to which gesture Lacey responded: 'For God's sake don't shoot!' And he added a few Anglo-Saxon words for emphasis. He landed not far away but the guard kept the shotgun on him. Lacey shouted that he was reaching for his identity card to prove he was English. The guard relaxed. 'I don't have to see your identity card; anyone who can swear like that couldn't possibly be a German.'

Lacey's face burns weren't bad and he covered the more serious ones on his legs with a new pair of trousers before reporting to his Commanding Officer, thus avoiding being taken off flying duty. But it had taken all day Saturday to get a new uniform and kit and to treat his legs privately. Exhausted, he had left a call with the station guard room for 4.30 next morning and had gone to bed early. Before first light in Surrey's eastern sky on Sunday morning, crewmen revved up and checked the 1,030 horsepower Merlin engines of 501 Squadron's Hurricanes. The roar shattered the quiet of the countryside for miles around. But it wasn't until a corporal came into his bedroom some time later and interupted his sleep that the day began for Lacey. 'Sign, please,' the corporal asked, holding the form that would relieve him of further responsibility. After Lacey had signed it, if he went back to sleep it was his problem. Lacey rolled over and signed and watched other pilots scramble for the washroom. He always waited for the rush to subside; he didn't eat breakfast and washed while the others were at the breakfast table. After they had gone he washed and dressed, in prickly (for summer) R.A.F. battle jacket and trousers and black leather flying boots, always polished. He came down as others were finishing breakfast, and all climbed aboard a Ford 1500 which had driven up the circular drive outside the front door. As the 1500 pulled away and started for the dispersal hut, centre of 501's operations, someone asked the time. It was 5.15.

At a square wooden building on the upper western edge of the field the lorry stopped, and pilots spilled into the main room of the squadron home. Inside were comfortable leather chairs from which the stuffing was protruding, a blackboard and several card tables. On one table just inside the doorway was a black field telephone, near it a gramophone and a few other furnishings. Flying equipment and flight jackets were scattered over the chairs. Lacey walked over to the blackboard. On it Squadron Leader H. Hogan had chalked in the names of those flying the first mission and the position they would fly. Lacey was Red Three, A Flight, which meant he would fly Hogan's wing. The flight of six, half the squadron, would fly in two vics. (The vics which made up the squadron were designated by colours—red, yellow, green, blue.) Since 501's radio code designation was 'Pinetree', Lacey would be Pinetree Red Three. He walked into a small room adjoining the main room, pulled on his yellow Mae West, picked up a brown leather flying helmet and parachute and was soon outside in conversation with fellow pilots.

In the east the sky was whitening, the light colouring the field's grass green and the virginia creeper on the old houses red. The still forms of three-bladed grey-green Hurricanes on the field's western edge, each with a battery cart beside it, emerged clearly out of the fading darkness. Lacey walked out to one of the nearest low-wing fighters. On the fuselage above the big belly air scoop were painted the letters SD, four feet high. Just behind the squadron letters, farther back on the fuselage, was a smaller F. (Lacey refused to have the F painted on after having been shot down on several occasions the day after it had been painted. It was chalked on.)

He greeted fitter and rigger, carefully laid his parachute on the tail elevator, straps properly arranged for the critical moment later when he would be dashing out from the dispersal hut. He climbed in the cockpit and checked the length of the rudder bar (adjusted by turning a spider wheel between the pedals). He set the tail elevator trim for take-off and opened the trap door on the gunsight directly in front to see if an extra bulb was in the clip. The little white bulbs which produced the light ring on the gunsight glass, all-important in combat, were scarce, and Lacey not only checked on the sight bulb and spare each morning but usually carried extras in his pocket. Bulbs in place, he hung his helmet on the right side of the gunsight and pushed the nozzle of the black rubber hose which protruded from it into the oxygen outlet, turning the nozzle to lock it in place. He plugged the lead wire from his helmet into a radio wire connection on the right-hand side of the cockpit floor. (It had a habit of coming out at embarrassing moments, causing loss of radio contact.) Then he signed form 700, the serviceability log, which, in effect, said he was satisfied the aircraft was fit to fly. Fitter and rigger signed before him.

There was no activity yet, and satisfied all was in order, Lacey chatted leisurely with crewmen about the night before —invariably the first topic of the morning. The sky was now fully lighted and he walked back to the dispersal hut. Pilots who were scheduled to fly, and some who were not, tried to relax; those not scheduled were noticeably more successful, many sleeping soundly. Lacey sank into a chair and tried to sleep but couldn't. The minutes passed, then an hour and then another. The morning was wearing on; the time came for tea-break. So far, 15 September had been an easy day.

The waiting resumes after the break. Clouds are beginning to drift in above the field, which takes some of the sting out of the sun's rays as they beat down on Lacey's fair and, in some places burned, skin. Minutes tick by and the clock moves from 11.30 past the half-hour. Over-casual glances and subdued tension are noticeable in the hut.

The telephone! Someone near the table picks up the receiver. All eyes focus on his every move. He is motioning pilots up. Scramble! Everyone is instantly in motion. Lacey bolts through the door shouting, 'Start up!' His fitter, a short distance away, leaps into the cockpit while the rigger runs to the battery cart. Crewmen at the other Hurricanes are also in action. Pilots don't know yet what enemy force they're scrambling to meet—they'll learn details by radio.

Lacey runs up just as the big Rolls-Merlin is coughing to a

start, smoke belching from its exhausts, propeller spinning. He grabs his chute, catches the half belt to his left at the safety box and holds the box to his stomach as he fits in the shoulder- and leg-straps and closes the catch. He jumps on the port wing as the fitter scrambles out on the starboard, and into the cockpit, pulling on his helmet as the fitter quickly lays the straps over his shoulders. He fits them and side-straps over the peg, fits in the pin. Now ready, he casts a glance right towards Squadron Leader Hogan's Hurricane. Hogan is ready. Lacey's fitter taps his right shoulder—he always does —shouts, 'Good Luck' and jumps off the wing. Hogan's fighter is taxi-ing out; Lacey pushes the throttle knob forward with his left hand, releases brakes, and amid the roar of the engine and wind the Hurricane begins to roll. Their clothes flapping in the propwash, fitter and rigger watch as the thundering fighter moves away gathering speed. Lacey taxies into position on Hogan's wing, and Hogan now applies full throttle. The fighters are taking off straight ahead and Lacey keeps his eyes on Hogan, about thirty feet ahead and right. He checks gauges in quick snatches . . . engine temperature, revolutions, oil pressure, boost, radiator shutter lever back . . . all in order. The Hurricane bounds forward and the Merlin's power pulls it faster and faster. The bumps are lighter . . . the wheels are off the ground. Lacey holds the stick back. He eases back a bit on boost (to avoid over-strain). The Squadron Leader's vic and Pinetree Red Three are airborne.

The three Hurricanes lean into a slight turn, lifting away from the field. Lacey retracts his undercarriage, flips the red handle on the right of the instrument-panel, raising the flaps, and pushes back the black knob on the cockpit floor to close the coolant shutters—never taking his eyes off Hogan for more than a second. He and Red Two are very close to Hogan; the other three vics, as they lift off, cut off the Squadron Leader in tighter turns and soon the two-flight squadron is tucked in neatly and climbing. Over the earphones comes Hogan's voice: 'Check in, Red Section.' 'Red

Take-off at 11.45 a.m. and landing shortly after 12.30 p.m.

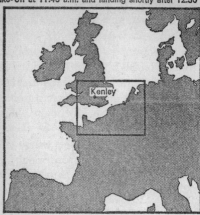

KENLEY

Lacey takes off in
scramble to intercept
large enemy gaggle
as "Red Three".
Squadron at maximum
climb attempts to get
above oncoming enemy

FIGHTER

HURRICANE

FIGHTER SQUADRON

501 SQUADRON

FIGHTER STATION

KENLEY

MISSION FLOWN BY

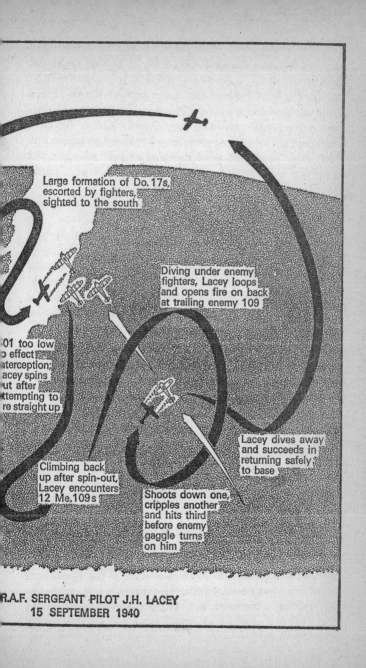

Large formation of Do. 17s, escorted by fighters, sighted to the south

Diving under enemy fighters, Lacey loops and opens fire on back at trailing enemy 109

...01 too low ...o effect ...terception; ...acey spins ...ut after ...ttempting to ...re straight up

Climbing back up after spin-out, Lacey encounters 12 Me.109s

Shoots down one, cripples another and hits third before enemy gaggle turns on him

Lacey dives away and succeeds in returning safely to base

R.A.F. SERGEANT PILOT J.H. LACEY
15 SEPTEMBER 1940

Two,' a voice replies. 'Red Three,' Lacey transmits. Then each pilot in the squadron checks in, in yellow, green and blue vics.

Now the vital information comes in over the earphones from the controller below: 'Pinetree Leader, vector one-three-zero, repeat one-three-zero. Angels fifteen. We have fifty-plus raid for you, approaching between Dungeness and Ramsgate.' Hogan acknowledges and a ripple of excitement permeates the squadron as it slants upwards into a partly cloudy south-eastern sky.

Lacey flips the gunsight switch; an orange circle appears in the middle of the sighting glass, which represents 100 m.p.h. in deflection shots (a two-circle lead for an aircraft flying perpendicularly at 200 m.p.h.). The space between the two bars on the glass can be widened or closed by adjusting the wing-span setter. An aircraft is within range from behind when the wing-tips touch the bars on each side. Lacey has had his eight ·303 Browning machine-guns harmonized for convergence at 150 yards, 100 yards closer than the normal firing pattern. His gun-belts are loaded with his own selection of ammunition: one De Wilde armour-piercing incendiary for every standard, the normal proportion being one to five. The De Wilde is what his armourer, Sergeant 'Dapper' Green, calls a 'dirty' loading. It has a tendency to foul the gun barrels but Lacey doesn't care whether barrels are fouled or not. Green, an admirer, reluctantly supplies the extra De Wilde ammunition—and almost weeps when he sees the guns after each combat.

The fighters reach higher and higher. The enemy will be high . . . controller directed Hogan to angels fifteen, which sounds like 15,000 feet—but 'fifteen' is a code word meaning 25,000. (Ten is automatically added to the controller's instruction.) The hope is to conceal from the Germans, who are often successful at monitoring R.A.F. radio conversations, how high R.A.F. fighters will be. If the Hurricanes surprise the faster enemy fighters from above, it is a considerable tactical advantage. But that is not easy to do from a scramble. The 109 has both a higher ceiling and a speed advantage.

Every pilot scans the sky ahead and above for the enemy gaggle as the Rolls-Merlins thrust the hump-backed R.A.F. fighters upwards at almost 200 m.p.h. The Hurricane, with its low wing loading of 27 pounds per square foot, outclimbs its R.A.F. partner, the Spitfire, which is otherwise the faster of the two. The Hurricane can also take more punishment. It has a top speed of about 330 (compared to the Spit's 367). Lacey is not envious of his comrades flying Spits, whom he refers to as 'glamour-boys'.

The squadron reaches 8,000 feet, 9,000, 10,000, course south-east. Ashford is in view below. The enemy should appear at any moment. The squadron obviously won't reach 25,000 before interception. Now the controller calls Hogan: bandits straight ahead, above! Lacey sweeps the sky ahead, sees nothing. Each pilot, silently and tensely, searches the sky, listening, checking his sight and guns. Altitude reaches 12,000 feet, 13,000, 14,000, the squadron still at maximum climb. Below it's close to lunch-time on the pleasant summer terraces of Kent and Sussex gardens.

'Bogies, twelve o'clock high!' The shout acts as an electric shock. 'Tally-ho,' Hogan responds. Lacey fixes his eyes ahead, and above . . . there they are . . . a big gaggle . . . 2,000 feet above, ahead. The enemy has the height advantage.

The dark shapes become larger by the second. Lacey's eyes stay on them. What aircraft? He sees two-engined bombers and also smaller shapes. Me.109s! Hogan pulls up towards them to make a head-on pass. Lacey pulls back on the spade-handle stick, forcing the nose of his Hurricane up. The whole squadron steepens its climb, but Lacey climbs more steeply than the rest and his speed slackens. The silhouettes of the German aircraft grow wider and they come on, above. The bombers—much larger—are Do.17s. The two forces are closing fast. Lacey realizes they'll pass too far overhead. Hogan can't get the squadron up high enough for a head-on pass! Desperate, Lacey pulls the stick handle back and the Hurricane climbs higher but airspeed slips. The Do.17s and Me.109s come on. The straining R.A.F. interceptors will miss them! The two formations flash together at 400 m.p.h. But the Germans are a thousand feet higher. Lacey's Hurricane almost stands on its tail. His eyes are locked on one of the Do.17s. Sighting almost straight up through the glass, as the enemy sweeps over above, he pulls the Hurricane straight up. Range 1,200 feet. Too far? His thumb presses the silver gun button. The eight Brownings roar. But the recoil and the angle of flight exert themselves. The Hurricane shudders. Lacey tries to dip the stick, recover. No response. He's lost flying speed, the nose won't dip. He stalls, falls off out of control to the right, into a spin.

Plunging towards the ground, he must forget the enemy and regain control. Momentarily thrown about the cockpit by violent buffeting and turning, he begins the all-important recovery procedure. Stick forward ... let her dive ... opposite rudder. Speed increases, the buffeting eases. The fighter straightens out, going straight down at great speed. Too long in a straight-down dive and a wing could come off. Pull it out! Lacey eases the stick back, throttle already back. A tremendous weight sits on his shoulders and he is pushed down harder and harder into the seat. But the green below begins to move backwards and the nose is moving towards the horizon. The Hurricane is coming out. The blood drains from his head and then the force of gravity, the multiplied weight which has pressed him downward, begins to ease. He is levelling off though he has lost 5,000 feet. The enemy and his comrades are out of sight.

He climbs to regain lost altitude, presses the microphone button just behind the throttle. 'Red Three to Red Leader. Where are you?' Over the receiver comes a reply: 'Red Leader to Red Three. Just north of Maidstone. Join up over Maidstone.' Lacey banks into a north-westerly heading to join up, eager to have company again. A lone fighter is easy prey. He gains steadily ... 12,000, 13,000, 14,000; twists his neck to check the sky behind him. No aircraft in sight. He can't be far from Pinetree squadron. The sky is empty and peaceful.

Then, ahead . . . straight ahead, north-west . . . specks . . . growing rapidly larger. Fighter squadron. Lacey studies the fast approaching bogies . . . single-engined aircraft . . . perhaps 501. They come on. He can see the spinners. Yellow! Me.109s! Coming head-on. Have they seen him? He must act. He's on a collision course with a dozen enemy fighters, each faster than the Hurricane. Instinctively, he pushes the stick handle forwards, the horizon rises and he dives to pass beneath them. But he won't run away. By all the rules of aerial combat he should. He continues his dive, gaining speed, and now the 109s are directly above.

The rush of air and the roar of the engine increase as speed increases. Now he hauls back hard on the stick handle. He pulls the nose into the straight-up position. This time he has the speed to avoid a stall and the Hurricane rockets upwards. Lacey is now zooming skywards almost directly below the last 109 in the formation, keeping the stick back. The Hurricane, coming over on its back, levels out at the top of a loop directly behind the last enemy fighter. Lacey is upside down, held firmly by seat straps, eyes fixed on the Messerschmitt ahead. 150 yards! Perfect firing range. His loop was timed to perfection. He has never shot at another aircraft on his back. The gunsight is adjusted for a normal drop in the trajectory of shells from an upright position. He will have to allow for this and fire well above the 109! He must act, speed is falling. The 109s are cruising homeward at about 240 m.p.h. and though he has built up speed in his dive, when he loses that momentum the 109s can pull away. So far they haven't seen the audacious approach. He lines up the enemy wing-span in the glass.

Now. Fire! His thumb (pointing earthwards) pushes the button. Eight machine-guns spit a stream of armour-piercing and incendiary shells. Lacey, head down, watches the effect. The roar of his guns and the vibration of the aircraft add to the strange sensation of attacking on his back. But he has compensated accurately. The 109 staggers from the blast of close, concentrated fire. Incendiaries crash into the engine and into the fuel tank behind the pilot and in seconds a black stream of smoke pours out. Complete tactical surprise! Now the 109 turns out of formation, falls off to the side and bursts into flame. It plunges straight down.

Finally, Lacey rolls over. The blood drains from his head and he sees more clearly the eleven dark enemy fighters, crosses on their wings, directly ahead. Still they haven't seen him—or the destruction of their comrade to the rear! He manœuvres in behind a 109 to the left... distance 250 yards, quickly he centres rudder and stick for proper altitude and lines him up in the sighting glass. Wingspan almost bar to bar, squarely in the orange circle. The firing button! For the third time the wing guns belch more than a hundred shells a second. Though the pattern of fire is not fully concentrated at 250 yards, shells strike the second Me.109 instantly, tearing pieces out of fuselage and wings. Lacey holds the button down. More shells find the mark. The second victim now begins to stream white smoke. Lacey knows he's hit the coolant. The 109 is doomed, for without coolant the Daimler-Benz will overheat.

Lacey takes his finger off the firing button. The pilot will have to jump—over England or the Channel. Suddenly anti-aircraft fire begins to dot the sky. It bursts uncomfortably close. And at this moment the remaining ten enemy fighters, at last aware of an impudent intruder, do what they should have done in the beginning. They split into two groups, half turning right and half left. They are coming around to get behind him. If he turns after one group, the other will curve in behind. His ammunition is low. They have a speed advantage. He is certain to be caught from the rear by one half or the other! Yet he still has a few rounds and one 109 in the group banking left is trailing behind. Perhaps he just has time to get him and still get away. It's a gamble. Left rudder, left stick. Lacey leans into a hard left bank to line up behind him. The group to his right banks more sharply to come around behind. No doubt the enemy pilots can clearly see blue and red circles on the top of the turning Hurricane's wings and no doubt they admire the tenacity of this interceptor, who should be running away from the battle—who should not have initiated it at all.

Lacey keeps stick handle back, standing on his port wing, and lines up behind the last 109. He's at maximum range. Time is precious. Fire! For a second the Hurricane's eight guns lash out in a staccato. Then firing becomes erratic. One gun empties after the other. All silent. No more ammunition! He sees white streaks ahead, in front, on both sides. He's in the trap. The 109s which banked right are behind. Dive! Instinctively, his right hand pushes the stick handle forward and he almost lunges off the seat as the fighter's nose dips and dives for earth. Luckily, the Hurricane has a high initial rate of dive, faster than the Spit, and—Lacey hopes—fast enough to escape the 109s. He steals a march on the enemy, diving first. His momentum increases; unless they dive simultaneously, they cannot immediately catch him, and the 109s have limited fuel. Lacey is utilizing the only advantage available under the circumstances—a good initial diving velocity. He spots a nearby cloud bank as he plummets downward. He'll slip into it and throw the 109s off if they're following him down.

Airspeed passes 300, 350, 400! Lacey plunges on, looking behind. He hurtles into the cloud bank . . . down through the milky white and out again at the bottom. He eases back on the stick, constantly looking behind. The Hurricane's nose comes up. He's down to 3,000 feet, still descending. He sees no one following! He reaches 1,000, goes on down to the tops of the trees, and sets course for Kenley, north-west. Since the field is in the opposite direction to the Luftwaffe bases, perhaps their leader chose not to turn back, or couldn't because of fuel limitations. Thus Lacey finds himself free from pursuit but vulnerable at low altitude without ammunition and alone. He tensely scans the sky behind . . . no enemy aircraft.

The lone fighter hurries along over the tree-tops.

For the first time since sighting the twelve enemy fighters Lacey begins to relax. Down below he recognizes familiar landmarks; he's not far from Kenley. He will claim one victory, one probable, and damage to a third, having engaged four aircraft in all. And today he hasn't been hit, even though after the last attack it was close. (Lacey has crash-landed and parachuted so often lately he's relieved that today, with burned legs, he'll walk away from the landing.) Raising his nose and increasing altitude slightly every so often to get navigational bearings, he flies straight to Kenley. The green of the big field comes into view and is an inviting welcome; he circles preparatory to landing. Cleared to come in, he eases back on the throttle, drops flaps and, as speed lessens, lowers his undercarriage. The Hurricane glides downward at 120 m.p.h. Just off the edge of the field he eases the nose upward and his speed comes back to 100.

The oil-spattered fighter touches down at 12.35 p.m. Pinetree Red Three is safely home. He slows the fighter and turns toward his revetment. His fitter and rigger are waiting, watching. Lacey, canopy open, brakes the Hurricane to a stop, pulls the throttle back. The engine continues to kick over and he reaches to two magneto switches at the bottom of the instrument panel and flips them off. The Rolls-Merlin dies. He pulls off his helmet, lifts himself out of the cockpit and begins to answer questions. He must tell the story—one enemy fighter surely shot down, one probable, attacks on another and a bomber! Congratulations come from all sides of a gathering which has quickly assembled. The petrol lorry arrives and immediately begins to refuel the fighter.

Lacey walks to the dispersal hut where returning pilots are gathered, discussing the flight. After a time the briefing officer asks casually: 'Anyone got anything to report?' Lacey is the only one who has. He hadn't mentioned it in the hut! He puts his combat report on paper and then is ready for lunch.

After eating, he comes back to the hut . . . and finds himself

Hurricane I's on the Western Front

Spitfire I's during the
Battle of Britain

Squadron Leader
R. R. S. Tuck

Squadron Leader
D. R. S. Bader

Hurricane II's in flight

Squadron Leader
J. H. Lacey

A formation of He.111's
on their way to England

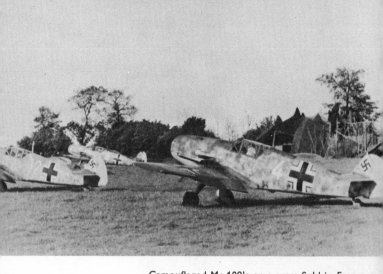

Camouflaged Me.109's on a grass field in France

An Me.109E shot down over southern England

Hans-Joachim Marseille

A Messerschmitt of J.G.27

Oberst Eduard Neumann in the Desert

Erich Hartmann

Messerschmitts of Mölders's J.G.51
on the Russian Front

Major Kurt Buehligen

Major Heinz Bär

again on readiness! He picks out a comfortable chair and tries to get some sleep, still thinking about shooting down an enemy fighter while on his back.

Later that afternoon the squadron was scrambled again. Once again Lacey was on the attack, intercepting a bomber force. Escorting 109s bounced the Hurricanes before they got into the bombers and in a dogfight with one Lacey shot the enemy's tail completely off with a concentrated pattern of fire. Shortly afterwards he caught one of the bombers (an He.111) and sent it down—his second kill of the afternoon. In the course of one day he had destroyed an Me.109 in the morning and probably another and then added two victories in the afternoon! When he landed at Kenley he was tired but satisfied. Four victories in a day. This spirit, personified so well by Lacey, was what made it clear to the Luftwaffe across the Channel that the assault against England would not be as easy as it once looked.

Lacey was shot down again on 17 September over Ashford, his parachute again saving his life. On the 27th he downed another 109, which raised his score to nineteen. (Shortly afterwards he was awarded a bar to his D.F.M.) In October he shot down three more 109s and crash-landed again, surviving another narrow escape.

Things were quieter after October. In recognition of his service and ability, Lacey was awarded a commission the following January. When fighter action increased somewhat in the summer of 1941, Lacey was back with 501, now as an officer, engaging in fighter sweeps over France. That summer he shot down three Me.109s before being posted to a training school as an instructor. (The R.A.F. customarily pulled its highest scorers out of action when they had done their share or had been on an extended period of combat duty.)

In 1942 he had just begun another tour of combat duty, with 602 Squadron, and had damaged three F.W.190s when he was suddenly transferred to a headquarters post. In 1943 he was posted to India. Only in the final months of the war did he return to operations, when he took command of 17 Squadron in Burma. On 19 February 1945 he encountered an Oscar II, a formidable Japanese fighter, and shot it down as his twenty-eight confirmed victim. It was his last.

After the war he remained in the R.A.F. and when I visited him in Hull he was about ready to retire after a full career in the Royal Air Force. He is still fair-haired (though thinning at the top), soft-spoken and mild-mannered: few suspect, as they engage him in conversation, that the Yorkshireman they are talking to is the top surviving scorer of the Battle of Britain. (And this quiet manner is found in many of the war's top pilots.) Speaking nostalgically of the Hurricane, he said: 'It was a collection of non-essential parts, you know—you could fire a bullet through it and never hit anything that mattered. But it could dive, and climb. And it could fly with anything shot off. . . .'

Ginger Lacey's quiet, bulldog tenacity was the essence of the British spirit which won the Battle of Britain—with all its consequences for the free world. But he possessed more than that. Perhaps no pilot in the R.A.F. was more sure in flying skill and aerobatic ability, and with this outstanding mastery at the controls Lacey combined expert marksmanship in the air. One wonders how many of the enemy he would have shot down, having scored over twenty victories in 1940 alone, if he had seen more extensive aerial combat in the last four years of the war. If he had survived—and he probably would have—he might well have been at the top of the R.A.F. list of aces.

# CHAPTER SEVEN

# THE CAMPAIGN IN AFRICA

THE FIGHTER struggle in Africa is one of the most interesting of the Second World War. As the numbers involved were not great, at least in the early stages, a fairly clear picture can be obtained. The basic consideration to be kept in mind, in summarizing this air campaign and looking at losses, is that the Luftwaffe possessed the better fighter.

German and Italian troops surrendered in Tunis in May 1943, ending the hostilities which had begun when Mussolini declared war on France and Britain in June 1940, hoping to get in on the spoils of Hitler's Continental victory. Thus the campaign lasted about thre  years. German participation began early in 1941, being undertaken to rescue Mussolini's forces from impending military disaster.

From the time German Me.109Es arrived in Tripoli, in April 1941, the Luftwaffe was better equipped in the air, and this superiority lasted until Spitfires at last reached the area in 1942—and even then Spitfires made up only a small percentage of the Allied fighter force. The R.A.F. enjoyed numerical superiority, but its Hurricanes, Curtiss Tomahawks and Kittyhawks were no match for the 109E, still less for the 109F, which arrived late in 1941. On the other hand, when R.A.F. fighters caught Stukas without a fighter escort (sometimes even with it), the German dive-bombers often suffered heavy losses. And, of course, R.A.F. pilots had enjoyed a technical edge over their Italian opponents until the Luftwaffe arrived in April 1941, and had destroyed far more aircraft than they had lost. (The British originally claimed that Italian losses in less than a year totalled more than 1,000, many of which were abandoned or strafed on the ground.) German losses in Africa did not become heavy until late in 1942, and reached a peak during the ill-fated Axis attempt to sustain beleaguered forces in Tunis from the air in 1943. Then, as Axis fields shrank in number and were crowded into a smaller and smaller area, and as transports attempted to cross the Mediterranean in desperate supply and evacuation efforts, Allied air superiority exacted a heavy toll.

Until the summer of 1942, however, about the time of the death of the great Hans-Joachim Marseille (of whom more later), Luftwaffe fighters often held the upper hand. Certainly from November 1941, when Jagdgeschwader 27 began to operate Me.109Fs, the technical superiority of the German fighters was pronounced—the arrival of a small number of Spitfires being inadequate to redress the balance. Thus one is led to the conclusion that in the fighter war in Africa quality triumphed over quantity, regarding both the British and Italians in the first year and the Germans and the British much of the time thereafter.

The first Luftwaffe fighters to be sent to Africa were some forty (one Gruppe) of J.G. 27, commanded by Eduard Neumann, in April 1941.[1] Later the Gruppe was expanded into the full Geschwader and finally an additional Gruppe from another Geschwader was sent in May 1942 (Gruppe III of J.G. 53). By 1943 about three Geschwader were operating —Hitler having rushed in reinforcements in the final months of the campaign. Thus German fighter strength in Africa in 1941 and 1942 is well known; it began at about 40 aircraft, rose to about 120 (Geschwader strength) and by 1942 exceeded 160,[2] though due to the poor serviceability rate of the Luftwaffe in Africa the number available for operations on any one day was usually no more than about

[1] From conversation with Eduard Neumann, Munich, Germany. Neumann was the commanding officer of the first Luftwaffe fighter Gruppe sent to Africa, and later became commander of the full Geschwader when it was expanded into three Gruppen as Geschwader 27.

[2] This estimate based on German records and confirmed by Neumann and Ring.

50 per cent of the total. (The R.A.F. serviceability rate was better, probably averaging about 66 per cent.) Maximum strength, in 1943, was several hundred aircraft.

R.A.F. strength was modest at the beginning of 1940, but was steadily built up during the campaign—though diversions to other fronts, such as that to Greece in 1940, sometimes interrupted the process. From 3 Gladiator squadrons, 6 of Blenheims, 21 Lysanders and 10 Sunderland flying-boats, with reserves of 100 per cent, as of the beginning of 1940 (Italy had not yet declared war), the figures moved upwards during that year, and during 1941 and 1942.[1] By the end of the summer of 1941 the Desert Air Force had grown to a fighter strength of 4 squadrons of Hurricanes, 4 of Tomahawks, 1 Royal Navy, 1 'army co-operation', and 6 others. At this time, Luftwaffe single-engined-fighter strength was still only about 40 aircraft (there were also 10 Me.110 long-range fighters).[2] By May 1942 the Desert Air Force contained 18 single-engined squadrons, among them 3 reconnaissance squadrons, 1 Hellenic and 1 Free French (these last two both Hurricanes).[3] One source reports that Desert Air Force fighter strength as of July 1942 was approximately 367 aircraft,[4] and that by the time of the Battle of El Alamain it was at least 24 squadrons—or about twice as many squadrons as the Luftwaffe had Staffeln.

If these are generally accurate estimates of the fighter

[1] Owen, *The Desert Air Force* (Hutchinson, 1948), Introduction to Book One. The author states that at the end of 1939 Italian strength opposing this force was at least double that of the R.A.F., the Italian fighters consisting of Breda 65s and C.R. 30s. By 1940, and the successful British offensive, Hurricanes had arrived in Africa. The Italians had, meanwhile, expanded their air forces, only to suffer a catastrophic defeat during General Wavell's 1940 drive to Cyrenaica.

[2] Owen, Appendix B.

[3] Based on official records.

[4] Owen, Chapter 16. This force consisted of 251 Hurricanes, 92 Kittyhawks and 24 Spitfires. Total Luftwaffe strength in Africa at this time was 310 aircraft of all types, not more than half of them fighters. Johnson, *Full Circle*, p. 201, estimates German-Italian air strength in the spring of 1942 at approximately 600 aircraft.

forces opposed, what were the losses? British loss statistics are not as easily obtained as the German (most of the 1941–2 German fighter losses are quickly obtainable from the records of J.G.27). German victory confirmations up to the time of Alamein (late October 1942) totalled 1,294. A breakdown of these shows that Luftwaffe pilots received credit for destroying 709 Curtiss (Tomahawk or Kittyhawk) fighters, 304 Hurricanes, 119 Spitfires and 162 others. Even confirmed claims, of course, are not accurate figures, and as to the types claimed, German pilots were notorious for confusing Allied types.

Official figures show that total R.A.F. losses from the beginning in the Middle East were higher than the number confirmed to German pilots, which is to be expected, for they cover losses to the Italians and to other causes. By September 1942 losses due to enemy action totalled 1,635 with another 1,648 damaged.[1] No doubt the figure was slightly higher by the time of the Battle of El Alamein and higher still at the conclusion of the African campaign in 1943. Thus it could be that German confirmations (1,294) were not excessive, though some British students of the desert war feel that Luftwaffe claims in Africa, especially in 1942, were not as reliable as their claims, for example, in Europe. In any event, of the 1,294 victories, 674 were confirmed to fifteen pilots! One fighter 'Experte', it is seen, was worth far more than several average pilots. The top scorer among all the German pilots in Africa (and among all who flew in the West for that matter) was Marseille, who died just before El Alamein with 158 confirmed victories (151 in Africa). He was not the only German pilot in Africa with a large number of kills. Werner Schroer, who ended the war with 114, scored 61 in Africa. And there were others who gained in the vicinity of 50 (Stahlschmidt, 59; Roedel, 52; Homuth, 46).

What were German losses in this period? Official records show that about 200 Me.109s were lost in air combat, with 31

[1] Table of Operations, R.A.F. Middle East Aircraft Casualties, 8 September 1942.

pilots killed, 30 missing (some probably killed), 28 captured and 25 wounded. These are interesting figures, and while we might partially discount the number of victories awarded to German fighter pilots (1,294), it would apparently take a considerable adjustment to bring R.A.F. losses down to a comparable total.

Fighter figures, of course, do not show the complete picture. For that one must take into account bomber losses. *Total* R.A.F. air claims—for aircraft of all types, both Italian and German—approximate to Luftwaffe confirmations, and it may be that the total number of Axis air losses, including Italian losses, Stukas, and so on, are about equal to British losses, as one researcher estimates.[1] On the other hand, in looking at the record of Luftwaffe versus R.A.F. fighters in Africa, one cannot escape the conclusion that the small number of Me.109s in the desert achieved outstanding results in 1941 and 1942. In the last six to eight months of the campaign German fighter losses sharply increased, in the rout and forced evacuation, as we have noted.

One indication that German confirmation figures as quoted above may not be too far wrong is the large number of fighters sent to the Desert by the R.A.F. Taking figures presented in English publications, it can be seen, for example, that between November 1941 and September 1942, 1,167 Hurricanes, 830 Kittyhawks, about 200 Spitfires and 7 Tomahawks were dispatched to the Desert Air Force. While a certain number were lost in accidents, some to ground fire, and others for different reasons, it would nevertheless seem that Luftwaffe fighter pilots accounted for a considerable number of them. And the Tomahawk and Kittyhawk seem to have taken a numerical thrashing in combat with the Me.109.

It should again be stressed that this is only the fighter-versus-fighter picture, and that therefore the glory of the Desert Air Force is not a false glory. There is no doubt that

[1] This is viewed a possibility by Christopher Shores, specialist on the African air war and author of *Aces High*.

in 1942 the teamwork exhibited by the Desert Air Force, co-operating with the Eighth Army, was a decisive factor in the rout of Axis forces. But just as R.A.F. fighters made short work of inferior Italian aircraft, so too did Me.109s win their own war against fighters of lesser performance. In the opinion of German pilots, American fighters which appeared in Algeria between November 1942 and the collapse of Axis resistance in May 1943 (P.39s and P.38s), were no match for the 109.

Certainly the record of J.G.27, in Africa until late in 1942, was an outstanding one. When the end became imminent, pilots of the two Geschwader then there were ordered to fly their fighters from bases in Tunis to Sicily. There was no means to evacuate crewmen but, as Allied forces closed in, pilots packed two and sometimes three crewmen into the tiny cockpits of the 109s (and F.W.190s which had also been sent to Africa), these cockpits being smaller than those in Spits or Hurricanes, and only about half the size of those in American fighters, and took off for Sicily. The unit served throughout the war, but it never again had such success, and suffered heavy losses in the last years when the best American fighters appeared over Germany in increasing numbers to challenge the celebrated Desert Geschwader with both quality and quantity.

# CHAPTER EIGHT

# THE LUFTWAFFE

THE GERMAN AIR FORCE, of course, was abolished in 1918, after a war in which it had produced the highest-scoring pilots, had held the upper hand over the fronts much of the time, and had introduced the first fighter with guns firing through the propeller. Army leaders, especially Colonel General Hans von Seeckt, realized that air power would be even more important in the future, and an air force was secretly organized and trained as a part of the Army.

As early as 1923 a secret agreement was concluded with Russia that led to the establishment in 1924 of a flying-training school deep inside Russia at Lipezk. It remained in operation for nine years, and most of the higher ranks of the then unborn Luftwaffe passed through it. (In addition another group of German pilots was sent to Italy years later, but this experiment was considered of limited value, and discontinued.)

To give young men flying training, the Deutscher Luft-sportverband was organized, and this organization conducted courses in glider flying all over Germany. Captain Kurt Student, head of the Reichswehr air technical branch, was its principal.

Aircraft manufacture likewise never entirely ceased in Germany after the First World War. The industry managed to progress by various means, some devious. A key man in its development was Erhard Milch, the head of Lufthansa and a friend of Hermann Göring, his deputy air commissioner in 1933 (there was still no military air organization). Lufthansa became a testing school for military pilots, and it was Lufthansa which developed the Lorenz beam system for approaches to airports, a system eventually used in the war to guide Luftwaffe bombers to British cities.

Though Milch had resisted joining the Nazis, Hitler gave him personal attention, probably at Göring's suggestion, and he was used by the Nazis with good effect in the building of both the German aviation industry and the new German Air Force in the early thirties. At first the Nazis did not admit existence of an air force, and therefore Milch was Göring's Secretary of State at the new Air Ministry. In 1935, however, Hitler announced the German Air Force as a *fait accompli*. The industry and the Luftwaffe expanded rapidly, though Milch's power was later to wane. (He had been nominated by Hitler to be Göring's successor in the early thirties.)

Milch preferred a thorough long-term build-up; Göring insisted on immediate results. Hitler demanded the biggest force in the shortest possible time.

The most glaring example of faulty planning in this rapid build-up concerned the heavy bomber. In 1935 the new German Air Force asked for prototypes of a long-range bomber, and Dornier and Junkers produced test models in 1936. The Junkers was probably the more promising. It could cruise at 200 m.p.h. (as fast as the Fortresses and Lancasters which were to wreck so much of Germany eight years later) and had a range of almost 1,000 miles. The man who had worked out the specifications for this four-engined bomber, and who, it is generally conceded, was destined to become the head of the Luftwaffe's heavy bomber arm, was General Walther Weaver, first Chief of Staff of the Luftwaffe. Unfortunately for the German Air Force, Weaver was killed in an air crash in 1936. Those who came after him, such as Albert Kesselring, who was later to serve so prominently in the war and to become a Field-Marshal, apparently did not share the strategic vision to push for a heavy bomber. It was Kesselring who signed the order early in 1937 which, in effect, cancelled the heavy bomber programme.[1]

Göring and Milch must share the responsibility, for Milch

[1] Wood, p. 45.

138

suggested that Germany did not have the capacity and resources to build the heavies, while Göring concluded that Hitler would be more impressed by large numbers of twin-engined bombers than by smaller numbers of four-engined craft.

When Göring made his comrade Ernst Udet, the famous First War fighter pilot, Colonel and Inspector of Fighter and Stuka (dive-bomber) Pilots, the effect was to weight the scales heavily in favour of reliance on the Stuka. Udet had purchased two of the American Curtiss dive-bombers which had made such an impression on the world, partly through films, and was sold on their potential. In the end, with argument and demonstration, he was able to win over the sceptics, and Germany embarked on what critics have felt was over-emphasis of the Stuka. (The Ju.87, built by Junkers, was selected in competitive trials with the He.118.) It is true that more was expected of the Stuka than it was able to perform against sophisticated opposition. But in the beginning, in Poland, France and the Low Countries, Africa and Russia, the Stuka did highly effective work with the Panzers. It is probably reasonable to say its development was well worth the cost and effort. When its use was attempted in a strategic campaign, the Battle of Britain, in which first-class fighter opposition was met, the Stuka proved far too slow, a sitting duck for enemy fighters. Though valuable as an army-co-operation dive-bomber, it was no substitute for other bombers, and could only be used when adequately protected by fighters.

Luftwaffe planners overestimated, as did those elsewhere, the defensive power of one or two rear-firing guns. Not only the Ju.87 but also the Me.110, the Do.17, the He.111 and the Ju.88 were under-armed and under-armoured for battle with modern fighters which carried eight ·303 Brownings or even 20 mm. cannon, or—in the case of U.S. fighters—six or eight ·50 calibre machine-guns. It was the heavier firepower of fighters in this war which upset the theories of the designers. The U.S.A.A.F. utilized the heaviest defensive armament yet seen, ten ·50 calibres, in the B.17 Flying Fortresses later in the war, and even these 'Forts', in tight-formation boxes, could not defy the fighter. Six or seven hundred American airmen went down in such bombers in a few hours—to the guns of German fighters—on several occasions.

The twin-engined-bomber concept in the Luftwaffe ruled out heavy bomb tonnages in strategic campaigns, such as those transported by heavy bombers of the R.A.F. and U.S.A.A.F.

As serious as the abandonment of the heavy bomber, in terms of cost to the nation and to the war effort, was the Luftwaffe's failure to stress the fighter. When the war began, bombers were being turned out at a faster rate than fighters. Fighter production didn't get into high gear until late 1943, and the first year in which it was really felt was 1944—when the war was already lost.[1] It will surprise many to learn that German aircraft production was less than that of Great Britain in the early years of the war, and remained comparatively low until well into 1942, a year after the attack on Russia. It reached a peak of about 40,000 planes[2] only in the last full year of the war. Over 25,000 of these were fighters. The emphasis placed on bombers was certainly Hitler's. As far as fighter production is concerned, in the opinion of many authorities a lack of organizational talent on the part of Udet was a limiting factor. Milch, who had been comparatively shunted aside by a jealous Göring, was called upon to set things right in mid-1942 after Udet's suicide, and had Germany produced early in the war the number of fighters that Milch or (later) Albert Speer managed to attain, the air war might have taken a different course. Speer, after replacing Milch, did the outstanding production job of the war for

[1] Galland, pp. 13–14. Bekker, *Angriffshöhe 4000*, p. 465, cites figures to show German bomber production exceeded fighter production in 1939 and 1940.

[2] Various sources estimate total German production at figures ranging from 44,000 to 38,000. Galland, p. 246, states that total production of aircraft of all types was 38,000. On p. 309 he gives the figure of 40,593. Bekker, p. 465, lists total 1944 German aircraft production as 40,593 units.

Germany, more than doubling Milch's figures.[1]

The other fascinating 'might have been' in the German fighter picture concerns the Me.262. Though many nations were working on the development of a jet-turbine aircraft, the first flown was in Germany, days before the invasion of Poland. This was the He.178.[2] But it was Willi Messerschmitt who persisted in this field, and who built the first practical jet fighter, the 262. He was, however, hindered in his work by Milch, and later by Hitler himself,[3] and it was

---

[1] Official German production figures, from numerous sources, show German fighter production, several hundred per month in 1940, rose only slowly, to between 300 and 400, in 1942, under Udet's direction, then under Milch to a figure of 1,000 per month, and by the autumn of 1944, under Speer, to 2,500 per month. See Galland, appendix chart (German edition); U.S. edition, p.14 and p. 246.

[2] Galland, p. 324.

[3] According to Messerschmitt (private conversation with me in June 1964) Milch came to Messerschmitt's home in 1941, just before the invasion of Russia, and strenuously objected to work Messerschmitt was doing on the Me.262. Milch's objections forced all Me.262 production work, or practically all, to a halt. Messerschmitt secretly continued to carry out what work he could on the project, begun in 1938. 'First we put a screw in the middle of the engines,' he recalls. 'In 1943 the late Major Opitz came to see me in Augsburg. He saw my pilot fly the Me.262, and wanted to fly it himself. I refused. Then he explained that there was a morale problem in the Lutwaffe, caused by the great number of U.S. planes, the heavy bombers and their armament. He said he couldn't get a permit to fly it. Finally, I relented. He flew it and said it was sensational. He called Galland. Galland also flew it. He talked to Göring, then they talked to Hitler. Then thousands were wanted right away. We produced them as fast as we could, in tunnels near Garmisch and elsewhere, but it was too late. They were shot up largely on the ground.' See also Galland, p. 325. (Galland sets the time of his flight as 22 May 1943). Galland also relates (pp. 326–31) how he received enthusiastic co-operation from Göring, Milch and others for the start of a crash building programme, after his initial Me.262 flight, and how Hitler, because of unfulfilled promises from Göring in the past, was sceptical. Hitler thereby held up the crash programme for six months. Yet the costliest delay, in Galland's opinion, was the order in late 1940 postponing all research (which Milch referred to in chastising Messerschmitt in 1941) and Galland estimates this order delayed development by two full years. The Luftwaffe also employed the world's first rocket fighter, the Me.163, in small numbers, but it played no major role in the war.

only late in 1943 that the go-ahead for a start in production came from the high authorities. And at that time Hitler was insisting that the jet be built as a bomber, labelling it the 'perfect blitz bomber' (which he intended to use against England).

When the 262 did go into action late in 1944 it quickly proved itself. But it was then too late and too few in numbers. Had several thousands been available in 1943 it is doubtful whether American piston-engined fighters could have won a clear-cut victory in German skies during the following year. The 262 was capable of a speed of 520 m.p.h., easily out-distancing Allies fighters when it was encountered in 1944 and 1945.[1]

As it turned out, the Me.109 and the F.W.190 served as standard German fighters throughout the war. Many models of both were produced, improvements being incorporated as the war progressed to increase performance. The 109 was chosen in competitive trials at Rechlin in the mid-thirties and became the standard Luftwaffe fighter. It served in the Spanish Civil War and was the only single-engined German fighter until 1941, when the Focke-Wulf was received by some units. The F.W.190 is generally rated the best conventional German fighter of the war, and certainly Allied fighter pilots held that opinion. But there are many German pilots, some who flew the Me.109 throughout the war, such as Erich Hartmann, who preferred the 109. Some are dedicated to the proposition that, handled properly, the latest 109s were a match for any conventional fighter throughout the war. No doubt their speed was greatly increased by various improved engines, and when the F series was introduced after the Battle of Britain many felt it held a performance edge over the Spit-fires then in use.[2] The 109 and 190 met American fighters in

[1] Galland, p. 326; also my own experience and that of every other Allied pilot who encountered the Me.262, comparatively few of which were destroyed in air-to-air combat.

[2] The F's performance against that of the Spitfire in 1941 is still debated. Windrow in *Profile Publications*, series No. 3 (London), states that Spitfire

Africa in late 1942 and 1943 on at least equal terms.

An early weakness of the 109 was its wing structure. With its light airframe and heavy engine, it was possible for pilots to tear its wings off when they pulled out of a dive.[1] The F.W.190, like the P.47, was radial-engined and air-cooled, and therefore could take more punishment than liquid-cooled engines, which without coolant would soon overheat or freeze. (The P.47 was perhaps the toughest of all the fighters in the Second World War, and this saved the lives of many strafing American pilots who often brought back their beloved 'seven-ton milk bottles' full of holes.) The F.W.190 was developed several years after the 109, and was the favourite of the majority of Luftwaffe fighter pilots. It was used for various tasks during the war—bombing, rocket-firing, and strafing—in addition to normal fighter-interceptor usage.

Morale among German fighter pilots during the war was unquestionably good. Yet it should be noted that during the Battle of Germany, in 1944 and 1945, the strain began to tell. There were, understandably, instances when gaggles fled in confusion, and others when fighter formations were almost destroyed in one day.[2] One reason for this was the inade-

---

Vs had a performance edge over Me.109 Fs until F.W.190s arrived in the summer of 1942. German authorities claim that the F was equal to the Spit V, and pilots disagree in their opinions.

[1] In private conversation with the author, 8 June 1966, Douglas Bader recalled: 'The square-winged 109 (the E which was used in the Battle of Britain) would lose its wings if a pilot pulled out of a long dive too sharply. We therefore had the advantage in pullouts. The Germans finally fitted the stick with weights, so that the pilot couldn't pull back on the stick so sharply, to reduce the chance of this happening.'

[2] Jagdgeschwader 27 and other units, on 2 November 1944 near Leuna-Mersburg, encountered American fighters and lost over 40 air-craft, 27 pilots killed and 11 wounded, in a fierce, short battle. The American Fighter Groups were 55 and 352. Hans Ring, in private conversation with me, February 1966, expressed the opinion that American long-range fighters in battles such as this 'broke the Fighter Arm's neck'. He cited yearly pilot loss figures of two Geschwader to show the effect of the appearance over Germany of long-range fighters: J.G. 26: 1940, 82; 1941, 72; 1942 69; 1943, 154; 1944, 293; 1945, 133. And J.G. 27:

quate training of Luftwaffe fighter pilots late in the war, caused by fuel shortages and by Germany's desperate need for pilots. Yet the accomplishment of German fighter pilots in general in the Battle of Germany, was considerable. Of 70,000 victory confirmations in the war, 25,000 came against the Western air forces, and, interestingly, more than half this number were shot down by less than 500 pilots.[1]

Luftwaffe fighter pilots enjoyed a comradeship akin to that in Fighter Command. On flying duty they usually led a good life, rest periods being provided during more normal times, though in Russia life was spartan. In spite of good morale, good equipment and courage, they paid a heavy price, being surrounded on all sides and fighting against odds. Approximately 8,500 of their number serving with operational units gave their lives during the war. Another 2,700 were captured, and 9,100 wounded. Twin-engined-fighter pilot losses (including those in night fighters) totalled approximately 3,600 killed and 3,100 lost from causes other than enemy action.[2]

The reader can get an idea of the great number of operational flights, and victories, of German fighter pilots by scanning the list in Appendixes 3 and 4. The flying records of the veterans reveal the demands made on them. While the top pilots tended to survive the war in most air forces, only about half the top hundred Germans survived. Many were lost after having achieved fifty, a hundred or a greater number of victories.

Non-commissioned officers flew as pilots in the Luftwaffe and, of approximately 560 pilots who won the Knight's Cross to the Iron Cross, about 300 began as enlisted men. Com-

---

1940, 73; 1941, 48; 1942, 73; 1943, 123 (Geschwader scattered); 1944, 380 (Geschwader in Germany); 1945, 126.

[1] Hans Ring, private conversation, 1965. Said Ring: 'We had, by English-American rules, 2,500 aces. But, of course, I say five victories is not an ace.'

[2] Obermaier, *Die Ritterkreuzträger der deutschen Jagdwaffe*, appendix; loss totals for Fighter Command and other R.A.F. commands, Macmillan, appendix. Others give slightly different R.A.F. losses.

missioned flying ranks in the Luftwaffe, beginning at the bottom, were as follows:

Leutnant
Oberleutnant
Hauptmann
Major
Oberstleutnant
Oberst
Generalmajor
Generalleutnant
Generaloberst
Generalfeldmarschall
Reichsmarschall

In the Luftwaffe, titles other than rank were used in certain positions, and had nothing to do with actual rank. Galland, for example, when a Generalleutnant, was General der Jagdflieger, and every Geschwader commander was called a 'Kommodore' regardless of his actual rank. Likewise a 'Kommandeur' commanded a Gruppe, and his rank could vary.

On another point there has been confusion since the war— the point system used by the Luftwaffe (only in the West). One of the first clear explanations seen in English, and in detail, is to be found in Toliver and Constable's *Fighter Aces*. In brief, points were awarded as incentives, and they counted towards decorations and promotions, and not as or towards aerial kills. German pilots did not share victories: they had to decide which was to get the victory if two or more were involved, or none would be credited. Points were awarded as follows: destruction of damaged twin-engined aircraft, $\frac{1}{2}$; single-engined fighter destroyed, twin-engined aircraft damaged or final destruction of damaged four-engined aircraft, 1; twin-engined aircraft destroyed, three- or four-engined aircraft damaged and separated from formation, 2; three- or four-engined aircraft destroyed, 3.

Germany called upon the young men of many countries, as did England, to fly her fighters. The Luftwaffe helped to train and supply the fighter forces of many Balkan countries in the war (the 'crusade' against Communism had an appeal among the devout in many cases), and many of Germany's allies, from Finland to Rumania, produced high-scoring pilots. Interestingly, too, more Luftwaffe pilots came from what is now East Germany than from the territory of the present Federal Republic.

Flight formations of Luftwaffe fighters began with the two-plane Rotte, two of which composed a Schwarm. A Staffel could consist of three four-fighter units or less, but was usually composed of eight to twelve aircraft. Three Staffeln comprised a Gruppe and three Gruppen (four as from 1943) made up a Geschwader.

# CHAPTER NINE

# THE STAR OF AFRICA OVER BIR HAKEIM

*6 June 1942—Oberleutnant Hans-Joachim Marseille, Luftwaffe*

OF ALL the German fighter pilots of the Second World War, the one who most thoroughly captured the imagination of his countrymen, and who has become a legend comparable to that of the R.A.F.'s Douglas Bader, was Hans-Joachim Marseille. He is looked upon today by such authorities as Adolf Galland, Hans Ring and comrades who flew with him in Africa as the greatest of the Luftwaffe's fighter pilots in the Second World War. Some of his feats were so incredible that sceptics in Allied countries for many years refused to accept records verifying them.

Those who watched him perform place him in a class by himself as an aerial marksman. So accurate was his shooting that his wing-man who verified his victories became known as the *'fliegendes Zahlwerk'* (Flying Adding Machine). His commanding officer in Africa, Oberst Eduard Neumann, ays of him: 'There was no one else like him. I could always pick him out by the way he flew.' His wingman, Reiner Pöttgen, says: 'He was the greatest of all our pilots.' Galland says: 'He was the unrivalled virtuoso among the fighter pilots of the Second World War. His achievements were previously thought to have been impossible.' Hans Ring, who has talked to a considerable number of German pilots who flew with Marseille, says he was the 'greatest' of the German *Experten*.

The Marseille mission described in this chapter is the only account in this book of a fighter action of a deceased pilot. It was only possible because there still existed so much detailed and eye-witness information about the action in question. His wingman survives and lives in Cologne. His commanding officer survives and lives in Munich. Both flew with him during the memorable episode related in this chapter and recall it today, even some of the words spoken. In addition, one of the men Marseille shot down that day confirms events from the other side. A check of R.A.F. losses on the day of the mission showed Marseille's claims to be reasonable. I have made use of German accounts of the combat and awards made on the basis of it. Suffice it to say that as a result of a not inconsiderable investigation I have come to the conclusion that the Marseille record has not been intentionally coloured. Where war records are concerned, of course, there is always the chance that information from the other side which becomes available after hostilities will somewhat alter the picture. The Marseille record should be accepted with this in mind, just as should that of every other fighter pilot.

Marseille's career was a short one. Born in 1919 in Berlin, he received his early schooling in the German capital and was nineteen when war broke out. His father served in the First War and was also a flier, and the family was of distinguished French Huguenot ancestry. Marseille had won his wings and was a young Leutnant on the Western Front when the German offensive against France and the Low Countries began on 10 May 1940. Serving with Jagdgeschwader 52 he shot down seven aircraft in the French campaign. After a brief period with Geschwader 5, he was posted to 27 on the eve of the departure of some of its pilots to Africa. He went with them, arriving in Africa in April 1941. In something over a year in combat he shot down 151 aircraft. His death on 30 September 1942 came at the high-water mark of the Luftwaffe effort in Africa. British aerial ascendancy was facilitated by it and it was probably a factor in the success of the Eighth Army. His value to the Luftwaffe and to the Afrika Korps can readily be seen in the fact that in his last four weeks of combat in September 1942 he shot down 57 enemy planes.

During this final month he had his greatest day—seventeen victories (in three missions). There has been post-war speculation concerning these confirmations and a brief look at this day is in order. Marseille claimed to have shot down two Spitfires and two Curtiss fighters on an early morning mission, eight Curtiss types (either Tomahawks or Kittyhawks) in a late morning mission over Alam el Halfa and five more Curtiss types late that afternoon south of Imayid. (He was said to have shot down the eight Curtiss types in ten minutes and the five that afternoon in six. The four in the morning required eleven minutes.) Such rapid, wholesale destruction had never before been achieved and questions were raised, in the Luftwaffe at the time and later in Allied countries. It was said after the war—and disputed on the German side—that the R.A.F. didn't lose as many fighters in the entire Middle East as were confirmed to Marseille that day. However, official records show the R.A.F. lost thirteen shot down, and that another six crash-landed after being hit, for a total of nineteen. Others were hit. Of the nineteen, two were Spitfires, eight Curtiss types and nine Hurricanes. Since German pilots often confused Hurricane and Curtiss, one would not want to be dogmatic until all R.A.F. squadron losses in the Middle East, and times and places, were carefully checked. Because Marseille on other occasions accounted for several Curtiss types in rapid order with a minimum expenditure of ammunition it would seem unwise to conclude that he could not shoot down a number of Curtiss fighters in a few minutes. The evidence indicates not only that he could but that he did on more than one occasion. In this connection, it should be remembered that the Me.109 Marseille was flying was a superior fighter to the Curtiss or Hurricane in the Middle East.

Luftwaffe confirmations, plus the agreement of those who flew with Marseille, are persuasive indications that the records should stand. If we are to begin altering individual records downwards, where do we stop? We learned after the war that Allied claims, and thus confirmations to individual pilots, totalled a greater number of aircraft than the enemy actually lost. Thus the scores of many British and American fighter pilots are obviously inflated, though not intentionally. No one seriously proposes that the confirmed wartime scores of Allied aces be reduced.

It is difficult, of course, to comprehend a talent for quick mass destruction. Only a few Allied pilots, among them David McCampbell of the U.S. Navy, and C. H. Dyson of the R.A.F., managed comparable destruction on one sortie. McCampbell shot down nine Zekes and damaged two more in one action in October 1944. Like Marseille, McCampbell was flying the superior fighter, an F.6F, and the Zekes adopted a defensive formation not unlike that used by Curtiss fighters in the Middle East against 109s and against which Marseille became so effective. Dyson, flying in the first Libyan campaign in Africa, in December of 1940, shot down six Fiat CR42s, one of them falling into an SM79 bomber and causing it to crash, giving him the R.A.F. high for one mission—seven. Successful in the First War, the Lufbery seems so have later been somewhat vulnerable as a defensive manœuvre against expert pilots in faster aircraft.

One of the principal reasons for Marseille's success, according to those who watched him develop, was the careful handling of his spirit and exuberance by his commanding officer in 27 Geschwader, Oberst Eduard Neumann. Marseille joined the Geschwader just prior to its departure for Africa. He had been something of a disciplinary problem in 2 and 5. Neumann, then Gruppenkommandeur and later Kommodore of the full Geschwader, was patient in handling the highly strung Marseille. Then twenty-one, Marseille was at that time, as he had been in school and in France, highly unorthodox in behaviour and in personal appearance. Likewise, he was unorthodox in flying tactics, often breaking accepted tactical rules. Individualistic in dress, a devotee of jazz, the latest dances and girls, he could have been a major disciplinary and morale problem. (He had once landed on an autobahn in Germany; and in Africa, in a fit of anger, he had once strafed the ground near the tent of a superior who had refused him combat assignments.) Speaking recently of

Marseille, in Munich, Neumann observed: 'Marseille could have been a problem character or a very great fighter pilot. At first his individuality—and his lack of discipline—alienated his comrades. However, after they realized his talent and skill, and saw the results he achieved, they became aware of his leadership and even magnetism, and looked up to him as to no other pilot.'

Neumann refused to step on the restless spirit and made a calculated effort to win Marseille's confidence and respect, which he succeeded in doing. As was the case with R.A.F. pilot Bob Tuck, saved from probable bowler-hatting at his first flying school by understanding superiors, Marseille's success was probably only because Neumann recognized his potential.

According to surviving comrades, Marseille's combat tactics were extremely daring. He would attack under conditions or circumstances universally accepted as unfavourable. When enemy pilots resorted to the Lufbery as a defensive tactic he didn't hesitate to attack. The accepted theory was that if one attacked any of the circling planes, his comrade behind would soon have the attacker in his sights. Marseille was so adept at gunnery that he delivered his attacks diving, or zooming up from below after a dive to gain speed, and very often knocked a victim out of the circling formation on the first pass with a burst of about two seconds. On some occasions he even joined the circle. Another formation he attacked in what was considered an extremely disadvantageous position was the V formation. He approached from behind, exposing himself to the fire of the trailing wings to reach the leading aircraft in the centre. He came in fast enough to escape the wrath of enemy fighters on the flanks and achieved victories with quick, accurate bursts, using this tactic on more than one occasion.

The key to Marseille's success was near-perfection in aerial gunnery. His kills were scored with a minimum expenditure of ammunition. Deflection shooting, while diving or zooming up from below, was his speciality. A constant practiser, he became so accurate (and confident) in turns, that he worked out a system in which he fired when the enemy aircraft (turning ahead) disappeared beneath his nose; after the short burst, he paid scant attention to the victim thereafter, concentrating on the next fighter in the turning circle ahead.

His flying skill, of course, was outstanding. In his last full year of combat, when he scored over 150 kills and became the highest German scorer against the West in the entire war, his aircraft was never hit. His movements were faster than average and though it sounds more legendary than factual, several surviving comrades insist that his Me.109 pulled vapour trails in quick turns (from the wing-tips) when no other fighter in the formation did so. Among those who confirm this are Neumann and Pöttgen.

His eyesight was extremly good (it is said he adapted his eyes to the desert by staring into the sun for long periods) and the fair weather and excellent visibility which usually prevailed in Africa enabled him to fly regularly and to perfect pinpoint markmanship. With a superior fighter and confidence, guided by a wise leader, Marseille used his talent to contribute a remarkable performance to his country's air effort.

Just as the German ground effort in Africa began as an emergency step to rescue Mussolini and the Italian forces from disaster, and was not a thoroughly prepared military effort, so too their air effort was limited and sporadic in nature, largely governed by the demands of the moment. In the beginning German air strength was limited to units of the Ju.87 (Stuka), which were sent to co-operate with ground forces. The Stuka did well at first, but then R.A.F. Hurricanes began to take a heavy toll of the slow dive-bombers. A call went out for fighter protection. The result was that a Gruppe of Me.109Es was dispatched to protect the dive-bombers. The 109s reached the front at the beginning of the first Rommel offensive, which began on 31 March 1941, and which would carry Rommel (who by-passed Tobruk) to the vicinity of Sidi Barani by the end of May. The Gruppe arrived with about thirty aircraft, though soon afterwards additional 109s arrived as reinforcement and replacement aircraft. This made it possible for Neumann to put perhaps forty fighters in the sky in a maximum-strength effort. Marseille was in Staffel 3.[1]

Leutnant Marseille began his flying in the desert normally enough. He was not yet the accurate marksman he later became. It was during the long summer of 1941 that he mastered gunnery and the flying techniques which were to make him famous. Fellow pilots, sometimes sympathetically and sometimes otherwise, were the victims of his constant practice gunnery passes as the Staffel returned from its missions. He practised incessantly, and slowly he worked out the split-second timing and sighting for accurate deflection shooting. It was not until late in September that he admitted to a comrade, Leutnant Hans-Arnold Stahl-schmidt, that he had found himself in the air. On that day, 24 September, he had shot down, for the first time in his career, five aircraft in a day—that morning a Martin-Maryland bomber and that afternoon four Hurricanes flying in a Lufbery defence between Sidi Barani and Halfaya Pass. These brought Marseille's total to 23. 'I believe I've now got it,' he told Stahlschmidt that evening. From that day on-ward, 'Gelbe 14' (Yellow 14, the number of Marseille's Me.109) became ever more famous in the desert.

By early 1942, though the British had meanwhile driven Rommel from Sidi Barani and back as far as Marsa el Brega, Marseille had pushed his total to 48 victories, for which he received the Knight's Cross. He was becoming known in Germany as the Pilot of Africa or Star of Africa, and was

[1] Written 3./J.G. 27 in the Luftwaffe. The Gruppe was not included in the designation because the nine staffels in a Geschwader were numbered consecutively, in arabic numerals, from one to nine. Thus the first three staffels would be in I Gruppe, the second three (4, 5 and 6) in II Gruppe, etc. The full designation, if it had been written as such, would have been 3./Gruppe I/J.G. 27.

beginning to share some of the publicity and glory accorded to Rommel in film and press.

In April he was promoted to Oberleutnant. On the first of June, 1942 he was given command of 3 Staffel, earning him the *title* (not rank) of Kapitän. This summer, or half of it—Marseille was on leave more than two months—his performance was to surpass anything yet seen. Rommel had struck back after the successful British offensive late in 1941, launching his attack in January of 1942. By April he was back as far as El Gazala. After a pause, he resumed his advance on 26 May, in what was to be his last successful offensive, and the closest approach of a German-Italian army to Alexandria. It is to one of Marseille's better days, in Rommel's last push to the east, that we now turn our attention.

A hundred miles to the north-west of the key fortress of Tobruk (still in British hands), dispersed about reddish-brown sand and rocks of the Cyrenian hills, lay the Luftwaffe fighter base of Martuba. The first light from the east to reach over the hills on Wednesday morning, 3 June, revealed a number of strange-looking half-circles, walls of petrol tins filled with sand. They were blast-proof revetments in which brownish-yellow Me.109Fs were protectively parked.

Luftwaffe fighters had only recently returned to the fighter station after its recapture from the British. In 1941 only part of J.G.27 had been operating in Africa, but now the Geschwader was at full strength—168 aircraft. In addition, a Gruppe from Jagdgeschwader 53—stationed in Sicily—had been flown to Africa. The newly appointed Kommodore of J.G.27, who had been Gruppenkommandeur, was Eduard Neumann. Hans-Joachim Marseille, at the time of the change, had been made Kapitän of 3 Staffel of Gruppe I whose Kommandeur was Hauptmann Homuth.

Rommel's last offensive had just begun and progress had been swift. However, several strongly held forts to the south, the capture of which was a strategic necessity, were holding out. They had to be taken before German-Italian forces could safely move on eastward. One holding out against strenuous Axis efforts was Bir Hakeim. Rommel was delaying the resumption of his Panzer offensive until this fort was taken. Only when it fell could the drive east be resumed and Tobruk assaulted with combined German-Italian ground and air strength. Bir Hakeim was manned by a determined Free French brigade under the command of General Joseph Koenig. Having withstood several spirited assaults, it was holding firm. Stukas were bombing it daily in an effort to reduce it to rubble and force its capitulation, and fighters from Martuba were escorting the Stukas. The distance from Martuba to Bir Hakeim in the south-east was short—seventy miles. The Stukas were based at Derna, a few miles north-west of Martuba on the coastal road. Thus pilots of Jagdgeschwader 27 knew that Stuka escort missions were likely that June morning. But the day began quietly.

Pilots lounged in summer khaki shirts. Marseille wore white socks and white tennis shoes, in which he always flew. In light shoes and lightweight khakis he was free of restrictive fur jackets, flying suits, G-suits and other equipment which encumbered pilots in colder climates and higher altitudes. Jagdgeschwader 27's fighter forces were outnumbered by the enemy but morale was high at Martuba and Marseille was one of the reasons for the confidence and aggressive spirit.

A hundred miles to the east, at the R.A.F. fighter station of Gambut, 5th South African Squadron was planning the day's flying operations. The P.40 Tomahawk pilots were told they would fly a late morning patrol over besieged Bir Hakeim. Crew chiefs checked the Curtiss fighters and pilots prepared for take off.

At Martuba flying orders came for a limited number of German fighters that morning. One group of six, led by Marseille, was to escort a force of Stukas bombing Bir Hakeim. Take-off would be at 11.30. Pilots of 1 and 2 Staffeln relaxed; the six selected from 3 Staffel, including Marseille and his wingman, Feldwebel (Sergeant) Reiner

Pöttgen, began to prepare for the mission.

The sun was hot and there was little wind but otherwise the weather was good. Marseille had very little to say in briefing his comrades. It was a routine mission. All had escorted Stukas. Shortly after eleven the six walked out to the can-walled revetments, where the long-nosed 109Fs were ready. Erste Wart Meyer (Marseille's crew chief) helped as he strapped himself in and closed the canopy. Exchanging a few words, he stood by on the starboard wing with the crank, awaiting Marseille's signal. Another crewman was on the left. The numerals 14, in figures several feet high, were painted in yellow just behind the canopy on both sides of the fuselage. Satisfied that the 109 was fit, Marseille gave a signal with his right hand and nodded. '*Los!*' he ordered, and the crew chief on the wing began to crank. The winding became louder and louder and Marseille waited until the momentum was high-pitched. He pulled the starter and the 1,500 horse-power Daimler-Benz coughed, shooting blasts of smoke out of the six exhausts of the engine nacelle, and roared. The three-bladed prop, whirling faster, became a smooth blur and wind rippled the crewmen's clothes. His crew chief jumped down and waved, Marseille waving back. Lengthening clouds of sand and dust swirled behind and he taxied the small, yellow-brown, low-winged fighter out of the revetment.

Out of their camouflaged can-walls five other 109s poke their noses, dust clouds spring up behind. Because dust is so heavy, J.G.27 pilots avoid taking off behind one another. Thus the six 109s will take off in twos, each Rotte (pair) a bit out to the side of the other, almost abreast. Marseille, who is 'Elbe One' in radio code, reaches the northern end of the field, the 109's yellow spinner pointing south-south-east. Two fighters are on his right, three to the left. He checks instruments, trim and radiator flaps—and eases the yellow knob on the throttle quadrant, left, all the way forward. The Daimler-Benz emits a roar heard several miles away and the loaded fighter leaps forward. Following a still louder roar, others begin to roll. The six fighters rumble faster and faster, almost hidden in the dust, and lift off the field. Marseille makes a slight bank while lifting his wheels and soon the six 109s become rapidly shrinking silhouettes in the morning, south-eastern sky. It is 11.32.

Because the Stukas will bomb from a low altitude, Marseille will not climb high. He checks guns—the 20 mm. nose cannon and two 7·9 machine-guns (the Me.109F had one cannon, the E two). A pale yellow sight ring appears on the sighting glass. Marseille searches the sky ahead for the Stukas, which he is to rendezvous with, then escort to Bir Hakeim. Across the African sky a hundred miles to the east, from the R.A.F. fighter field at Gambut, 5th South African Squadron is taking off. Fourteen to sixteen Tomahawks (P.40s) set course south-west for Bir Hakeim. Instead of crosses atop their wings are painted blue and red circles; on the bottom, blue, white and red.

Marseille soon sights the Stukas in the assigned area. He spreads his fighters to afford them as much protection as possible. The Stukas, loaded with bombs, are slow. The 109s throttle back slightly and S-turn to stay in escort position without losing too much speed, thereby becoming vulnerable to surprise attack. Marseille and Pöttgen knife upwards into the sky above the larger Ju.87s. The Stukas are low, about 4,000 feet, Marseille a thousand feet higher. Minutes tick by. Pilots search the skies ahead; all clear. The Cyrenian hills are now disappearing below. Flatter land stretches out ahead. To the left Gazala comes in view. The Staffel flies on, due south-east. Time: 12 noon. Bir Hakeim is twenty minutes away.

The Stukas, with bomb load, two-man crew and 45-foot wingspan, cruise at only 160 m.p.h.; thus Marseille and the other fighters zig-zag to maintain a reasonable speed in case of a bounce. But no enemy fighters come in view. It is 12.10. Fifty miles to the east, about twelve minutes from Bir Hakeim, fly the Curtiss fighters to their Bir Hakeim rendez-

Take-off at approximately 11.30 a.m. and landing shortly
after 12.30 p.m.

Derna
Martuba    Tobruk
Bir Hakeim

Tomahawks go int[o]
defensive Lufbery-t[ype]
defensive circle

### FIGHTER

Me.109

### FIGHTER GESCHWADER

J.G. 27

### FIGHTER STATION

MARTUBA (AFRICA)

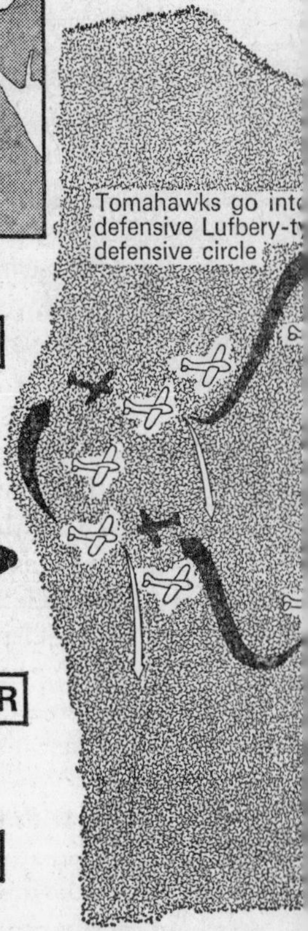

**MISSION FLOWN B[Y]**

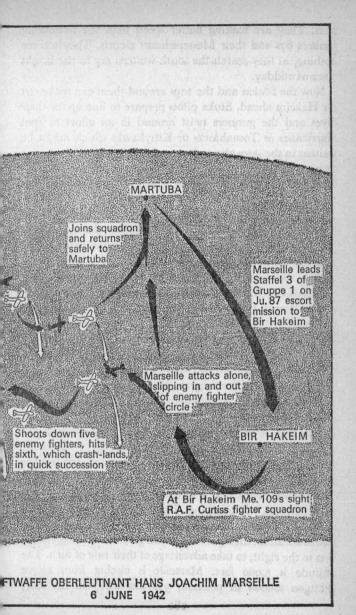

FTWAFFE OBERLEUTNANT HANS JOACHIM MARSEILLE
6 JUNE 1942

vous. They are making better speed than the lumbering Junkers 87s and their Messerschmitt escorts. They too see nothing, as they search the south-western sky in the bright glare of midday.

Now the Stukas and the 109s around them can make out Bir Hakeim ahead. Stuka pilots prepare to line up for their dives and the gunners twist around in an effort to spot Hurricanes or Tomahawks or Kittyhawks which might be waiting in the skies above. But as the Stukas and the six 109s fly on, getting ever closer, it's obvious that no R.A.F. fighters are over Bir Hakeim. Perhaps it will be an easy operation after all, even though this is the second Stuka attack of the morning and the German-Italian pressure on Bir Hakeim has been constant. The Stukas approach the target and prepare to wing over in dives . . . pilots manœuvre to get into line for the bomb run. Marseille and the 109s are now slightly west of Bir Hakeim. It is 12.21.

'*Horridoh!*' The shout comes in like a jolt over the mike of every German fighter pilot. 'Indians—from behind,' some-one shouts. Marseille turns and sees the Tomahawks. They're above and coming on from behind. It's 5th South African Squadron. The Ju.87s are already in dive-bombing runs, and bombs begin to crash down on Bir Hakeim, from which only light anti-aircraft fire returns. Marseille pulls the nose up, and the Me.109s automatically separate into pairs, Marseille and Pöttgen the highest of the three. The Tomahawks, a slightly deeper brown and making good speed come on—as if to bounce the Stukas. Now they see the 109s! Some of the R.A.F. fighters alter course, and pilots on each side feel the tension.

Marseille banks into a closing course. He's now at the enemy's level, still climbing. The Stukas are pulling out of dives and lining up on a north-westerly course. The Toma-hawks ahead lift their port wings and go into a circling forma-tion to the right, to take advantage of their rate of turn. The altitude is 5,000 feet. Marseille is closing from above (Pöttgen follows in position, 350 feet away to his left), measuring the enemy fighters as they circle. Gelbe 14 will dive into the Lufbery-type formation. The Tomahawks, as they circle, are not more than 200 feet behind each other, starboard wings pointing downward in a tight turn.

Marseille pushes his stick forward, his nose drops and he is diving. Pöttgen stays up.

The diving Me.109, gaining speed, approaches the Lufbery, reaches its level, continues downward; then Marseille pulls back on the stick. The yellow-nosed 109 curves back up, towards the circle, Marseille's eyes fixed on one Tomahawk. The P.40's wing-span grows wider, wider . . . touches the yellow light-circle rim. Marseille, only 150 feet from the victim, coming up in a climbing right turn from behind, presses both triggers on the black stick grip. The cannon and machine-guns explode into noise and vibration. The short burst strikes the engine, the pattern of fire moving quickly back. Marseille is in and out, now pulling up again above the circling formation. The P.40 streams smoke, turns out of the circle and plunges downward. The pass required only seconds. Marseille levels out as he reaches the top of his climbing arc. The mortally-wounded Tomahawk plunges straight down, leaving a vertical column of smoke, strikes the ground, explodes. The Tomahawks continue their defensive manœuvre, which keeps off most would-be attackers—but not Marseille. He pushes the stick forward, banks right and down, again, to pull in behind another. Speed increases as he eyes the next victim.

With split-second manœuvring he pulls out of the dive, banks sharply right, coming down just behind another victim in the circle. Marseille is so fast that the fighter behind hasn't got a good shot at him. He swoops in, for seconds, dead on target, presses the buttons. The guns roar again. Again a short stream of metal—150 feet—smashes in concentrated pattern into the engine ahead. (As Marseille later explained, his system of sighting was to fire as soon as the enemy fighter disappeared beneath his nose. The entire burst, fired at the correct lead, very close, usually found its way to the enemy's engine or cockpit.) The second enemy fighter emits smoke, falls out of the formation. Pöttgen watches in admiration. Marseille is down and pulling out, roaring back up, approaching the Lufbery again, much quicker than after the first firing pass. The second victim is diving vertically for the earth below, only 3,500 feet; the circling fighters are steadily losing altitude. Marseille keeps his fingers ready on the triggers, his eyes on the sighting glass, and is banking right into the circle for the third time. He times his entry so that he enters just behind a third victim, moving up and through the circle, then slows a bit, is just a second or two in firing position. At that moment the guns from the lone yellow-nosed 109 spurt shells again. They strike home for the third consecutive time. Victim number three begins to stream smoke.

Marseille is above the Lufbery formation now, scans the scene below, and is winging over, seeking a fourth victim. This dive is even faster than the last. As the third victim pours smoke, in a steady descent out of the circle, the 109 is curving back into the Tomahawks again. Standing on his right wing, descending, in a sharp turn, Marseille estimates time and distance and the fourth victims' wing-span widens into the circle, then beyond. The enemy fighter disappears beneath the 109's nose. He presses the buttons. The cannon is not firing! Ammunition stoppage! Nevertheless, the two machine-guns spurt a pattern that converges on the same top section of the Tomahawk. Pieces fly backward, the engine streaks black and white smoke, and the long-nosed fighter wobbles as a wing goes up and falls out of formation. Marseille has hardly looked back at his victims—usually a cardinal sin in fighter combat. So certain is he of his aim he takes only a quick glance and concentrates on the next victim. Pöttgen, fascinated, watches the third fighter crash and explode. The fourth begins its last descent.

Marseille is again quick to return to the Lufbery and, in another hard turn to the right, is shortly manoeuvring stick and rudder to slip in behind number five. The enemy pilots, apparently under the impression that a number of fighters are attacking, or unaware of what is happening so quickly, continue circling. It is 12.28: six minutes since the first P.40 was shot down. In seconds Marseille is back in position, curving in from slightly above, as if he were one of the R.A.F. circle. He presses the triggers . . . only the machine-guns fire. They reach out and smash the fifth victim, from engine to cockpit again . . . a very short burst, dead on. Marseille lifts his finger. Now he is out and away, and the fifth victim is falling out of formation, smoke streaming backward. Pöttgen sees number four crash. The formation is far lower now. With every turn a little altitude has been lost. Marseille watches from a distance now and takes stock. His cannon is not firing. He has shot five enemy fighters out of the formation, hasn't been hit . . . an incredible, lightning-fast performance. Above, Pöttgen circles. Marseille sees the Tomahawks spiral lower and lower. His 109 still runs smoothly. He has more ammunition. Airborne an hour, he still has fuel. He eases the yellow throttle knob forward to slip into the spiral once more.

Eyes fixed on victim number six, Marseille manœuvres his rudder pedals and stick to make his last flashing entry into the circle. He picks his spot between two circling Tomahawks, wings over and down, pulls out and into the turning circle, coming on fast. He has the longer P.40 wing-span in the yellow light ring, now eases back on the stick, his right wing pointing directly earthwards. The 109's nose moves forward from the cockpit to the engine of the fighter ahead, in the turn. Then the victim disappears from view. Fire! Marseille's guns roar, shake the smaller Me.109 for the sixth time. Machine-gun shells smash into victim number six, Marseille whips over and out of formation and down and away. The sixth victim emits smoke from its exhausts, turns out of the circle. and begins its descent. Marseille has knocked six of the enemy out of the formation! Elated, excited, he presses the mike button: 'Elbe One to Elbe Two—*Hast du den Aufschlag gesehen?*' (Did you see them crash?). Pöttgen replies: 'Elbe Two to Elbe One—Victor, Victor.' Marseille waggles his wings, zooms back up towards Pöttgen, unmolested. Then over his earphones, Marseille hears a surprise congratulation. Kommodore Eduard Neumann has arrived above the scene in time to witness the combat. 'Bravo, Joachim!' he shouts. There are other calls of congratulations—from other pilots. Marseille is elated. The battle is suddenly over. The other 109s, only a few of whom managed to mix with the enemy, are turning for Martuba. The Tomahawks have headed homewards, Marseille's sixth victim steadily losing height. The triumphant Staffel points its yellow noses north-west, Marseille's heart beating hard. It's the first time he's knocked down six fighters in one sortie. It's taken him eleven minutes!

The time passes slowly on the homeward flight, but finally Martuba looms in view ahead. Marseille will swoop over the field and roll to signify his victories. Below, crewmen, some of whom regularly bet on Marseille's probable kills, are sitting and waiting. Shortly the hum of fighters, to the south-east, reaches their ears. The Staffel comes into view, Marseille leading. As he approaches the field, Gelbe 14 drops lower and comes on fast. He roars over tents and huts and the buildings scattered over the brownish-red surface, and rolls—once, twice, three times—and then is over and gone. Crewmen cheer, especially Marseille's crew. Three victories! Marseille banks into a turn at the far end of the field, the top of his wings visible as he turns vertically, low, and comes back. Down he comes, and as he reaches the edge of the field he begins to roll again. One, two, three rolls . . . and then is off and banking upwards and into a landing pattern. Crewmen, pilots and other personel on the field are stirred by the aerial announcement. They know six in one mission is a new record, even for Marseille.

Marseille eases back on the throttle, opens the radiator flaps, lowers his landing gear. His propeller turns easily, the engine moans low and he glides in to land. Airspeed 200 k.p.h., 190, 180, 170. Only feet above the gravel. Thump! Gelbe 14 is down and rolling. Pöttgen is 150 yards behind, to the side. At the end of the roll, Marseille turns his 109 to the left and taxies to the revetment, where crewmen are waiting in great excitement. Pöttgen taxies in behind. Marseille pulls up to the walls of sand-filled cans and guns his engine, turns and cuts the throttle. Several crewmen around him instinctively give a cheer. His crew chief smiles: '*Gratulieren!*'

Pöttgen parks sixty yards away, is soon out of the cockpit and bounding over to the Marseille parking area, where a crowd fast assembles. Marseille is tired, but he talks to crewmen and pilots who shower him with smiles and congratulations. As Pöttgen comes up, Marseille again asks him if he saw the victims. Pöttgen, repeats again—he saw them all. Crewmen examining the guns are amazed when the cannon housing is opened. Marseille fired only ten rounds from his 20 mm. cannon! The belt caught, jammed the gun. And a check of the machine-guns shows he fired only a few hundred shells from each. The crowd continues to increase. Marseille remains with his aircraft perhaps ten minutes, to answer questions, accept congratulations. He jokes with all who come to get a glimpse of the Pilot of Africa. Then he must head for a near-by command tent—to file the required intelligence report, and see Neumann.

At the tent he smokes a cigarette, more of a ritual than anything else (he's not a heavy smoker) and writes a report of the action for the intelligence officer. Though only Kapitäne usually report to the tent, Marseille's whole Staffel is with him. Once more congratulations are in order. There is a toast—red wine. Kommodore Neumann then arrives to deliver his congratulations in person. There will be a celebration in his honour that night, he says. Marseille begins to relax.

The struggle over Bir Hakeim continued and Marseille was to have another big day over the fort on 10 June. Though Rommel had, since 3 June, assaulted the fort several times, it still held out. Stuka losses had been heavy—and would have been heavier had it not been for the Me. 109s protecting them. Stuka Geschwader 3 had lost fourteen Ju.87s in a week.

Field-Marshal Albert Kesselring finally called in Ju.88 bombers based in Greece and Crete. On the 10th the combined weight of all the Luftwaffe strength that could be brought to bear was thrown into the air assault on Bir Hakeim. All during the day 124 Stukas pounded the fort, supported by 76 Ju.88s. The bombers were protected by the full fighter strength of Neumann's J.G.27. On that day Marseille shot down four fighters, his 78th, 79th, 80th and 81st victories.

Next morning a white flag flew over Bir Hakeim, and the fall of the fort at last freed Rommel's rear, allowing him to continue his successful push toward the Nile. Kesselring himself presented Marseille with the Knight's Cross to the Iron Cross the day after his six victories at Bir Hakeim, and Marseille's star continued to rise. After his four victories on 10 June, he continued to fly daily. On the 15th, near El Adem, he was credited with four kills to bring his total to 91. By this time his comrades were openly speculating when he would reach the magic number of 100. No one had seen anything quite like it, and Marseille was already a legend. On the evening of the 15th a comrade asked him when he would shoot down his hundredth victim. Marseille laughed and said it would happen the afternoon of the day after the next. They were prophetic words—and such incidents add colour to the legend which has survived. The next day, the 16th, he shot down four, and on the 17th, with everyone in the Geschwader aware of what might happen, Marseille and six other comrades in 3 Staffel took off to counter persistent R.A.F. strafing attacks, which were especially disturbing 21st Panzer Division. At 12.35 he was back over the field—and did six rolls. He had run his total to 101 ! The entire field came to greet him as he landed. When Meyer opened the canopy, however, everyone could see the strain was beginning to tell. His complexion was ash-grey. He had probably pushed himself too hard to live up to a prediction.

Neumann ordered him off operations, in spite of protests from Marseille, who was eager to participate in the attack on

Tobruk. Not only was he grounded; he was to report back to the homeland. There he was personally decorated with the oak leaves and swords to the Knight's Cross of the Iron Cross by Hitler. While in Germany he was honoured by high officials, interviewed for propaganda purposes and welcomed as a national hero. But he never boasted of his exploits. One report of an interview with him in Germany reveals his unassuming nature. He was asked if it was hot in Africa. 'Yes.' Was there a lot of sand in the desert? 'Yes.' Were the British there? 'Yes.' Were they good in combat? 'Yes.' Did he shoot them down? 'Yes.' Everyone, by this time, began to laugh except Marseille, who apparently didn't know what the joke was.

He returned to Africa, after more than two months' leave, as the youngest captain in the Luftwaffe at 22, and again took command of 3 Staffel. Rommel, during his absence, had pushed as far as El Alamein, only to be checked there, and the front had stabilized. For a week Marseille did nothing spectacular and then, on 1 September, he achieved his greatest score of the war, the highest of any German pilot in a single day against the Allies—seventeen confirmed kills in three flights (about which so much speculation abounded after the war). Two days later, in recognition, he was awarded the swords and diamonds to the Knight's Cross of the Iron Cross. When, on 15 September, he scored kill number 150, he became the first German fighter pilot to reach this total on any front. On 26 September he scored his 158th kill: his last. On 30 September, flying a new Me.109 on his 482nd sortie, with seven comrades, his luck deserted him. The Staffel had escorted Stukas and had then searched the skies unsuccessfully for the enemy. On the way back to German lines (the base had by then been moved to Fuka), Marseille's engine suddenly caught fire. He was heard to call on the radio: 'I've got thick smoke in the cabin. I can't see.' Pöttgen and others closed in, watching helplessly. The Staffel was still over British-held territory. Pöttgen called: 'Just three minutes to El Alamein!' Then two minutes, then one.

Marseille tried to stick it out until he was over German territory. Perhaps he waited too long, or perhaps he was the victim of bad luck. In any event, the eight Me.109s were at last over German lines, four miles past the white mosque that marked the front, one smoking badly. Marseille's last call was: 'I must get out now.' He rolled the smoking 109 over, the canopy flew backward and he dropped out. But the 109's nose dipped, the rudder probably striking him in the back as he fell free. All waited, horror-striken, for his chute to billow open, in vain. Marseille hit the ground, chute still unopened. As fast as his comrades could reach the scene after landing (in a car driven by 1 Staffel's Kapitän, Hauptmann Ludwig Franzisket), they recovered his body.

He was given a military burial in the desert. His Staffel was never again the same, and his death affected the entire Luftwaffe in Africa, so aggressive and indestructible had he seemed. In all, his score of 158 included the following types: 101 Curtiss Tomahawks and Kittyhawks; 30 Hurricanes; 16 Spitfires; and 4 bombers—all but four were fighters. Higher totals were to be scored by German pilots in the East, but Marseille's was the highest of any German fighter pilot flying against the Western powers, even though he died more than two and a half years before the end of the war, and his score of seventeen in one day was only once equalled or surpassed during the war by a Luftwaffe fighter pilot. (Captain Emil Lang shot down eighteen Russian aircraft in one day on the Russian Front.)

Since 1945, Germans and others probing the air war have slowly begun to realize the magnitude of Marseille's performance. In 1957 his achievements were recalled in a full-length film, well received in Germany, even though for many years after the war the German public shied away from war films and war heroes, remembering the horrors of the Nazi regime and the devastation it brought. Only in recent years has the public in the United States and England begun to show an interest in Marseille. The inevitable conclusion is that he mastered the art of quick attack and the science of aerial gunnery, especially in deflection shooting, to a degree seldom equalled in aerial combat. He may well have been 'the unrivalled virtuoso among fighter pilots of the Second World War'.

# CHAPTER TEN

# THE BLACK DEVIL OVER KURSK

*7 July 1943—Leutnant Erich Hartmann, Luftwaffe*

GERMANY'S TOP *Experte* of the Second World War, and the highest-scoring fighter pilot in history, Erich Hartmann, was a schoolboy in 1939 and reached the Front only during the third year of the war. He was credited with the astonishing number of 352 kills, practially all of them, admittedly, on the Eastern Front. And though victories in the East were not altogether comparable to victories in the West, his record nevertheless makes him history's top-scoring fighter pilot.

Hartmann was a steady, methodical hunter in the air and an easy-tempered and happy pilot on the ground. He quite often flew several sorties a day, week after week and month after month, against large formations of low-flying Russian bombers and fighters. His opportunities to encounter the enemy were almost continual and he usually had a number of enemy aircraft to choose from as targets. But he didn't try to shoot them all down on every mission. On one occasion, 24 August 1944, he shot down six, but normally he was content with less. He flew 1,425 sorties, engaging the enemy in 800 of them. The reputation of the 'Black Devil of the Ukraine' was appreciated on both sides and his value to the Luftwaffe and also to the German Army was incalculable.

Considering the number of his victories, it is tempting to discount his achievement by evaluating Russian Front kills lightly, by assuming they came easily. There are several considerations which should be remembered, however, in arriving at an accurate evaluation. First of all, German pilots on the Russian Front had vast opportunities to score kills. The very number of Russian aircraft was a factor. Secondly, the style of flying on that front was well-suited to the fighter interceptor which usually flew in a Rotte or a Schwarm (that is, in twos or fours) in 'free chase' of low-flying Russian formations. German fighters thus enjoyed the flexibility and freedom to determine how and when to attack and what formations to attack—a major tactical advantage in fighter combat, especially with faster aircraft. (Luftwaffe pilots exploiting this tactical advantage against the numerous foe shot down an estimated 44,000 Russian aircraft during the war. Another 16,000 were lost to the forces of Germany's allies.)

Also, the German pilot in the East was not engaged in a strategic offensive campaign against Russia requiring long high-altitude flights. On the contrary, he was usually cast in the role of an interceptor of boxes of slower Russian bombers and fighters striking targets in German-held territory. Thus German fighter pilots could easily fly three or four quick low-altitude interception missions a day, never ascending to great height and not straying far from base. That this provided many and constant opportunities for kills can be seen from the individual flying records of German pilots in the East. Hartmann's is convincing on this point. He scored an average of one victory in every four flights, one every second or third time in combat. When viewed in this context, his victory total can be more easily comprehended. In the Allied air forces, pilots who flew 500 sorties were exceptional. A top R.A.F. fighter pilot, Johnnie Johnson (who, like Hartmann, began to run up a score against the enemy several years after the outbreak of the war), was on operations, off and on, throughout the war and flew 515 combat sorties.

Hartmann's victory total is brought into better perspective when one realizes that over 100 Germans scored more than 100 victories. More than ninety per cent of these served on the Russian Front. Two Luftwaffe pilots reached the total of 300 kills. The totals of some of the other top scorers on the Russian Front were: Barkhorn, 301; Rall, 275; Kittel, 267; Nowotny, 258; Batz, 237; Rudorffer, 222—136 in the East and 86 in the West; and so on.

Against the air forces of the Western democracies the scores of the top German fighter aces were not so high. But there were at least eight who scored more than a hundred victories in the west—the top scorer being of course Marseille. Others were Bär (124—220 in all), Buehligen (112), Galland (104) Schroer (102—114 in all), Mayer 102, Müncheberg (102—135 in all), and Priller (101). The complete list of German aces with more than 100 kills totals 104.

Hartmann's victories on the Russian Front were not achieved in the first year of the war, the period in which German pilots found it easiest to down their opponents. He scored his first kill in October of 1942 and was credited with less than twenty victories as late as the summer of 1943. It was during that summer (the events related in this chapter took place at this time) that he began to accumulate victories more rapidly.

Shot down many times, it was after one of those experiences that he was briefly captured. While riding with his captors in a truck he suddenly struck the nearest, 'baled out' over the side and ran for the woods. He evaded his pursuers and reached his own lines. German pilots, in general, were something less than keen about getting shot down over Russian territory, being less than keen about having their throats cut. Therefore many of them were conscientious about staying over their own lines or behind them—with the result that quite a number who were shot down or who baled out returned within hours to their units to fly and fight again and to add to their scores. Though downed many times, Hartmann served to the very last and claimed his 352nd victory on the final day of the war. The Russian victim was executing a victory roll!

Thus Hartmann's score is impressive by any standard of measurement. It can be partially attributed to the great number of enemy aircraft (targets), to the nature of the air war in the East, to the number of missions and combats engaged in and to the superior performance of his Me.109.

But it must also be attributed to Hartmann and is a prodigious and unprecedented achievement.

How would Eastern Front pilots have done against the air forces of the Western democracies? That is one of the most frequently asked questions about the fighter war. A study of the records indicates that they would not have done badly. Not flying as often, however, they would not have achieved as many kills. Hartmann had that opportunity for a short time when transferred to Rumania in the summer of 1944. Flying the same 109 he preferred throughout the war, during this short period he shot down five P.51s (probably the best American fighter of the war).

The experience of other Eastern Front pilots and entire Geschwader indicates that it would be unwise to draw too many conclusions about the ease of scoring kills on the Russian Front. One example is that of Major Joachim Müncheberg, one of only eight German pilots to score more than 100 victories in the West. Müncheberg was transferred to the Eastern Front for a few weeks in 1942 and was shot down three times in that period. Another example concerns Jagdgeschwader I, successful in the West and transferred to the East. The Geschwader had no success; in three weeks it was practically destroyed as a fighting unit and was returned to the West. Conditions on the two fronts were vastly different and the Eastern Front pilot, suddenly transferred to the West, dreaded high-altitude attacks against heavily-defended, close-flying boxes of American bombers and did not initially do well in such actions. So, too, Western Front pilots transferred to the East had to acclimatize themselves to conditions on the Russian Front, where ground fire brought down more German aircraft than enemy pilots, and where the low-level style of fighting was altogether different.

Hartmann's Geschwader was the most successful in the entire Luftwaffe, scoring 177 victories in the West before moving to the East where it scored almost 11,000 more. The great number of kills registered by this one Geschwader is another statistical indication of the opportunities German fighter pilots had. It is interesting to note, in this connection, that the *Experten* (the Germans didn't use the word ace or think five victories earned a pilot special distinction) accounted for more than half the Russian total. Of the 44,000 German victories in the East, Hans Ring estimates that 30,000 were shared by 300 pilots! Thus the veteran German pilot on the Russian Front was often a highly effective professional who frequently ran up a high score. For the novice it was not easy. One Geschwader in the East which experienced the loss of eighty pilots in a certain period found that sixty had scored no kills.

The war in the East was, then, a war against vast numbers of Russian aircraft over a vast front. But there can be no exact comparison with the air war in the West, nor need there be. To what extent higher scores of German fighter pilots in the East were attributable to their greater number of adversaries, their superiority in equipment or their advantageous role is debatable. Conditions undoubtedly produced more opportunities and often it was somewhat easier to score a kill; on the other hand, it seems likely that the scores of the top German aces in the East deserve more respect than some have accorded them in the post-war years.

Erich Hartmann was born in Weissach, Württemberg, in 1922, four years after the end of the Great War. When the Second War began he was seventeen and still at school. He joined the Luftwaffe during the second year of the war, and after successfully completing pilot training was posted to the Eastern Front late in 1942. He was just over twenty. His first operational flights gave little indication that he was to become the top fighter pilot of the war. In fact, until the summer of 1943 his flying record and score against the enemy, while respectable, were not unusual compared to those of some of his comrades. During this time he was working out the tactical techniques which were to dispose of so many opponents. One was, when attacked from behind, to send his wingman down and ahead to lure the enemy in front of his guns. If his wingman was very young he sometimes let him fly top cover while he dived below the enemy, pulled up and into him and fired a very quick and accurate burst as he climbed through the formation and out of range (not unlike one of Marseille's tactics). Hartmann usually closed 'until the enemy aircraft filled my windscreen' before opening fire. Normally, his bursts were short and very accurate and he apparently didn't make the mistake of overplaying his hand, trying to shoot down too many aircraft in one action. He was usually content to shoot down one and score another victory another day, which was probably why he was there again another day. Like most fighter pilots, he was not a large man, and not muscle-bound. But he possessed the prerequisites of success—quick reflexes and co-ordination, good eyesight, an aggressive spirit, coolness in action—to such a degree that they added up to 352 enemy aircraft in two and a half years.

Ironically, his first really big day came in the German summer offensive of 1943, the last and quick-dying hope for Germany on the Eastern Front. It was the final German summer effort in the war against Russia, Operation 'Zitadelle', an advance which made initial progress, stalled, and then turned into a massive withdrawal. For the first time since Hitler had attacked Russia, his armies found themselves in retreat along a broad front in midsummer.

The offensive began on 5 July. General Heinz Guderian recalls in *Panzer Leader* (he was then Inspector General of Armoured Troops) that everything the German Army could muster in the way of attacking strength was committed. For the pincer attack which was to seal off and trap Russian forces in a prominent salient west of Kursk, ten Panzer, one Panzergrenadier and seven infantry divisions were employed in the south (in the Bielgorod area), and seven Panzer, two Panzergrenadier and nine infantry in the north (in the Orel area). The Germans were using new panther and tiger tanks and placed great hope in them—though they were destined to be severely handled by Russian Il.II fighter-bombers newly equipped with two long-barrelled 37 mm. P.11/37 cannon.[1]

The Luftwaffe was to co-operate in breaking Russian resistance in the opening days of the offensive and squadrons were secretly moved up to front-line bases late on the afternoon of 4 July. Transports (Ju.52s) arrived during the night with fuel and maintenance equipment. The squadrons were due to attack at dawn next morning. Staffel 7 of Jagdgeschwader 52, of which Leutnant Hartmann was a member, moved up to Ugrim (14 kilometres behind the launching point of the southern arm of the pincer attack) late on the afternoon of the 4th. During the night of the 4th, tanks, which would begin their push at dawn, moved into position on all sides and transport aircraft with squadron supplies landed on the field. At first light on the 5th the offensive began and German tanks went straight through the Russian lines. But Ugrim pilots were in for a shock. The first four fighters, including the Deputy Staffelkapitän, did not return. Yet there was no appreciable enemy opposition. Unusually large deposits of iron in the earth, it was found, were causing compasses to fluctuate wildly; needles often strayed sixty to seventy degrees and pilots soon became lost. After the loss of the first Schwarm of 109s and the Deputy Staffel leader, Hartmann was given command of 7 Staffel. Next day the German offensive continued. The disturbing feature of the advance was that the Panzers were encountering a new defence line every kilometre or two as they drove forward. Obviously the Russians had prepared thoroughly for the German offensive and had anticipated its direction.

Fighters at Ugrim meanwhile began to master the strange magnetic variations and become orientated. Russian air opposition was still almost nil. Fighter pilots of 7 Staffel had no way of knowing that things would be different next day, as

[1] William Green describes the development of the Il.II in two articles in *Flying Review International*, August-September 1965. The new cannon were devastating, he reports, knocking out 70 tanks of the 90th Panzer division alone in 20 minutes near Kursk.

they went to bed on the night of the 6th, in their small, hastily erected tents pitched in the deep summer grass of southern Russia.

Two hundred and fifty miles north of the Crimea, in the slightly rolling Ukraine north-west of Kharkov, the first rays of light crossed the grass field at Ugrim shortly before 3 a.m. It was Wednesday, 7 July 1943. Scattered about in foot-and-a-half high grass, without cover, were parked the blue-green Me.109G10s of 7 Staffel. On one of the low, white-nosed fighters a heart containing the name *Usch* was painted on the fuselage. In the distance on all sides stretched a gently rolling landscape of birch, oak and pines—all green. The sky was again clear. For two days the German offensive had continued in the good summer weather.

On the edge of the grass were seven or eight large camouflaged tents and a number of small sleeping tents. The sleeping tents were six feet long and three wide, just large enough to cover an air mattress. Into one of the smaller tents an enlisted man poked his head: '*Leutnant, aufstehen.*' Erich Hartmann awoke, replied, and began to get dressed. He put on blue-grey trousers, a grey shirt and grey sports shoes with rubber soles. After pulling on his clothes he walked down to a small stream nearby and washed and shaved in the fresh water. Then he walked to the 'Bar'—one of the larger tents in which pilots ate and lounged. In one corner was the squadron operations section and in another a stove where two Russian girls were cooking breakfast. '*Was gibt's?*' he asked. Nothing was reported. All quiet. It was just before 3 a.m. and Hartmann was one of four pilots already in the tent; he and three of the others were to escort the early morning reconnaissance plane, which would take off shortly after three. Each morning this plane took off at first light to report front line observations and each morning four pilots flew the unpopular early-morning escort. This morning was Hartmann's turn. He ate a good breakfast, two *gebackene* (fried) eggs, bread and butter and two or three cups of coffee. It was almost time for the

F.W.89 to take off on reconnaissance. Hartmann gave the word and the four started out to their aircraft.

Not far from the Bar waits Hartmann's 109 and crew chief 'Bimel' Merten. *'Ist der Bock klar?'* (Is the goat ready?) Hartmann jests. Merten reports all in order and helps Hartmann with his straps in the dim light after he lowers himself into the cockpit. Soon he is ready. Aircraft clocks show 3.04; the eastern sky is whitening and it is time to go. The F.W. has started. Hartmann rolls one of two grey wheels behind to his left to one-third flaps, the other to take-off trim. After opening the shutters and checking the fuel, he pumps the yellow primer handle on the left side of the cockpit floor and opens the throttle, nodding to Merten. Merten, standing on the starboard wing, begins to crank. Slowly the whine increases in tempo. Now it is enough. Hartmann waves him away and Merten shouts: *'Frei!' 'Frei,'* Hartmann replies and pulls the small black handle just below the magazine switch on the instrument panel. The 1,450 horsepower Daimler-Benz coughs several times and heavy smoke shoots out of the six exhausts. Then it catches up, the smoke thinning into nothing as the prop begins to whirl smoothly.

Not far from Hartmann three other 109s roar into life. The Schwarm is ready to taxi out. With his right hand Hartmann signals several times in the poor light and then releases his brakes and begins to taxi to take-off position. Merten waves good luck. The blue-green 109s are soon in a line of four, the blast from the propellers flattening the high grass behind as they taxi out. At the edge of the field, a few yards from the landing cross, Hartmann checks engine gauges and glances at the other fighters. They hold, braked, near by, while props whirl and engines roar and shatter the early-morning stillness of the countryside for miles around.

He signals that he's going, releases his brakes and pushes the yellow throttle knob on the left all the way forward. The 109 leaps and bounds ahead and other pilots release brakes at full throttle and begin to roll—some thirty to forty feet between each, slightly behind Hartmann. Hartmann gathers speed rapidly and after 300 yards the prop is pulling the light fighter over the grass at 160 kilometres an hour. He eases the stick back as speed continues to increase, keeping the nose straight by manœuvring rudder pedals. The wheels lift off and Hartmann is airborne at 3.06. The other three fighters lift off in succession and soon the four Messerschmitts are banking left out of the field, landing gears retracting slowly. Hartmann eases the throttle, closes the radiator flaps and checks engine gauges. The other three fighters are closing in and the F.W.89 is just ahead. Soon the snooper and its four protecting hawks are climbing gently into the north-eastern sky, a sky gradually turning light.

Hartmann checks his guns and the electric light image on the sight—a circle and bars to denote distance from a target and range from behind. Working. His guns are loaded with four types of ammunition—*Panzer, Panzerspreng, Panzerbrand* and *Panzermine*—armour-piercing, heavy armour-piercing, incendiary and explosive. Altitude increases to 2,000, 3,000, 4,000 feet. German aircraft must stay at a respectable height or ground fire—from either side—is likely to seek them out. The fighters continue into the north-east and Hartmann occasionally glances below and sees many vehicles, including tanks. He scans the eastern horizon, at the same time keeping an eye on the near-by reconnaissance plane. There has been little Russian air activity the past two days and pilots subconsciously expect no action. Hartmann checks in with operations by radio. Nothing reported in the area. The flight continues.

The reconnaissance aircraft makes a turn, and the white-nosed fighters bank outside their charge in a now rapidly lightening sky, the light clearly revealing the big figure 1 painted a yard high on the side of Hartmann's fuselage, behind the cockpit. Below the cockpit, in white, is the name of his sweetheart, Usch, inside a red heart pierced by an arrow. (Hartmann writes to Usch Paetch every day and after the war the letters are to become a valuable source of

Take-off at 03.05 a.m. and landing shortly after 04.00 a.m.

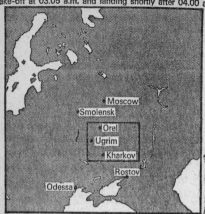

FIGHTER

Me.109

FIGHTER GESCHWADER

J.G. 52

FIGHTER STATION

UGRIM (RUSSIA)

Hartmann leads four Me.109s off on early reconnaissance flight over front

UGRIM

Later in day flew two more missions, shooting down IL.11 bomber and Lagg 3 fighter on first, three fighters on second for total of 7 victories in day

MISSION FLOWN BY

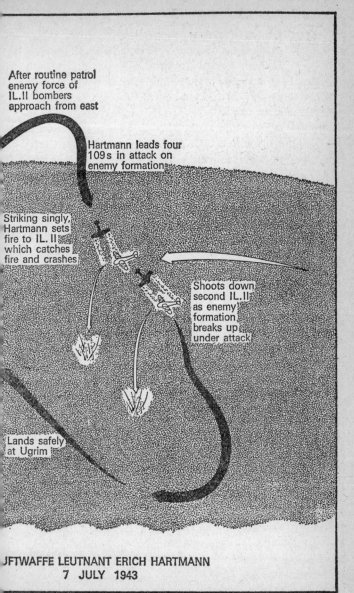

After routine patrol
enemy force of
IL.II bombers
approach from east

Hartmann leads four
109s in attack on
enemy formation

Striking singly,
Hartmann sets
fire to IL.II
which catches
fire and crashes

Shoots down
second IL.II
as enemy
formation
breaks up
under attack

Lands safely
at Ugrim

LUFTWAFFE LEUTNANT ERICH HARTMANN
7 JULY 1943

day-by-day information, since his log book for the last year of the war was lost.)

The flight proceeds uneventfully for some time. Finally the F.W.89 heads back toward Ugrim.

Operations at Ugrim at this moment gets a report from an *Adler* (Eagle) post! *Adler* posts are scattered about the countryside and consist of an observer in a car with a pair of powerful glasses and a radio telephone. The front-line area is charted on a graph with numbers on one side and letters across the top. Operations and the various *Adler* posts have copies of the chart. When an observer hears or sees enemy aircraft he immediately calls in to report his observation and the position. Now Ops calls Hartmann and relays the report: enemy aircraft heading west—position *Berta neun* (B.9). Ten to twenty Russian planes, flying low.

Hartmann's circulation speeds up as he looks at his chart— the *Schwarm* is very close to B.9. He scans the sky to the east, sees nothing and banks in the direction from which the enemy might come. He climbs the four 109s on interception course at increased throttle setting. All is quiet but tension grows. The four pilots carefully sweep the sky ahead, watching, searching . . . for small dots far distant. But minutes pass and nothing comes into view. The four 109s fly on.

Hartmann's earphones vibrate. '*Achtung! Sehen Sie links, vor uns, dicke Mobelwagen!*' (Attention! To the left, ahead, fighter-bombers!) It is one of the Staffel. Hartmann glances to the left at once and sees a number of dots to the east. 'Victor,' he replies. He eases the throttle forward and pulls back on the stick, to prepare the four 109s for an attack. Meanwhile the F.W.89 disappears into the south-west, on its way back to Ugrim. He studies the silhouettes of the oncoming armada . . . too large for fighters . . . Il.II bombers, probably on their way to attack German ground targets. The Il.II is heavily armoured and hard to shoot down except when hit from beneath in the large oil radiator. Once hit there, it rapidly catches fire.

Now the red star on the enemy rudders becomes visible,

and their rear-firing guns. The enemy aircraft come straight on. Hartmann, above, banks to make a pass. The heavily-armoured Il.IIs are dark-green and flying at 3,000 to 4,000 feet. Hartmann is at 6,000, now squarely in front of the on-coming box. His pilots know what to do; each is to attack at will. Hartmann, eyes fixed on the enemy, presses the mike button of his helmet: '*Wir griefen an!*' (We attack!) One of his wings flashes up and he peels off in a dive at the oncoming enemy formation.

The engine roars, his airspeed accelerates and soon he is down to 5,000 feet, 4,000—on down. He eases back on the stick and stands on a wing to come around and up from be-hind one of the Il.IIs. The fighter-bomber formation flies straight on. Sighting carefully through the rectangular glass in front of his face and the reflected orange light ring and bars, he selects a big green victim and manœuvres with stick and pedals to approach fast from behind and beneath. The 109 is doing 600 k.p.h. after the dive, streaking up swiftly. But Hartmann waits. The enemy's dark green wing-span widens rapidly in the glass. The pilot of the ill-fated aircraft flies on straight and level, unaware of what is behind him. The rear gunner can't see in the blind spot area beneath the tail. Now the wing-span fills the space between the sighting bars. Hartmann still waits. The sleek fighter is 200 yards out, 150 yards; Hartmann points his guns towards the big oil radiator beneath the nose. Now 100 yards. Fire!

His right forefinger presses the silver-coloured trigger and his thumb the cannon trigger and the two 12 mm. machine-guns and the 20 mm. cannon spit metal at very short range, shells which immediately smash into the *Shtolmovik*. Hart-mann is gaining at such speed that he can fire only a second or two; then he is past his victim and pulling up above the formation. At this instant a short blue flame reaches back from the Il.IIs radiator. The other 109s flash into the forma-tion, select victims and open fire. Many of the Russians, as they often do, fly on and hold ranks. Others attempt to take on the four attacking 109s. Hartmann looks back down on the enemy gaggle. The Il.II he attacked is streaming heavy smoke and falling out of the formation. The distance to the ground is short. As the plane plunges it billows flames which cover the whole engine. It dives straight into the ground and explodes. Victim number one for 7 July; it is his 22nd of the war! Climbing back up, Hartmann prepares to make another attack.

The Russian formation is now beginning to separate into pairs and singles. Once more he peels off, starts down and again builds up great speed. He dives below the Russians and pulls up under them from behind. He has plenty of ammunition. Checking his rear regularly, he zeros in on the Il.II, juggling controls to make the Me.109 a stabilized gun platform for accurate firing. (Yawing or skidding distorts aim.) Working up rapidly from behind and watching the lengthening wings in his gunsight glass, Hartmann prepares to open up on his second victim. Now, however, the pilot ahead sees the Luftwaffe fighter behind. He suddenly pulls up and turns—a tactic (not a good one) of many Russian pilots. Hartmann has practised long at deflection gunnery and is a master at judging the proper lead turning behind. Instantly he banks in behind the turning, climbing Il.II, and is at once on him. A quick glance into the sight, estimating lead. Range 250 metres ... 200 ... 150. He pulls the trigger! He is very close to his opponent and his aim is accurate. Deflection fire smashes into the dark-green bomber and pieces and debris fly out and back. Then ... the telltale blue fire and smoke! The oil radiator again. Hartmann pulls up sharply above the box, now scattering wildly, looking down and behind. The second victim is falling out of formation. Other Il.IIIs are burning; the four-plane attack is a success.

The Russians are shattered and heading east. Suddenly Hartmann realizes the sky is almost empty. He will collect the Staffel; he presses the mike button and announces that he will set course for Ugrim. His wingman has kept him in sight and soon the Schwarm is together again, headed south-west. Hartmann reports the action to operations. It is only 3.50!

He has two victories before the day has begun for most pilots.

Ugrim is fifteen minutes distant and the Messerschmitts cruise homeward at 5,000 feet. Passing over German formations they see orange rockets below—the signal from German units telling them where the line is. They fly on for fifteen minutes and the field becomes visible ahead. Hartmann will waggle his wings to announce his victories, a traditional gesture. He lowers the nose and gains speed as he approaches, levels out and roars across the field at low altitude. As he crosses over he dips one wing and then the other; then he comes back and gives the field a second salute. Victories 22 and 23. Soon the Staffel is banking into a landing approach, wheels down, and the low-winged, white-nosed fighters descend steadily. They level out just above the tall grass . . . bump down. Hartmann holds the stick all the way back, rolling normally, and after she slows turns towards the parking area and Merten who, of course, has seen the victory passes. Several others are gathered at his parking area. He leads the fighters in, turns and taxies into position, cuts the throttle and switches off.

Merten smiles as he jumps on the wing and shouts: '*Gratulieren!*' Hartmann must answer many questions about the early-morning fight, what he saw, how many Il. IIs there were, and so on. He leaves his parachute in the aircraft and after more questions and answers, and congratulations, walks to the big tent. For Merten the two kills mean a painting job. On the rudder he paints a small yellow bar about three inches long for each victory. Already there are twenty-one bars on the rudder. Hartmann is hoping one day he can have the letters *hundert* painted there—the word representing a hundred yellow bars. (By the end of the war he will have earned three 'hundreds' and over fifty yellow bars.)

As soon as he is in the big tent Hartmann talks to III Gruppe Operations by telephone, reporting the action. Early morning activity indicates the day will be different from the 5th and 6th, when the German offensive rolled forward against scarcely any aerial opposition. There are other reports of Russian air activity.[1] Hartmann, who has located the exact position of his interception on the graph, accepts congratulations from pilots just rousing themselves from bed and writes out a *Gefechtsbericht* (Combat Report). When this is finished, he eats another breakfast (two more eggs) and walks back out to his aircraft. Near by four pilots sit in their aircraft on the alert. As soon as Hartmann landed at 4.05 the four climbed into their cockpits. They are on maximum alert and ready to take off at a moment's notice. They can be airborne in forty seconds should an *Adler* report produce an alarm. In a scramble, the entire Staffel rushes into the air but the four stand-by fighters will be the first Schwarm airborne. The scramble signal is a rocket shell over the field exploding into about fifteen white stars with a loud explosion, which pilots refer to as a '*Radieschen*' (radish). One or two red rockets fired aloft is the signal for the four pilots on alert to take off immediately.

The sun is up—it is 5.15 and Hartmann is tired! Chatting for a few minutes with Merten, who has refuelled and re-armed his 109, Hartmann lies down on the grass and falls asleep. His first sortie of 7 July had been eventful. The rest of the day will be even more eventful. And the months of July and August, just beginning, are to be the first in which his ability as one of the war's greatest fighter pilots will make itself evident.

Hartmann slept for only a few minutes before the spell was broken. Orders came for another '*frei*' chase over the battle area. An hour and forty-five minutes after landing he found himself leading another 109 flight into the north-east. It was to be his second eventful sortie of the day. Not too far from Ugrim the 109s encountered the suddenly plentiful enemy—another formation of Il.IIs, this time with fighter escort.

[1] This is the day Il.IIs launched massive attacks which destroyed 70 8th Panzer Division tanks in 20 minutes. And two hours of Il.II attacks were to cost 3rd Panzer Division 270 tanks and almost 2,000 casualties. 17th Panzer lost 240 vehicles out of 300.

Hartmann led the Staffel in to attack and in a battle with both fighter-bombers and fighters shot down one of each. The Russian fighter victim was a Lagg III. The two additional victories gave him four for the day and made his total 25! The flight lasted about an hour and Hartmann was down at 6.45. Once again he reported by telephone on the air battle and filled out another report—to be sent that night to 52 Geschwader headquarters.

With the two encounters, and four victories in a day, Hartmann was well satisfied. Lunch came, and afternoon. Then orders for another 'frei' chase over the battle area. At seven minutes after five that afternoon the new Staffel Leader pushed the throttle full forward and the Staffel lifted off the field again into the north-east. And not long afterwards it found the enemy again, this time in the form of a large gaggle of Russian Lagg III fighters. A spirited dog-fight between the two fighter formations erupted and Russian aircraft fell rapidly from the sky. Leading the white-nosed 109s for the third time that day was Hartmann. When it was over and the sky suddenly empty, Hartmann had shot down three fighters—victories number 26, 27 and 28 and his fifth, sixth and seventh victims on 7 July! It was the biggest day he had had in aerial combat. Air fighting had been heavy over the entire front that day. Jagdgeschwader 52 passed the 6,000-mark in Geschwader victories, and the Luftwaffe claimed 193 Russian aircraft destroyed.

This day was the beginning of Hartmann's meteoric rise among German fighter pilots in the East. In the months of July and August he shot down 78 enemy aircraft—more than three times the number he had accounted for in his first nine months in action. And his victories never ceased after that. All through 1943 and 1944 his pace of destruction was rapid— though the Luftwaffe couldn't turn the tide on the Eastern Front. By 20 September he had scored his ninetieth kill (this was the day the Russians captured and lost him). As the German front fell back the number of enemy aircraft steadily increased and so too did Hartmann's score. He was the fourth German pilot to reach 250 kills but the first to reach 300 and the only one to reach 350. As victories came rapidly one after another, he received award after award. Finally Hitler called him home and personally decorated him with the swords and diamonds to the Knight's Cross of the Iron Cross. Only twenty-eight were awarded during the war.

It was not Hartmann's fault that Germany lost the war in the East. Had the Germans produced many more like him, the task of the Russians and the Western Allies would have been more difficult. And though his first great day in the air came in 1943, after which the fortunes of his country were ever afterwards on the decline, his flying record reveals increasing effort and greater and greater achievement until the last days of the war.

Operation 'Zitadelle' proved a short-lived success. At great cost German Panzers drove forward from south-west and north-west toward the projected meeting point behind enemy lines, the city of Tim. The northern pincer advanced some ten miles before bogging down in multiple defence lines and under heavy air attack. The southern attack (in Hartmann's area) drove forward some forty miles. But this was short of the meeting point, and the attacks were so costly, in men and tanks, that after the first week it was clear that Hitler's last summer offensive had failed. Hartmann and other pilots of the Staffel saw how things were going, flying daily over the battlefield. They witnessed days of fierce tank battles north-east of Ugrim. For two or three days the tanks met on a vast plain. Hartmann still recalls the battle: 'Tanks were lined up for many kilometres. The battle went backwards and forwards for days. Finally, the Russians brought up fresh reserves of tanks. We had no more.' (J. F. C. Fuller, the military author writing in *The Second World War*, estimates the defeat of the attack at Kursk as being as disastrous to the Germans as the defeat at Stalingrad.)

On 15 July the Russians themselves attacked just to the north of the German assault and, the German lines having been weakened to gather together formations for the push in the south, broke through. By the 22nd the German pincers which had been moving toward Tim were withdrawn. But this failed to restore the situation. On 4 August Orel was evacuated and the Germans were pushed back by a general offensive all along the southern front. It was the first time since the war began that Hitler's armies had been repulsed and driven back in defeat after launching a carefully-planned summer offensive. This noticeable change in the fortunes of the war sent a chill down the spines of Germans to the west and their allies in the Balkans, for it was an ominous warning that the Red Army could not be held, even in summer and by Hitler's best formations.

The 'Black Devil of the Ukraine' and his comrades thus began moving ever so often westward, a trek that was to carry them—with stops here and there as the lines temporarily held—all the way into the arms of the United States Army advancing eastwards. By then Hartmann had been shot down sixteen times and had baled out twice in what must certainly be one of the remarkable individual performances in the history of warfare.

Hartmann surrendered to American forces in Czechoslovakia (hoping to avoid capture by the Russians) in May 1945. But because of political naïveté and a prior agreement with the Communists, the Army turned him over to Russian units advancing from the east. At the hands of the Russians, Hartmann was treated as a criminal. He was tried in a Communist court and sentenced to prison, where he remained for ten years. But as he had survived the tests of war so he mastered the post-war years. Released from Russian prison, and returned to his homeland, he was reunited with Usch, whom he had married eight months before the end of the war. Once more he joined the German Air Force. When the new Luftwaffe acquired American jets Hartmann checked out in them. He was last posted to the United States for a tour of duty and became a jet instructor. He is serving as an Oberstleutnant (Wing Commander) in the German

Air Force as this book goes to press.

Now forty-three, Hartmann is one of the enigmatic personalities among the great fighter pilots to survive the war. He is still easy going and happy on the ground, and cool in the air. If he has nerves no evidence of them is visible. Too young for command in the Second World War, neither intense fighting in 'cannon-fodder' rank on the Eastern Front for two and a half years nor more than ten years in a Russian prison have left a lasting effect upon his personality. In fact, he is today more relaxed, more 'one of the boys', than most of the younger pilots. Such steady indestructability throughout the last twenty-five years is remarkable testimony to self-discipline.

It may be that Hartmann took better care of himself during the war than most. He was a milk and cocoa drinker, an early-to-bed pilot. The fact that he wrote to Usch every day during all the trials on the Eastern Front provides a clue to his character. Yet meeting and questioning him after studying his record—as is the case with so many of the wars' greatest fighter pilots—it is hard to imagine him as the deadly aerial virtuoso who became the top-scoring fighter pilot in history.

# CHAPTER ELEVEN

# THE LUFTWAFFE *EXPERTEN*

THE OFFENSIVE at Kursk, in support of which Hartmann flew on 7 July 1943, was the last German offensive in the East. On the first two days of the attack Luftwaffe pilots saw few Russian aircraft but on the 7th and thereafter the picture changed. Before the summer was over the Russians employed an estimated 10,000 aircraft on the front. Luftwaffe pilots found themselves confronting steadily growing numbers. But despite the unequal odds they faced, 1943 was a record year for many German pilots, and Luftwaffe fighters shot down an astounding number of Russian aircraft. Scattered thinly along the vast north-south front, the German fighters usually flew in Schwärme and Rotten (four and two aircraft).

Hartmann was not alone in his sweep through eastern skies. He was the top scorer, but not, as has already been seen, the only German *Experte* with a conspicuous number of kills. Fourteen other Luftwaffe fighter *Experten* scored more than 300 and all served in the East; only one scored a proportion of his kills in the West. Hartmann of course, was just beginning in 1943. So were some of the others, whose records are almost equally impressive, but about whom comparatively little has been written.

There was Major Gerhard Barkhorn, an East Prussian, the only other pilot of the war to score more than 300 victories, who once scored 7 victories in one day. He flew some 300 fewer operational sorties than Hartmann—1,104—and in these he shot down 301 aircraft. He flew 120 times before scoring his first kill, and although transferred to the Western Front later in the war (where he wouldn't change from an

Me.109 to an F.W.190) all his kills came on the Eastern Front. He was shot down once—by a P.39—and in his best month he scored 38 victories. He must be considered one of the war's greatest.

Major Günther Rall, third highest-scoring German pilot, was credited with 275 victories. Of these, 3 came in the West, 272 in the East. Whereas Barkhorn's ratio of kills to flights was better than Hartmann's, Rall did better than either. He scored his 200th victory on his 555th sortie! Like Barkhorn he served in Jagdgeschwader 52, and like both the two highest-scoring *Experten* in the East he survived the war. He was a native of Swabia.

After Rall came Oberleutnant Otto Kittel from the Sudetenland. Kittel had 267 confirmed victories, all in the East. He had risen from the rank of corporal and flew F.W.190s. At one period he was captured by the Russians, and served fourteen days in a Russian prisoner-of-war camp. He escaped and rejoined German forces. In February of 1945 he shot down an Il.II and followed it for a moment, only to be caught and killed by another Il.II which had followed him. His ratio of successes was even better than those above him in victories—267 victories in 583 flights.

Major Walther Nowotny, an Austrian, also achieved a vast number of kills in the East—255. He began flying Me.109s, then changed over to F.W.190s and was the first German pilot to reach 250 victories. In 1943, when he began his spectacular rise, he shot down 167 Russians in four months! He was pulled back from the front and given command of the first Me.262 jet wing near Osnabruck (otherwise his score on the Russian Front would almost certainly have been higher). In November 1944, flying the Me.262, he was killed in an air battle over his base after shooting down an American bomber. At that time Group Commander Harry Broadhurst and his Tempests, and P.51s also, were almost constantly over the jet station, seeking to shoot down the fast Me.262s as they landed.

An interesting record is that of Major Wilhelm Batz, a

The Me.109

The Spitfire V

Adolf Galland
(right, fore-
ground) with
Reichsmarschal
Hermann Göri

Wing Commander J. E. Johnson

Lieutenant
R. C. Johnson

The Focke-Wulf 190

The three American
fighters that flew from
England—left to right,
the P.47, P.38 and P.51

A formation of P.51's over England

A B.24 Liberator breaking up during the Battle of Germany

The death of the Luftwaffe—aircraft burning on the ground in 1945

A captured Me.109 at Salzburg dwarfed by a colossal F.W.200, thought to have been used by Hitler

This luncheon given in the Capitol to
celebrate the publication of the author's
*American Aces* brought together ten of the
top twelve surviving U.S.A.A.F. fighter
pilots. Also in the picture are the late
President Kennedy (centre, back row),
and Nathan F. Twining (extreme right),
then Chairman of the Joint Chiefs of
Staff. The author is third from right

Franconian from Bavaria. He was comparatively old, having been an instructor, when he managed to reach the Front in 1943, the fourth year of the war. It is said that younger pilots were at first sceptical of his value because of his age and gruff personality. Yet from the time he began combat operations with Jagdgeschwader 52, in March 1943, he bettered the success ratios of the top pilots. In 455 flights he scored 237 kills. He had 3 kills in the West (2 Liberator bombers and 1 Spitfire). On one day (13 May 1944) he shot down 15 Russian aircraft in seven sorties. In addition to his confirmed victories he had about 50 which were unconfirmed. He flew the 109.

Major Erich Rudorffer, from Leipzig in Saxony, had perhaps the most remarkable record of all Luftwaffe's fighter *Experten* because his 222 confirmed victories were fairly evenly divided between East and West. He had 86 victories in the West and 136 in the East and flew 109s, F.W.190s and the Me.262 in achieving them. He scored 14 kills against the Russians in one day, and 13 on one occasion in seventeen minutes! He is said to have flown down the streets of London early in the war, when flying with Jagdgeschwader 2 (Richthofen). He scored 12 kills in the West with the Me.262 and during his wartime flying career was shot down sixteen times (six times over water) and baled out nine times. He began as a flight sergeant, survived the war and is now a farmer in Holstein.

Another remarkable record was that of Oberstleutnant Heinrich Bär, also a Saxon from Leipzig. Bär received confirmations for 220 victories in service on practically all fronts. He was the top scorer against the U.S.A.A.F. and R.A.F. in Europe and served in France, in the Battle of Britain, in Russia, Africa, Italy and in the defence of Germany. He began as a flight sergeant and scored his first kill in September of 1939. Of his 220 victories, less than half—96—were in the East; he had over 40 kills in Africa and shot down more than 20 four-engined bombers over Germany. He survived the dangers of war, but died some years afterwards.

Oberst Hermann Graf, of Jagdgeschwader 52, was credited with 211 victories, 202 of them in the East. He scored his first kill in August 1941, and thereafter he accumulated victories so rapidly that by 2 October 1942 he had scored his 200th! He was withdrawn from the front because of his amazing record, and in an attempt to prevent his loss or death, though later he went back on operations, adding 11 additional victories. All his flying was in a 109, and he survived the war. He was somewhat old when he entered combat—almost thirty—and his thirtieth year, 1942 was his most successful. He was a native of Swabia, from the Lake Constance area.

Major Theodor Weissenberger, the most famous pilot of Jagdgeschwader 5 (operating from the north of Norway) scored 208 victories, most of them in Me.109s, but he also flew an F.W. 190 in the West, where he scored over thirty victories. His first 23 victories were scored in an Me110 in Russia. A native of Frankfurt, he flew some 500 sorties, thus his ratios of kills per sortie was one of the best in the Luftwaffe. He was transferred to the West when the Allies invaded France in June 1944, and shot down 25 Allied aircraft in three weeks, a notable personal success, while the Luftwaffe was failing miserably as a whole. He survived the war, but lost his life shortly afterwards in a racing accident.

Leutnant Walther Schuck, of the Saar, scored 206 victories, most of them in the East but several on other fronts. His service was all in Me109s, and one day he scored 12 kills. He was transferred to Me.262s late in the war and was credited with 8 victories in the jet fighter. He began as a flight sergeant, scored his first kill in 1942, served throughout the war and survived.

Oberstleutnant Hans Philipp, a Saxon, flew both the 109 and the 190 and was also credited with 206 victories—25 of them in the West. He was the Kommodore of Jagdgeschwader 1 and his big year was in 1943. In that year he was withdrawn from the Russian Front to help in the Battle of Germany, and met his death on 8 October 1943 in a dogfight with P.47s.

Major Heinrich Ehrler, a Swabian from Baden, scored

204 victories. He was the Kommodore of Jagdgeschwader 5, and of his victories only 4 were achieved against the Western powers. He was blamed by some high officials as a scapegoat for the loss of the *Tirpitz*, and died in April 1945, when his fighter is thought to have crashed into a bomber. He flew only in 109s.

Oberleutnant Anton Hafner was credited with 204 victories in 795 flights on three fronts: the West, the East and Africa. He flew both 109s and F.W.190s, and despite his score did a considerable amount of ground strafing. He was also Swabian and was shot down and killed on the Eastern Front in October 1944, when Yak IXs caught and wiped out his entire Schwarm over East Prussia.

Captain Helmut Lipfert, of Türingen, was an officer in the labour forces and disliked his work. He succeeded in transferring to the Luftwaffe and was twenty-seven when he scored his first kill. In 700 missions he was credited with 203 victories, 5 of them coming in one day. Thirteen times he was shot down by Russian ground fire but was never wounded. He shot down several American four-engined bombers over Romania and one P.51.

All these *Experten* scored more than 200 victories—and all served on the Eastern Front. Counting Hartmann, there were fifteen German pilots with more than 200 kills, and nine of them survived the war.

The high individual scores in the East are not so surprising when one considers conditions on the front. In 1943, for example, opposing the Russian hordes were only four Geschwader—from the Baltic to the Caucasus. Each German pilot had therefore ample opportunity to meet the enemy. On that 2,000-mile front were deployed Jagdgeschwader 5 (two Gruppen), 54, 52 and 51. These all accumulated massive scores. J.G.52 was the most successful, with 11,000 victories. Next came 54 with 9,500 and then 51 with 9,000. Hans Ring estimates that these confirmations were not more than ten per cent in error.

An indication of how the Luftwaffe command appraised

victories in the East, compared to the West, is seen in the decorations system effective at this time—1943. A Luftwaffe fighter pilot generally received the Iron Cross, Second Class for 2 or 3 kills in the East. After 8 kills he was likely to receive the First Class. The German Cross was awarded at about 30 kills, and at about 75 the pilot in the East could expect the Knight's Cross. For those who scored between 100 and 120 the Oak Leaves to the Kight's Cross; above 200, the Oak Leaves with Swords; and above 250 the Oak Leaves with Swords and Diamonds.

On the Western Front at this time, pilots could win the Knight's Cross with Between 40 and 50 points,[1] so that 15 bombers in the West could earn the same recognition as 75 victories to the East.

German pilots who served in the East agree that victories came rather easily in 1941, rather less easily in 1942, and in 1943–4 became more difficult as Russian aircraft improved and pilots gained experience.

The Russian Air Force used the Rata extensively in 1941, and also the I.19. In the winter the Lagg III appeared. Though this was considered a good fighter, by then many of the best Russian pilots had been killed. The J.12 was also used by the Russians, and in 1942 the MiG I and II appeared. In the same year the P.39 put in its appearance, as did another American fighter, the P.40. Hurricanes appeared in the north in 1942, and also Spitfires (around Leningrad), supplied by the British. In 1943 the Lagg V was introduced on the Front, and also the Yak IX. These fighters were almost as fast as the Me.109, and highly manœuvrable. When the later model Yaks and the Lagg VII were produced they were even faster, but it seems that German pilots in the 109 and 190 maintained an edge over the Russians in whichever fighters they flew. (The Lagg III, interestingly, was derived from the He.112, which had been sold to Russia and Japan before the war.)

The fighter-bombers used most extensively by the Russians

[1] See p. 145.

were, of course, the Il.II and Il.IIm.3, the latter with a rear gunner. German pilots were high in their praise of these gunners, who often fired until their falling machines struck the ground. Many German pilots are said to have been killed because they approached too close behind a burning, falling Il.II, only to be hit by the rear gunner seconds before the aircraft hit the ground and the gunner met his death. Other bombers were used, of course, and among them were Martins, Bostons and Mitchells from the United States.

There were eight Luftwaffe fighter pilots who scored more than 100 victories on the Western Front, which indicates that a number of Germans did achieve remarkable results by any standard. There are those, among them some famous R.A.F. fighter pilots, who do not accept these records as accurate; however, in the last few years writers and historians have generally accepted them, with the reservation that the scores might be slightly inaccurate, like all individual tallies, but no more than is customary in such tabulations.

Among the Luftwaffe's top scorers in the West, we have already discussed Marseille. His victories in Africa, of course, were probably a little less difficult than a comparable number against the West in Europe. If that is true there was one German fighter pilot whose record earned him a special distinction. He was Heinrich Bär, mentioned earlier in this chapter as one with more than 200 victories.

Of Bär's 220 victories, most came in the West, not the East: he is the only one of the top fifteen Luftwaffe scorers of whom that can be said. He received confirmation for 124 victories against the Western democracies in Europe, 12 more than the next highest-scoring *Experte* in the West (other than Africa), Kurt Buehligen with 112. Thus Bär's 220 victories, even in comparison with higher totals, are considered by some to constitute the most impressive accomplishment of any fighter pilot in the Luftwaffe in the Second World War.

Buehligen's record is impressive not only because he shot

down the second highest number of Allied aircraft in Western Europe, but because he shot down 24 American four-engined bombers. Galland's total of 104 ranks him third among pilots operating against the Western powers in Europe. It is noteworthy because Galland was taken off operations when he became General of the Fighter Arm in 1941. Had he remained with J.G. 26—and survived—there seems little doubt that he would have become the highest scoring German fighter pilot in Western Europe. Therefore both Galland and Bär have their champions in the question of who was the outstanding fighter *Experte* in the West in the Second World War.

Major Joachim Müncheberg's record of 102 kills against the Western air forces in Europe and 135 kills in all theatres is an impressive one. Major Werner Schroer's total of 114, of which 102 were against the Western powers, is likewise remarkable. Schroer, among those who flew with Marseille in Africa, is said to have learned some of Marseille's tactics.

As for Marseille, his commanding officer, Neumann, is not inclined to think his total was high primarily because he was not up against the best British or American fighters in Africa. Neumann and Galland, and others who flew with Marseille, think he would have been a high scorer on any front. Neumann's appraisal of Luftwaffe *Experten* must be given weight because he was recognized as one of the great Geschwader leaders, even though his own record of thirteen victories is not a high score in the Luftwaffe. (His role was perhaps somewhat comparable to that of Colonel Don Blakeslee of the 4th Fighter Group in the 8th U.S. Army Air Force.) Neumann led a Gruppe of German fighters in Spain in 1937 and 1938, flying the He.51 against Loyalists in the Rata or the Russian-built Curtiss. He recalls a day early in 1937, when Ratas shot down seven He.51s. The defeat ended aerial combat between the two aircraft, the Germans waiting for the arrival of the Me.109 to renew the contest—and gain superiority. Neumann, a Rata and a Curtiss to his credit, was recalled to Germany in 1938.

When a commander was needed to lead a small group of pilots in Africa, being dispatched to aid General Rommel and his Afrika Korps, Neumann was selected. In the desert, strafing Hurricane IIDs had been causing Rommel's troops considerable trouble and were also making life miserable for Stuka pilots. The 109s were sent to relieve the situation; Neumann had orders (direct from Göring) to report to Rommel upon arrival, which he did on his first day in Africa—after a combat mission in his first hour.

The appearance of the 109s had an immediate effect, and Neumann recalls the system then used to avoid being surprised by the R.A.F. There was no camouflage but lookouts were posted to the east. Two to four pilots were kept sitting in fighters on the field at all times. With five minutes' warning the 109s could be over 20,000 feet above the base, and usually they had five minutes, often more.

In speaking of Marseille specifically, and of fighter pilots in general, Neumann is firmly of the opinion that Marseille was the most talented fighter pilot in the Luftwaffe, one reason being that he imparted to his Staffel, the Gruppe and J.G. 27 as well, a highly contagious combat spirit.

Marseille stood out among his comrades, for the next highest score after his 151 in Africa was Werner Schroer's 61. The controversy over the validity of Marseille's confirmations should not concern us too much at this late date, It was fashionable for a time to dismiss his score as propaganda or exaggeration, and it could be that the actual total is not a hundred per cent correct. The fact is, however, that the claims were confirmed and that the German confirmation system was generally responsible.[1]

Other German fighter aces achieved records worthy of

[1] The most serious doubt about any Marseille claim rose concerning 1 September 1942, which we discussed briefly in Chapter 9, on which day he claimed 17 victories in three sorties—claims which were confirmed. The Table of Operations, Middle East, shows R.A.F. aircraft losses—as reported in Chapter 9—were 13 fighters shot down or listed missing and another six which had crash-landed. This leaves the question open until researchers check exact times, squadrons, and so on. The author was,

mention. Some were specialists against heavy bombers of the U.S.A.A.F. One of these was Oberleutnant Herbert Rollwag, who began as a flight sergeant and was awarded 132 points for the destruction of 44 bombers! He survived the war, having scored a total of 102 victories in all, and is alive today. Another bomber specialist was Major George Eder, shot down seventeen times and wounded on twelve occasions! Eder, who also survived the war, shot down 36 bombers.

In this brief summary of the achievements of German fighter pilots we have not attempted to probe the field of night fighters. The Luftwaffe (like the R.A.F.) developed a highly trained night-fighter force. Two of these pilots scored over 100 victories against the R.A.F. at night. Major Heinz-Wolfgang Schnanfer was credited with 121 kills (9 in one night—21 February 1945) and Oberst Helmut Lent had 102 confirmed night victories, plus 8 day victories, which gave them the distinction of being the highest-scoring night fighter pilots of the war.

There were other German fighter pilots who accomplished what sounds almost unbelievable. On the Western Front, Leutnant Willi Unger scored 22 victories, 19 of them being four-engined bombers, in 37 flights. Oberfeldwebel Walther Loos was credited with 38 kills, 22 of which were four-engined bombers, in 66 flights. And Oberleutnant Kurt Welter, in only 40 flights, scored 33 kills, among them 21 four-engined bombers and 7 Mosquitoes, one of which he rammed. In his first 11 sorties he scored 14 kills and was shot down nine times!

Many of the expanding records of Luftwaffe fighter aces, and the relatively easy missions, came to an end in the bitter and massive struggle of the Battle of Germany. Here the Luftwaffe was beaten, even though fighter production was ample (approximately 20,000 fighters produced in 1944 alone). The average German fighter pilot in these last years

---

however, able to confirm the victories of Marseille's memorable flight on 6 June 1942, on the Allied side.

was probably not up to the average in either the R.A.F. or the U.S.A.A.F. Training had become chaotic in Germany and there were shortages of fuel. The veterans surviving may have been the best, but they were few.

The latest-model British and American fighters, models which had been built and introduced during the war, also enjoyed technical superiority. Luftwaffe pilots were thus often green and outclassed technically and sometimes suffered heavy defeats. In the two years Luftwaffe fighter losses soared, reversing the ratio which had prevailed over the Western Front during the early years of the war. These heavy losses might, in fact, give a distorted picture of the German fighter to one unfamiliar with the performance in 1940–3.

Many of the highest-scoring *Experten* were recalled from other fronts to join the homeland's defence, some joining new jet squadrons, and many were killed in the contest—a struggle against quantity and quality. For the first time in the air fighting, Me.109s and F.W.190s were now unable to dive away from opposing fighters. The P.47s and P.51s followed them to the deck and fought it out at tree-top level if necessary, where they could out-turn the German fighters. They were also faster.

Luftwaffe fighter gaggles seeking to intercept American bomber boxes often numbered more than sixty planes and sometimes as many as ninety. Various weapons were introduced in an effort to turn back the bombing assault, including jets (the Arado 234 and the Me.262—and a few He.162s, the so-called People's Fighter), the rocket fighter (Me.163), heavier guns, rockets slung under the wings of conventional fighters, long-range guns, bombs dropped from aircraft above the bomber boxes, and even a special unit to ram the bombers.

One of the fascinating might-have-beens of the Luftwaffe fighter effort at this critical stage is the question of what would have happened had Galland succeeded in staging the much-discussed and planned *grosse Schlag* (big strike). The idea was to assemble 2,000 German fighters in an all-out effort to smash an American bomber force so badly that the disaster would halt the daylight bombing offensive. The number of fighters was actually assembled toward the end of 1944 and training for the great day undertaken. Galland was willing to accept the loss of 400 or 500 fighters if he could bring down an equal number of bombers. (Had he done so, that would have meant the loss of 5,000 American airmen in a few hours.)

German accounts say the weather was never right for the big blow before the German counter-attack began in the Ardennes, when many of the assembled units were suddenly transferred to the West to support the Panzer offensive. One English authority has suggested that November battles with American fighter escorts produced German defeats so heavy that they pointed clearly to an ominous outcome for such an effort. Whatever the result would have been, this great confrontation—which promised to be history's biggest— never took place. Many fighter units transferred to the West were decimated, their aircraft strafed on the ground, lost in combat or in bad-weather accidents.

Though the *grosse Schlag* didn't come off, the fighter battles between escort fighters of the Eighth Air Force and defending Luftwaffe fighters were nevertheless the biggest of the war.

# CHAPTER TWELVE

# THE CAMPAIGN OF 1941-2

THE POPULAR conception of a one-sided British victory over German fighters as well as bombers in the Battle of Britain, plus R.A.F. claims at Dunkirk in May and June, had produced a widespread belief that the Spitfire and the Hurricane were vastly superior to the Me.109. As a result, some people were in for a rude awakening in 1941 and 1942. It was not then generally known that British pilots had claimed three times as many aircraft over Dunkirk as they had actually destroyed.[1] Nor was it generally known that R.A.F. fighter losses in the Battle of Britain had been substantially higher than 109 losses.

It was thought, rather, that pronounced superiority of the British fighters in these engagements had meant the salvation of the evacuating army in the first instance, and the salvation of Britain in the second. And the tendency of pilots to over-claim continued, apparently in 1941 and 1942. This is a common failing amongst pilots and crews of all nations (and reached sublime proportions in the case of American heavy-bomber gunners). Hans Ring, however, rates the claims of American fighter pilots as closer to the mark than those of their R.A.F. counterparts.[2]

## The Non-Stop Offensive

After 1940 and the Battle of Britain, the roles of R.A.F. and Luftwaffe fighters were reversed. In 1941 the R.A.F.

---

[1] *Full Circle*, p. 122.
[2] Private conversation with author; Ring rates the accuracy of U.S. fighter pilot claims as 'excellent' with the exception of claims against the Me.262, the jet fighter which appeared in 1944.

went over to the offensive. The Luftwaffe—most of its strength having been transferred east for the attack on Russia—was forced into a defensive role. R.A.F. fighters found themselves on sweeps and bomber-escort flights over France while Luftwaffe pilots now enjoyed the advantages of the defensive, better combat formations, and, generally, fighters of superior performance (in these years they were equipped with the Me.109F and the F.W.190).

The R.A.F. was superior numerically, for after June there were only two Jagdgeschwader left in France—2 and 26—and part of one in Holland, which established German fighter strength at about 275 aircraft.[1] R.A.F. fighter pilots flew under the handicap of having to escort bombers, often in obsolete flying formations, and they were now at a further disadvantage in being over enemy territory.

Looking back over results of these two years, the record of the Luftwaffe Geschwader is an impressive one, even considering the advantage of defence. The confirmed claims of all German fighter units in the West in 1941 totalled about 950

[1] In 1943 the strength of Geschwader was increased by the addition of a fourth Gruppe. Prior to 1943, a Geschwader contained three Gruppen, each with three Staffeln, these numbering nine to twelve aircraft each. By adding another Gruppe, the average strength of Geschwader, including a headquarters Schwarm of four and a few aircraft in reserve, was increased from about 120 to 160 aircraft. As can be seen, U.S.A.A.F. fighter squadrons were larger than either R.A.F. squadrons or Luftwaffe Staffeln, since they were normally composed of sixteen fighters, whereas the R.A.F. squadron numbered twelve and the Luftwaffe Staffel eight to twelve. The American organization table used the designation 'Group' for a unit of several squadrons, usually three, while the R.A.F. called this a Wing. R.A.F. Groups were large fighter organizations sometimes consisting of many Wings. (There were only four Groups in 1940 for the entire country.) The American designation for organizations composed of Groups was the Wing. The Luftwaffe table of organization was not comparable because three squadrons, or Staffeln, formed a Gruppe, but the Gruppe was not an entity as in the American sense, but part of a three-Gruppe Geschwader, the strength of which was greater than a U.S.A.A.F. Group or an R.A.F. Wing. Some units of J.G. 52 were in Holland, and there were about four training Staffeln in the West, in addition to 2 and 26. On 26 July 1941 the combined strength of all was 238 fighters, according to official records.

aircraft, and it would appear that those claims were reasonably accurate. According to accepted British sources, Fighter Command lost 849 fighters in 1941. Bomber Command losses were even higher (1,328), but these involved night operations to a large degree. Coastal Command lost 339.

British claims were optimistic. Fighter pilots received confirmation for 909 victories during 1941.[1] German records show that actual losses from all causes in France and the Low Countries during the year were 183.[2]

If British fighter pilots overclaimed by the ratio indicated above, it would appear that in 1942 they were not quite so optimistic. The strength of the German fighter defence did not change. The R.A.F. continued its offensive. German fighters received confirmations for 972 victories during the year. Accepted British sources place Fighter Command's losses in 1942 at between 890 and 915, Bomber Command's at 1,616 and Coastal Command's at 352. Again, German claims do not seem unreasonable. However, German records show that Luftwaffe losses in all day-fighter units in the West during 1942 were only 272, while the number of confirmations awarded to British fighter pilots was about 500.

The records of Geschwader 2 and 26 in these two years are interesting. They shot down about 750 of the 950 Luftwaffe confirmations in 1941 and about 930 of the 972 in 1942. The pilot losses of J.G. 26 according to the records of the Quartermaster General of the Luftwaffe, were, in 1941: 50 killed in action, 14 killed in accidents, and 6 lost as prisoners. In 1942 the Geschwader lost three less—the total for 1941 and 1942 combined being 141.

We must bear it in mind here that German fighters which were hit, or slightly damaged, or which performed the standard trick of emitting smoke and diving away, were probably sometimes claimed by R.A.F. pilots. And some of those which were hit were undoubtedly only slightly damaged

[1] From private tabulation of squadron records.
[2] Official records, confirmed by Luftwaffe historian.

and not reported.

The impressive fact shown by these figures is that, in the two years, German fighters in the West apparently shot down over 1,500 aircraft, the vast majority of them fighters, while losing less than 500.

One must conclude, from these figures, that the 1941–2 battle in the West was a successful one for the Luftwaffe. And from a comparison between R.A.F. claims and indicated German losses, the former were obviously still running high, as they had in 1940. This estimate is reinforced by exact figures which have become available for certain specific air battles during the period. That at Dieppe is an example. In that intense encounter on 19 August 1942 (an episode described later in this book takes place on that day) Allied claims were considerably more optimistic than the German. R.A.F. claims for the day were 91 victories and 44 probables. Official German records show Luftwaffe losses were actually 48 aircraft from all causes, 20 being fighters.

German claims that day were 112 victories. R.A.F. losses admitted totalled 108.[1] Thus the Luftwaffe won this encounter by a better than two-to-one margin. The comparative strength of forces committed was as follows: R.A.F., 48 Spitfire squadrons, 6 Hurricane squadrons, 4 Mustang reconnaissance squadrons, 3 U.S. Eagle squadrons (Spitfires), plus 8 additional squadrons, including fighter-bombers. Luftwaffe strength comprised a limited number of bombers, plus the two fighter Geschwader in the west, each of nine Staffeln.

If such indications are of value in assessing the fighter battle in 1941 and 1942, what about Germain claims in 1940? There were clashes in the Battle of Britian in which Luftwaffe pilots claimed a number of aircraft but in which the R.A.F. has admitted no losses. One of them, which still puzzles some German students, is a clash which occurred on 15 August, the

[1] Hans Ring, in conversation with author. Johnson in *Wing Leader*, Chapter 9, says the 'Luftwaffe shot down R.A.F. fighters by more than two for one' in the Dieppe air battle.

day of the maximum Luftwaffe effort against England. On that day Luftflotte 5, in Norway, joined in the assault, and R.A.F. pilots intercepted the Scandinavian-based bombers and long-range fighters off the coast, shooting down seven Me.110s and sixteen twin-engined bombers. German pilots, in return, claimed twelve British Spitfires. But the R.A.F. announced that no Spitfires were lost and none hit. A recent partial check of squadron records shows that seven squadrons engaged the enemy formations, claiming over forty destroyed and a number of probables. From these individual records (41, 72, 73, 79, 264, 605, 607 and 616 Squadrons) it appears that, from 605 Squadron, one pilot crashed and one force-landed. From 79 Squadron one aircraft was badly shot up. This would indicate perhaps that the R.A.F. score for the day was incorrect, though it also indicates a one-sided R.A.F. victory. Perhaps the reason some German sources question the 'no losses' assessment of the R.A.F. for the clash with Norway-based squadrons is that some of the German claims for that day were confirmed by two eye-witnesses. (Of the twelve Spitfires claimed by German pilots in the battle, the Abschusskommission confirmed six.)

In this battle, of course, the R.A.F. was employing fighters and the Luftwaffe had no single-engined aircraft in its formations, so the advantage in equipment was with the R.A.F. and the one-sided victory is understandable. On the other hand, since the Germans had no single-engined fighters in the battle, German eye-witnesses who reported seeing Spitfires hit should not have found aircraft identification as difficult as would have been the case if fighters from both sides had been engaged. We must accept official R.A.F. loss figures, of course, unless they should be corrected.

In the case of victory claims, practically all have been corrected, and this is the case for 15 August 1940. Originally the R.A.F. claimed 182 destroyed on that day, admitting 34 losses. Claims were later scaled down to 75, but losses admitted remained the same. German records show 55 Luftwaffe aircraft were lost due to enemy action, 20 more from other causes, and others damaged.

In summary, looking back over the fighter campaign of 1941 and 1942, the non-stop offensive, it would seem certain that the defenders had the better of it, and by a good margin, even though their numbers were few. They enjoyed, of course, the defensive advantage, good tactical formations and aircraft with superior performance, in many cases, while the attackers were escorting bombers. British fighter losses for the two years were not much higher than for 1940 alone, but British bomber losses were about double 1940 losses in 1941 and still more in 1942. German fighter losses, on the other hand, were far less than in 1940, as were bomber losses.

# CHAPTER THIRTEEN

# SPITFIRES GET THE KOMMODORE

*21 June 1941—Oberst Adolf Galland, Luftwaffe*

THE MOST FAMOUS—in many ways the greatest—of the German fighter pilots in the Second World War was Adolf Galland. Galland shot down 104 Allied planes, all in the West, which made him one of the highest scorers among German fighter pilots flying against the English and Americans, and he achieved this score though forbidden to fly in combat from December 1941 to the end of 1944!

He was a natural leader who rose to the rank of General of the Fighter Arm at thirty, then the youngest general in the German Armed Forces. He saw combat in Spain, Poland, France, Sicily, Italy and Germany and won his country's highest decorations; he was the first to win Germany's highest award. He was one of the few acquainted with the air war at both the front-line and command levels.

Galland was born in the town of Westerholt in Westphalia in March 1912, and was one of four brothers, three of whom became unusually successful fighter pilots in the Second World War. Their father was bailiff to Count von Westerholt, a post held by the Galland family for close to a hundred and eighty years. (The original Galland came to Westphalia as a French Huguenot fleeing religious persecution, settling in Germany in about 1742.)

Adolf attended elementary school in Westerholt, finished advanced schooling in Buer and, impressed by the glider flying then in vogue, decided to become a commercial pilot. With his father's consent, he made his first flight at seventeen. Initially he experienced difficulties mastering flying techniques, as did many of the war's greatest fighter pilots, but he overcame them. Soon afterwards he entered a glider-flying contest and did well. He completed glider school training at Wasser in Rhön in 1931, when he was nineteen. By that time he had achieved impressive successes in glider contests and had become a glider instructor.

He soon owned his own glider and, after establishing a regional flight endurance record, stood the examination for admission to Lufthansa's commercial pilot training school. Of thousands who applied and stood the examinations, only eighteen or twenty were accepted. Galland was one of them. Successfully completing Lufthansa's pilot training school in 1932, he applied for admission to the armed forces (the small German Air Force was *sub rosa* at this time). He was accepted.

In 1934 he was sent to Italy for secret flying training after which he attended a military flight training school in Dresden where he was taught aerobatics. In 1935 he was assigned to the 2nd Fighter Wing of the Luftwaffe, which was being rapidly expanded by Chancellor Adolf Hitler.

Being an experienced pilot, he quickly rose to prominence in the Luftwaffe. He was one of the group of German volunteers Hitler sent to Spain to help the Insurgents overthrow the Republican Government. He didn't become famous as a fighter in Spain in 1937 and 1938 as did another famed German fighter pilot, Werver Mölders, but flew three hundred sorties in an He.51 and learned much about direct air support. He won the Cross of Honour for the Spanish Campaign in gold with diamonds—only fourteen of which were awarded.

During the Polish campaign in 1939 he flew seventy sorties in twenty-seven days and was promoted to Hauptmann (Captain). Stationed on the Western Front when Hitler launched his armies against France and the Low Countries on 10 May 1940, he scored his first kill in this theatre on 12 May, downing an R.A.F. pilot flying a Hurricane.

That was the beginning of a highly successful career against the R.A.F. and the U.S. Army Air Corps, in which Galland was shot down on many occasions, forced to parachute out of burning planes, wounded several times by enemy gunfire, grounded by a personal order from Hitler and, in recognition of his 96 victories, in December 1941, promoted to General of the Fighter Arm. He had emerged from the Battle of Britain in 1940 the highest-scoring German fighter pilot— 57 victories.

Although Galland himself points to Hans-Joachim Marseille (both became wartime idols of the German people) as the greatest German fighter pilot of the war, there are many who feel he had no peer. His combat flying ceased, except for occasional missions, in December 1941. Thus his score of 104 aircraft is more impressive than it appears among the list of top-scoring German aces. That he was an exceptional pilot (as was indicated in early glider contests) and one of the best marksmen in the Luftwaffe is undoubted. In addition, he had no superior in determination and aggressiveness. When grounded he was always miserable, biding his time until he could fly again, and in the final days of the war he returned to action and led a jet fighter squadron against overwhelming odds.

In 1941 Galland was Kommodore of one of the two German fighter Geschwader left in the West to oppose the R.A.F.— most of the Luftwaffe having been transferred to the East for the offensive against Russia. His Geschwader was distributed over various fields in the Pas de Calais and in those days he often led his fighters against the R.A.F. He came to know the names of some of the R.A.F. aces, several of whom he met when they were shot down over France and accepted his invitation to dinner. German fighter pilots in 1941 were confident and capable and their fighters were perhaps the best in the world. Morale was good and Galland led his squadrons whenever he could. And it is with this period, and a memorable day for Galland, that we are now concerned.

Saturday, 21 June 1941, was warm and sunny over the Straits

of Dover. Close to the coast of Kent, and the French coast between Calais and Boulogne (the Pas de Calais) were the strategically located advanced fighter fields of the R.A.F. and the Luftwaffe.

The two air forces, flying from the same bases, had met in all-out battle in the summer of the preceding year, when the German Air Force had failed to subdue the R.A.F. and bomb England into submission. At the conclusion of that struggle, the Luftwaffe discontinued massed daylight bomber attacks and bombed England largely by night. In the summer of 1941 it was the R.A.F. which had gone over to the offensive in an effort to relieve pressure on Russian armies in the East and R.A.F. fighters and bombers were carrying out daylight attacks on targets in France. Because the escorting fighters (Spitfires and Hurricanes) had limited range, targets bombed by the R.A.F. were usually close to the coast. German fighters, which a year before had often flown as bomber escorts over England and London, were now playing an opposite role—attacking R.A.F. bombers over France.

On the French side of the Straits, midway between Calais and Boulogne and a few miles east of Cap Gris Nez, sprawled the Luftwaffe fighter station of Wissant, named after the French coastal village. On a clear day German pilots could see the chalk cliffs of Dover across the Straits, and, higher, the radar and radio towers which stood out clearly on the green Kentish shore. The distance was twenty-two miles.

At the beginning of this summer of 1941 only two Luftwaffe Geschwader, 2 and 26, defended France and Occupied Europe against the R.A.F. assault, then being referred to in the Allied press as the 'non-stop' offensive. Kommodore (Commander) of Jagdgeschwader 26, which had its head-quarters at near-by Audembert in a farm house, was Oberstleutnant Adolf Galland.

The morning of the 21st began without a hint of action. There were no reports of enemy activity. The breeze steadily increased from the Straits as the morning wore on, and the rising sun warmed the green, rolling Calais hills. Galland was nervous. The weather was too good.

His Geschwader was composed of three Gruppen, each containing three Staffeln. The normal flying strength of squadrons was from eight to twelve fighters. Thus, using all nine squadrons, Galland could send up more than a hundred fighters. He also had a Stabschwarm (staff schwarm) of four, with which he normally flew as leader. (In general, a Geschwader's strength at this time could be estimated at 120 aircraft.) One squadron was based at Audembert with Galland; the other eight were stationed at three other nearby fields. Galland rotated the nine squadrons in and out of Audembert, where they remained two weeks, to become personally acquainted with as many of the pilots as possible.

All 26 Geschwader squadrons were equipped with Me.109s in 1940. But in 1941 one group—three squadrons—were reequipped with F.W.190s. The 109Es hidden under wooden camouflage sheds just south of the field at Audembert were painted grey or light blue beneath, which blended with the sky viewed from the ground. They were powered by 1,150 horsepower Daimler-Benz inline (DB605 inverted V=A) engines, turning three-blade propellers producing a speed of better than 350 m.p.h. at 12,000 feet. Luftwaffe fighter pilots were confident the 109s—smaller than Hurricanes or Spitfires—were faster than the R.A.F.'s fastest. (The Mark I Spit was rated at 355 m.p.h., but at 19,000 feet. At about this time the R.A.F. was equipping its squadrons with the Mark II Spit, which could achieve 370 m.p.h., and the Luftwaffe was introducing the Me.109F, about 20 m.p.h. faster than the E.)

The double row of sheds housing the 109s at Audembert were effectively camouflaged to blend inconspicuously into the roll of surrounding farmland. Trees were painted on sides, netting was used extensively, and from only a moderate height installations became indiscernible. A few hundred feet west of the sheds, just south of the grass take-off area, stood a white masonry chalet.

At 7.30 that morning Galland was awakened in one of its

five bedrooms. He washed and shaved and dressed in black, sheep's wool flying boots and flying suit and a brown R.A.F. flying jacket. The first officer to report to him was the weather officer, who confirmed what he already had seen—flying conditions were excellent. He was also briefed on the latest information gleaned from intercepted radio traffic and prisoners-of-war. (The German Signal Corps supplied valuable information about R.A.F. activities, down to detailed facts such as which squadron leaders had gone on leave.) For breakfast Galland drank a mixture of raw eggs and red wine. He could never eat much in the mornings. In spite of his nervousness, nothing was apparently happening on the other side of the Straits.

He resigned himself to paper-work relating to Friday's activities. The morning progressed and soon it was ten o'clock, then eleven. Outside, it grew warmer. Apart from an occasional roaring start-up, of one of the 109s by a crewman, the only sounds through the open farm-house window this summer morning were those of breezes, birds and insects. But Galland couldn't relax. It was a quarter past eleven.

The telephone rang. It was an officer in the plotting room, a wooden building a few hundred feet from the front door, left. '*Viele, über Kent,*' the voice said. Galland answered: '*Komme sofort.*' In sixty seconds he was hurrying through the door of a ninety-by-ninety-foot plotting-room. Inside the curved-roofed building, which was covered with green netting stretching away to each side, were a number of tables on which were charted plots from Freya radar stations on the coast. Galland went from one to another, scanned the situation map where all the data was combined into a single picture. The picture was clear enough; he immediately ordered an alert and a briefing and hastily departed, leaving instructions that he be informed of any change in the developing picture.

Time was very short, for the distance was not great. Crewmen hurriedly began checking the 109s to have engines warm and ready to go. The distant roar permeated the countryside and frenzied activity on all sides betrayed the sudden change of pace of the fighter station; an atmosphere of imminent action had fastened its grip on the field. Galland meanwhile was explaining the prospect to hurriedly assembled pilots at the farm-house. 'We have detected three wings of bombers, probably with fighter protection, at three thousand metres. We expect them to penetrate the coast a few kilometres west of Dunkirk.' Using a map, he continued: 'We expect to intercept between here and here' (he indicated an area to the east, slightly inland). 'All squadrons are assembling. If there's time, I will lead them all in a concentrated formation; if not, we'll attack in separate groups.'

There were few questions, little time. Galland, wrapping a yellow scarf around his neck, and fifteen other pilots ran towards their 109s. Galland would lead the staff Schwarm of four, in addition to the Staffel of twelve. Since the *Gefechts-alarm* (battle alert) had sounded, all crewmen were present at their 109s. Galland greeted his crew chief, Unteroffizier Meyer, bounded into the cockpit of the ready 109 F.2 and, after strapping himself in, started the engine by pulling the start button.

After quickly checking instruments and gauges, he signalled ready. A crewman standing nearby pointed a flare pistol into the air and fired. A small green ball of fire shot up a hundred feet. Galland closed his canopy, released the brakes, eased the yellow knob on the left of the cockpit wall forward with his left hand; the Daimler-Benz howled louder as the prop pulled the fighter forward. Other pilots—only a short distance back—taxied out behind. Galland taxied north to the southern edge of the field, turned right to reach the eastern edge, and halted. Close to him were three other fighters, the rest of the Schwarm. Behind the Schwarm, in twos and fours, came the Staffel, now all taxi-ing rapidly into position. It was 12.24 and Galland opened the throttle all the way. The 109 began to gather speed, leaping and lunging over the grass as all the power of the big engine thrust the light (5,500 pounds) aircraft faster and faster. Sleek, pointed-

Take-off at approximately 12.24 a.m. and crash-landing less than an hour later

Wissant
St. Omer

109s climb rapidly to gain altitude advantag

Galland lead
squadron on
scramble to
intercept R.A
bomber-fight
force

WISSA

| FIGHTER |

Me. 109

| FIGHTER GESCHWADER |

J.G. 26

| FIGHTER STATION |

WISSANT (FRANCE)

MISSION FLOWN B

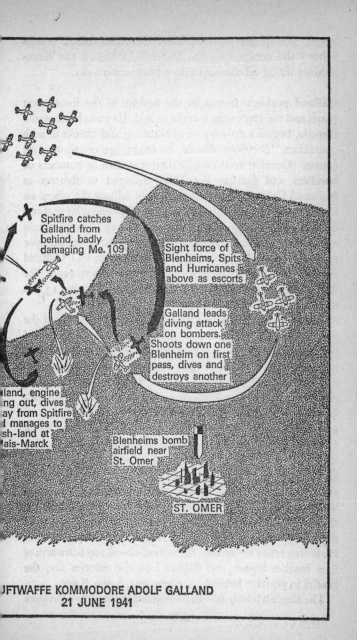

Spitfire catches Galland from behind, badly damaging Me.109

Sight force of Blenheims, Spits and Hurricanes above as escorts

Galland leads diving attack on bombers. Shoots down one Blenheim on first pass, dives and destroys another

...land, engine ...ng out, dives ...ay from Spitfire ...d manages to ...sh-land at ...ais-Marck

Blenheims bomb airfield near St. Omer

ST. OMER

LUFTWAFFE KOMMODORE ADOLF GALLAND
21 JUNE 1941

nosed, grey-green fighters, with three-foot black crosses behind the cockpits on the fuselages, followed the Kommodore lifting off the field into a blue western sky.

Galland pushes a button at the bottom of the instrument panel and the 109's wheels begin to fold. He eases back on the throttle, begins a slow turn still climbing and checks in with operations. '*Die dicken Hunde*', he hears, are continuing on course. (German controllers called a stream of bombers or bombers and fighters Fat Dogs, referred to fighters as Indians.) Galland closes the air scoop, adjusts the wheel on the left of the cockpit floor for proper climbing trim and sets course at 110 degrees. His 109—with Mickey Mouse insignia on the side of its canopy—climbs initially at 3,000 feet per minute. (As the air gets thinner, the rate slows.) Galland estimates it will take a little over five minutes to reach the desired height above the oncoming bombers—about 13,000 or 14,000 feet.

The airspeed needle at the bottom of the right side of the panel shows a climbing speed of close to 400 k.p.h. (top speed indicated on the dial is 750). Galland checks to be sure his engine and oil temperatures are within limits. The German system is easy. Water lines and gauges are painted in green, oil in brown, air in blue, fuel in yellow. The fire-extinguisher is red. He flips the stick cover lid to ready his guns and cannon and switches on the electrical gun-sight button. Directly in front of his face, on a glass rectangle measuring four inches high and two wide, a yellow-white electric light circle appears. At a hundred metres a Spitfire's wing-span (thirty-six feet) fills the circle. Galland can fire his two 20-millimetre wing cannon by depressing an uncovered button on top of the stick with his thumb and can fire two 7·8 machine-guns by depressing the front of the black, hand-shaped stick handle. He is now ready for action; the yellow-nosed 109 Schwarm of four reaches higher and higher into the eastern sky, the Staffel in position behind . . . 6,000 feet, 7,000, 8,000.

The English bombers—twin-engined Blenheims—prepare

to go into their bombing runs over an airfield. It is at Arques, near St Omer. The Blenheims, Galland is informed by radio, are already east (ahead) of Galland's climbing yellow-noses so there will be no time for Galland to assemble the Geschwader. The controller at Wissant also reports large formations of R.A.F. fighters located above the bombers. Galland acknowledges, continues his climb. Altitude 9,000, 10,000, 11,000 feet. He follows a course furnished by the plotters below, points slightly south of due east. He should be seeing the enemy formation and scans the sky ahead. Nothing is in sight. He checks the sky behind, continues on course. Up ahead ... he can see St Omer. Then ... just past St Omer on a road leading south-west he sees the airfield—and bombs bursting! It's under attack. The R.A.F. bombers—he calls them in—are over Arques at 11,000 feet. A pack of escorting Hurricanes and Spitfires are above. Galland and all the German pilots feel the tension of impending battle upon seeing the enemy; they move their throttles all the way forward and steepen their climb. Galland will get above the R.A.F. fighters and into position to make a diving attack. The 109s roar upward higher and higher above the bombers, now off to the right. Galland leans into a wide right turn, keeps his stick back climbing and pulls up above the escorting fighters and well above the enemy bombers, still below, right. The Blenheims appear to have finished their bombing and are turning homewards.

His Staffel is in position. But English fighters are between the 109s and the bombers. Can he get through the escort to get to the bombers? No other German fighters are yet attacking. He must dive through the escort, presses the mike button of his brown helmet: '*Angriff!*' Diving pass to the right. His port wing flips up, exposing a black and white cross, and the 109 accelerates downwards and right as Galland pushes stick forwards and applies right rudder. The 109s quickly stretch out in the dive. Airspeed rapidly increases. Galland keeps the nose well down and peers ahead and down through the gunsight glass. The Spits and Hurricanes, above the Blenheims, appear to be rushing up to meet him as they bank above their larger comrades but Galland pays them no attention. He is suddenly on them, flashes through the enemy fighter formation at 400 m.p.h. Taken by surprise, the R.A.F. fighters bank sharply to take on the 109s. But so fast are the German fighters diving that they are now down and far away from the enemy fighters and approaching the Fat Dogs.

Galland eases back on the stick, feels the drain of blood from his head, but keeps his eyes fixed on the Blenheim formation. One of the twin-engined bombers is off to the right, trailing behind the formation. Galland manœuvres feet and stick, levelling the 109, still hurtling forward at great speed, and rushes up from directly behind. The distance rapidly closes in a straight-from-behind approach. The dorsal turret gunner hasn't seen him. Galland keeps his eyes on the electric light circle, his fingers on the trigger buttons . . . closer . . . closer. The wing-span of the Blenheim spreads wider and wider, now a line of diameter. Galland is on him. Thumb and forefinger down! Cannon and machine-guns roar amid vibration. Aim is dead on. Shells rake the bomber and the Blenheim staggers under the sudden barrage. Pieces fly backwards and there is a flash of flame—high octane! Galland is so close he must bank away to avoid fiery death. He veers to the side and the Blenheim wings over and plunges . . . smoke pouring back behind streaks of flame. A parachute opens, then another. Two of the three-man crew are out. There is no return fire from victory number 68 for Galland.

In the attack he has lost his comrades who have selected targets of their own. Most of the Staffel seems occupied with enemy fighters but Galland is alone, scans the sky and climbs at full power back above the bombers. He will come down again in another diving attack if enemy fighters don't interfere. Gradually the lone 109 out to the side pulls above the boxes and milling fighters around them. Galland manages to stay out of the mêlée and now, back at 12,000 feet, is ready to make a second pass. He checks the rear . . . clear behind. A little higher . . . over 12,000 feet now, above the enemy fighters. Once more he dips stick and starts down in a diving pass. His speed quickly accelerates and down he flashes through the fighters again. But this time one of the R.A.F. pilots spots the diving Messerschmitt, stands his Spitfire on a wing, opens the Rolls-Merlin engine wide and starts down after him. Galland is diving faster, however, and pulls away, eyeing the bombers below through his sighting glass. Rapidly closing them as he levels out at great speed, he decides to attack the lead bomber, then make his way out and away in front of the formation. He has the necessary speed, man-œuvres rudder pedals and stick to bring the 109 in dead astern of the leading Blenheim. The bomber grows larger and larger in his sights as he comes on fast. The rear gunner hasn't time to take him under fire. The wing-span is stretch-ing across the circle. Galland presses the buttons. Again cannon and gun shells streak straight into the victim, Galland so close behind he can't miss. His firing pattern concentrates in the starboard wing and from the starboard engine dark smoke streams backward. Galland takes a second to watch as he pulls off to the side. The Blenheim begins to yaw . . . it's falling out of formation to the right, leaving a dark trail of smoke. Once again the crew, or some of them, get out. Galland sees one 'chute, then a second. Victim number two. His 69th victim of the war.

Whump! Whump! Tracers, streaking by above, to the side. A second for the new situation to register. Smoke! He's hit. Fighter behind! Instantly he kicks rudder, dips stick and does a diving turn down and away. The fuel injection of the Daimler-Benz again proved its worth. He dives into a patch of haze and this and his quick change of direction save him. (The Me.109s enjoy a tactical advantage over Spits and Hurricanes in a sudden dive, when centrifugal force mo-mentarily interrupts the flow of fuel to the engine; the Daimler-Benz is equipped with fuel injection and in such dives continues to perform normally. That brief moment, the distance gained, is enough to enable Galland to get away. British pilots often attempted to nullify the German advantage by rolling or half-rolling as they dived in pursuit.)

Galland checks behind. He has evaded the Spit but has lost much altitude. And smoke leaves a long, white, funnel-like trail behind his F.2. He can see his right radiator is shot up and coolant is pouring out. The engine is certain to overheat. He pushes his stick down, looks behind again, and begins to search the landscape below for a place to get down. The engine begins to run roughly. Engine temperature steadily rises. No more coolant. The liquid-cooled engine will soon be finished. Directly below, he sees an open place in the land-scape, two miles east of Calais. He looks carefully ... airfield. Calais-Marck! He was so busy fighting he hadn't known his position. The engine is now throbbing and clanking, louder and louder. Galland eases back on the yellow throttle knob, but at that very moment the Daimler-Benz stops completely. The whirling three-blade prop out front turns slower and slower and then freezes. No power!

The airfield is just below, fortunately. Checking behind, thankful no enemy fighter has spotted his crippled 109, Galland circles to stay directly over the field. He will circle until very low and then bank in a last turn which will take him out and around to its edge when he is down to a few hundred feet. Silently the Messerschmitt circles downwards. The whistling of the wind and the billow of white smoke accompany him as he calls on his own training as a glider pilot. No wheels. He will belly in, canopy open. He prepares to jump out as soon as the 109 stops sliding. Fast descending, he glides out to the field's edge and makes the last turn, levels the wings, dips the stick and noses her down over the grass. Stick back, slower and slower, 75 feet, 50, 25 . . . solid bumping, sliding, crunching. The 109 rushes over the ground, sliding straight, slows and comes to a halt. Galland is up and out of the cockpit as soon as the fighter stops. Men are rushing out from all directions. He is down safely on a German field.

His first request to onrushing field personnel is that they radio Audembert for a light plane to come and pick him up, which is done immediately. (Audembert is only ten miles down the coast to the south-west.) He walks around the battered 109. The prop is bent under, belly thoroughly skinned and the right radiator, about two feet back from the propeller under the nose, is badly shot up. The Spit must have come up from behind and low!

Galland answers questions about the action and tells of his two victories. Field personnel prepare to move his damaged 109 and an Me.108 looms into sight in the western sky. It is from Audembert and Galland is soon on his way back to the base—in time for a late lunch. There he learns his wingman, Hegenauer, has been shot down too. It has been a hard day ... two victories in a few minutes but both he and his wingman shot down. The action is thoroughly discussed by excited German pilots.

After lunch, Galland—with no injuries—returns to his desk and paper-work and red tape. The weather is still perfect ... but surely the R.A.F. has had enough for one day. He works on until three o'clock. Half past the hour, and then four. And then ...

The telephone. Plotting house. Large formations once again assembling across the Straits. Galland hurries over and soon is among the tables looking at radar plots ... enemy formations, several heading towards France. From the plots it appears they'll cross in fifteen to twenty miles south. For the second time that day Galland sounds the *Gefechtsalarm* and pilots hurry into action. With whom shall he fly? His wingman is missing. He hasn't had time to arrange things. For one of the few times in his career Galland decides to take off alone. It's against the rules of fighter combat. Perhaps he can join one of his Gruppen when airborne. And so, without waiting to find a wingman, Galland races out to his other Me.109 which has been made ready (two aircraft are always at his disposal) and is soon leaving a cloud of dust in his wake as he taxies out to take off. The lone, roaring 109 soon lifts off the grass into the still-blue western sky. It is minutes after 4 p.m. Galland banks left into the south, toward the area where the enemy will cross in. Retracting landing gear, he makes a quick cockpit check, turns on his guns and sight—all in order—and continues a solitary climb into the south. He soon reaches 10,000 feet, then 11,000 and then 12,000. He checks with control . . . enemy formations should be a few miles ahead, a bit higher, and are thought to be fighters. He can't make them out but below, forward, he sees Boulogne. The Daimler, at maximum climb, continues to pull the 109 upward into the south and he reaches 15,000, 16,000 then 17,000 feet and is approaching Boulogne off to his right, still climbing. He searches the sky ahead . . . wants to find friends before the enemy. South-east of Boulogne . . . dots . . . aircraft. His eyes remain fixed on the approaching specks . . . fighters. He can distinguish the silhouettes . . . Me. 109s! It's Gruppe I of his Geschwader! He will join them. He's up to 20,000 feet, levels out, points the yellow nose of his fighter in the direction of his comrades. Then off to the left of the 109s he sees another formation of fighters . . . Spitfires! He sees only six and they're at lower altitude. He has the altitude advantage and, quickly changing his mind, stands the 109 on its left wing to curve in above them. Perhaps he can dive down at speed, utilizing the element of surprise and bring down the last in the formation, get away before the others turn.

The Spits are now ahead and below and Galland noses down into a dive which will bring him into position behind the sixth enemy fighter. He must get in and out quickly. Airspeed increases as he holds the nose down, carefully sighting through the glass. The trailing Spit is in view . . . still small in the pale yellow light circle. He eases slightly back on the stick as the 109 approaches 700 k.p.h., levels out and comes in behind the enemy. Blood drains from his head, he is pressed down hard in his seat as he pulls stick back further, fast coming in from behind on the Spit, now growing bigger and bigger in the sighting circle.

The R.A.F. fighter stays in the same flying altitude just long enough. The thirty-six-foot wing-span widens, now fills the circle. A hundred metres. Galland presses both buttons. The cannon and 7·8 shells smash into the larger Spitfire.

Debris flies backward. Smoke streaks from the engine. Almost at once Galland knows his foe is finished. The enemy pilot probably didn't know what hit him. The Spit's wing goes up and over he flips, the roaring Merlin engine points earthwards and down plunges Galland's 70th victim—his third of the day. Galland dives away to avoid the flight path of other Spits. He checks behind, sees nothing, and watches the falling Spitfire plunge to the ground a few miles south-east of Boulogne. Unlike his regular 109, which he flew in the morning, this one has no camera and he wants to see where the Spitfire crashes.

But he pays the price for a lone wolf attack. For the second time in the day he is startled by ominous sounds. Whumph! Whumph! Whumph! Whumph! He can hear, feel the 109 taking hits . . . many hits. A sudden pain in his head, his right arm! Desperate, trapped, Galland rams the stick forward, dives straight down, down—and pulls out, banking. At last he's out of the line of fire, but too late. The 109 is mortally crippled and Galland is bleeding profusely. His frantic evasive action has shaken off the pursuing fighter but the engine is banging loudly and vibrating heavily. Soon it will be finished. Galland switches it off to lessen chances of fire, which all pilots dread, especially 109 pilots who sit in front of the fuel tank. The 109 begins its glide downwards silently, just as another did earlier that morning.

On the right side of the cockpit and fuselage is a large gaping hole, through which the wind rushes in; there are holes in the wings. The enemy fighter's aim was deadly accurate. But the 109 responds to the controls and Galland feels he can make another belly landing. He is still high, over 17,000 feet, and points the nose northwards. Ominously, fuel and coolant begin leaking into the cockpit floor. Galland, head and arm bleeding, notices the liquid on the cockpit floor and realizes his danger. Then, whumph! The enemy again? He looks back. Flames stretch out behind. The tank, behind, is afire! His breath almost stops as he notices small streams of liquid fire running between his legs from behind the seat into the cockpit. He must get out!

Galland jerks off his seat-straps, reaches up with his left hand to release the top of the canopy. The *Kabinennotabwurf* doesn't work! The top won't fly off, is jammed! He pushes up hard with both hands. No movement. The fire is hotter. He must get out or burn to death. He pushes with all his strength, straight up. Flames now reach up from the bottom of the cockpit. He has seconds. Still he can't open the canopy. With all his strength in a desperate leap he throws his whole body against the roof. The front section of the top finally lifts, is caught by the wind and hurtles back and away in the slip-stream. Galland at the same time pulls back on the stick, stands in his seat, and tries to spring out of the cockpit as the 109 stands on its nose. He gets part of the way out, but his parachute, on which he sits, catches on the back part of the canopy which hasn't dropped away as it should have. And as he stands struggling, half in and half out in the biting wind, the 109 stalls, falls down and away on a wing and goes into a spin. Galland, still caught, falls with the burning plane. The force of the wind pushes his body backwards against the very part of the cockpit from which he needs to free himself. His parachute is stuck into it. Desperately, he tries with hands and feet as he turns and falls to pull free, but he's stuck fast. The fighter falls on downwards, his feet burning, his body violently buffeted as the 109 spins. For some strange, un-explainable reason Galland's mind turns to his electric train set—he has an elaborate installation at Audembert and he received two new engines that morning. Through his mind at this critical second flashes the thought he won't be able to try them out. Strange how the mind works!

With hand reaching out and gripping the aerial mast and feet kicking, Galland makes a final desperate effort to free himself. And then, without knowing how it happens, he is falling free. He's alone, hurtling downwards, turning over and over as he falls. With relief, but suffering shock, Galland grips the release handle of his chute! With a start, he realizes what he's doing just in time. He's about to get out of his parachute harness, in mid-air! If he had pulled the *Schnell-trennschloss*, he would have fallen free without his chute. Shaken, he carefully grips the ripcord handle (*Aufreissgriff*), pulls. For a moment he fears his chute is not working. Then, with a jolt that straightens him up, feet downwards, the 'chute opens and he is oscillating back and forth, softly and noiselessly floating down.

It's quite a contrast to the desperation and terror of only seconds ago. He is still high. Below a green summer landscape stretches in all directions. He notices his burning Me.109 smash into the ground about a mile away, thinks how close he came to going in with it. Then a Spitfire looms in view, flashing through the sky ahead, and apparently takes some pictures of him descending. Others are farther away and he hears them firing. Boulogne is easily visible to the west. He is coming down on top of a big forest . . . the wind is taking him towards the edge. He mustn't land in the trees . . . down, down; the wind carries him towards the edge; it will be close. He's over the forest, drifts towards a hedgerow. A large poplar tree is directly in his path. He passed below but the canopy of his chute strikes the limbs and collapses. As the air spills out his descent quickens and he strikes the ground falling too fast. A sharp pain stabs him in the left ankle. Luckily the ground is wet and soft—a meadow—or he would certainly have been hurt badly. Even as it is, he's not in good condition.

Until now he hasn't realized he is badly burned but lying on the ground, bleeding from the head and right arm, his ankle dislocated, burned over the bottom part of his body, he begins to realize his condition. He makes an effort but can't stand up. His ankle is swelling rapidly, energy draining away. He can hardly move. He can feel pieces of metal in his head. He just lies there, glances around half dazed. At some distance he notices a French farmer, and then another, and slowly they approach. Galland is helpless and at their mercy. Soon there are several others with them but they are extremely cautious and approach slowly. Galland speaks: 'I'm

German and I'm wounded. Please help me.' One of the French onlookers is a woman; all are elderly. Another man speaks: 'He will die very soon. We must call the Germans. If he dies before the Germans come, they will say we killed him.'

Galland, understanding the conversation, replies: *'Ich werde nicht sterben. Ich bin sehr kräftig.'* (I will not die. I am very strong.) The Frenchmen look at him in surprise. Several reach down and begin to drag him to a near-by farm house. When they finally arrive at the house, Galland asks: *'Haben Sie etwas Cognac?'* They have none but they have some eau-de-vie. It's in a dirty bottle but Galland takes a long drink. One of the old men starts down the road to inform a group of German Todt Organization workers, the nearest Germans.

In a few minutes a car approaches. Galland can see they're Germans and is relieved. Quickly they ask: *'Wohin sollen wir Sie bringen?'* Galland tells them to take him to his fighter station. They tell him he should go to the hospital. Galland insists and they help him into their car and drive him to Audembert, 26 Geschwader headquarters. At his arrival there is excitement and relief. Galland even has a cognac and a cigar and feels somewhat better. But they soon pack him off to the nearby naval hospital at Hardingham, where his good friend, Dr Heim, removes various pieces of metal from his head and patches him up. Heim suggests he stay a few days at the hospital. Galland, however, refuses to remain and is soon back at headquarters; he will remain in command, if necessary from the ground!

The Geschwader claimed fourteen enemy aircraft shot down that day, a considerable victory. Galland had scored three of the kills, which brought his total to seventy. Thus quite a celebration was in progress by nightfall (though Galland was swathed in bandages) in honour of his 70th kill. High-ranking officers and friends flew in for the celebration. His friend, General Osterkamp, flew in from Le Touquet with a surprise. From the *Führerhauptquartier* later came the official confirmation of what Osterkamp told him. The message read: 'I bestow upon you as the first officer of the German Armes Forces the oak leaves with swords to the Knight's Cross of the Iron Cross,' and was signed, 'Adolf Hitler'. Galland thus became the first German to win the oak leaves with swords. He had already won the oak leaves. At that time it wasn't known whether there would be a higher award in the war. With the award came an order: Galland was not to fly again without Hitler's express permission. That took some of the pleasure out of the evening for him.

He remained grounded only ten days. No change in his grounding order was received so he began to toy with the idea of 'testing' a 109 when a hostile formation was overhead. On 2 July, when interception of a major enemy force was getting under way, he took off on such a 'test' flight. The enemy formation was again Blenheims, protected by Hurricanes and Spits, and again Galland plunged alone into the attack. It was a dangerous tactic—as he should have known—but he had not flown for ten days and was bursting with frustration. He dived into the bombers, shot down one and engaged a Spitfire, which he also hit. At that moment, however, the lone 109 was hit by another Spit from behind. Once again he was in serious trouble, badly wounded. Only armour protection behind, which he didn't know had been installed, saved his life. He managed to get away and land, but collapsed from shock and loss of blood after climbing out of the cockpit.

The news soon reached Air Fleet Headquarters and was transmitted to Berlin. By that time Galland was in the hospital where the surgeon remarked as he entered: '*Jetzt werden wir Sie für eine Weile nicht mehr fliegen lassen.*' (Now we'll stop you flying for a while.) Reichsmarschall Göring heard of Galland's disobedience and the news also reached Hitler. Göring telephoned to ask why he had disobeyed the Führer's specific order and Galland replied unconvincingly he was only testing a 109. '*Sagen Sie es Hitler,*' Göring told him. That was the first indication he had that he was to see the Führer. It was July and the great German offensive against Russia was in progress in the East but Galland was ordered to report to Hitler at Rastenberg, in East Prussia. He flew to the Führer's headquarters.

Hitler greeted him with a smile. '*Bitte, wir lieben Sie; wir können Sie nicht verlieren. Ich habe versucht, Sie zu schützen. Sie haben gegen meine Befehle gehandelt, aber ich kann Sie verstehen. Wir haben nur Angst, Sie zu verlieren. Seien Sie vorsichtig!*' (Please, we love you. We can't lose you. I tried to protect you. You have acted against my orders, but I can understand you. We only fear to lose you. Be careful.) That was the reprimand. Hitler personally pinned the oak leaves and swords on him. He was Göring's guest for several days before returning to the Front.

Galland's victory total rose steadily from 71 as of 2 July to over 90 by the end of 1941. It was while he was pushing his score into the nineties in the last half of 1941 that Wing Commander Douglas Bader was shot down near Galland's fighter base one day in August. Galland sent a car to fetch him to tea and received him as an honoured foe. When pressed to say how many victories he had achieved (22½), Bader—according to Galland—was reluctant to give a figure. Galland remembers Bader's reply—that his total, compared to the score of Galland and Mölders, was comparatively modest. Galland escorted Bader around the Luftwaffe fighter station even let him sit in the cockpit of his own Me.109, explaining the controls. Galland—at Bader's request—introduced a young pilot as the one who had downed Bader—though he was not finally sure about it and had that day shot down two Spits himself.

This encounter was repeated, with Bader and Galland in reverse roles after the war—Galland was then a prisoner-of-war, Bader interviewing him. Bader repaid some of Galland's hospitality by presenting him with a box of cigars.

At the end of 1941 Galland's score had risen to 94 and at this time the death of the General of the Fighter Arm, Werner Mölders, another of Germany's greatest fighter pilots, caused his recall from the front. Göring appointed him Mölders's successor. He became Germany's youngest general at thirty and was soon decorated again by Hitler, this time with the diamonds to the oak leaves and swords to the Knight's Cross of the Iron Cross—received by less than thirty members of the German armed services during the war.

Galland was not completely happy at his desk job. He undertook special assignments which put him at the Front from time to time. He personally led the fighters which protected German warships in their successful dash up the English Channel in 1942. In 1943 he personally led the fighters defending Sicily. He was one of the first to fly the new German jets and helped influence fighter armament and production in 1943 and 1944. However, his blunt reports of unpleasant truths, which indirectly reflected on Reichsmarschall Hermann Göring, and on what Göring said, brought him into conflict with Hitler and the Reichsmarschall, who dismissed him from his post at the end of 1944.

It was Hitler who put an end to 'this nonsense', as he called it, after Göring had banished him from his post and severely reprimanded him. In the end, Göring also relented. However, this was in the final days of Germany's collapse. Galland began his last assignment in January, 1945. He organized a special fighter unit (T.V.44) equipped with new Me.262 jets, selecting expert pilots from all fronts. The aircraft mounted new and highly effective heavy rockets and cannon and achieved notable successes against formations of bombers and fighters then swarming daily over Germany. Galland fought to the last—his book is entitled *The First and the Last*—and was wounded in these air battles again. Having flown his jet fighters from Munich to Salzburg to escape capture in the last days of the war, he set the prized aircraft afire as U.S. tanks appeared on the outskirts of Salzburg. He was captured, held for two years as a prisoner-of-war, and released. A year later he made his way to Argentina, where a position in aviation awaited him. In January 1955, he returned to his homeland and today he is a consultant and representative of several aerospace companies, some of them American, in Bonn. He is also president of a commercial airline and an executive officer in several other businesses, including an insurance company.

He travels widely in his private Beechcraft, constantly encountering former friends and foes in various countries and enjoys reminiscing about the war when he has time. He and Wing Commander Bob Tuck have met on many occasions since the end of the war.

Had Galland not been recalled from the Front in late 1941 it seems probable he would have scored a far greater number of kills, though his appointment as General of the Fighter Arm might also have spared his life, so aggressive was he in combat. (Two of his three brothers who followed him into the Luftwaffe as fighter pilots were killed during the war—having scored 51 and 17 victories.) There is no doubt he was one of Germany's greatest Second World War fighter pilots, and considering his talent as a leader, administrator and pilot, he is probably the outstanding surviving *Experte* of the Luftwaffe.

# CHAPTER FOURTEEN

# DUEL OVER DIEPPE

*19 August 1942—Squadron Leader J. E. Johnson, R.A.F.*

THE ALLIED fighter pilot officially credited with shooting down the greatest number of Germans is an Englishman from Leicestershire who was almost turned down by the R.A.F.—James Edgar Johnson. Air Vice-Marshal Johnson was born in Loughborough in 1915 and attended Loughborough School and then Nottingham University. At twenty-two—when he first sought to join the R.A.F.—he was enjoying a promising start in life as a fully qualified civil engineer with an appointment at Loughton.

His application refused, he joined the mounted Leicestershire Yeomanry in which he served until 1939, when he received a query from the Air Ministry. If he were still interested in flying, the letter said, he should be at the Store Street, London, headquarters of the Royal Air Force Volunteer Reserve two days later for a medical. Johnson was still interested; he was waiting when the doors opened, and he passed the medical that morning. After lunch he was sworn in as a flight-sergeant R.A.F.V.R. The war was only months away, but it was to be two years before he scored his first victory against the Luftwaffe. He was posted to Stapleford Tawney, a flying training school in Essex, where he flew Tiger Moths at weekends. He attended evening classes twice weekly in London, at which he learned navigation, armament, signals, and the other essential theory of flying.

With the outbreak of war, the Volunteer Reserve was mobilized immediately. Johnson was posted to Cambridge, where he continued to train in Tiger Moths. He remained there until the spring of 1940, when he left for Sealand Training School near Chester, having logged eighty-four hours of flying. At Sealand, where he flew the Miles Master, he was one of the few in his class to be made officer-cadets. At this time the war exploded into its full fury on the Continent and Johnson, still in training, had to be content with newspaper accounts of the air action. During this summer Johnson experienced his first narrow escape, when he went solo at night in poor weather. He became lost in heavy cloud and experienced vertigo, but finally descended successfully and found the dimly lit landing strip under a 600-foot ceiling.

Johnson won his commission as Pilot Officer at Sealand and was posted to near-by Hawarden to be checked out in the Spitfire. He was progressing satisfactorily flying the best and fastest fighter in the R.A.F. (as the Battle of Britain was beginning) when ordered to deliver a packet of official papers to Sealand. The field was short and, trying to drop the Spit in just over the fence at the beginning of the landing area, Johnson allowed speed to drop too quickly while still high, fell out with a jolt and ground-looped, crumpling the undercarriage. It was not a very happy return to Sealand. Though not officially reprimanded or washed out, he was thereafter on probation and had to watch his step. One more prang and he would be out. Meanwhile, the Battle of Britain rose to a high intensity, with Johnson still out of it.

Finally, towards the end of August, he was called into the adjutant's office and told to pack and report to 19 Squadron at Duxford, near Cambridge! At that time he had 205 hours in his logbook, just 23 in Spitfires. He was, presumably, now to take on the Me.109. Arriving at Duxford with two other replacement pilots, Johnson soon found the veterans of 19 Squadron unwilling to send him (or the other replacements) up against the Luftwaffe. He was keenly disappointed at the time, but the decision was undoubtedly the right one, for 19 Squadron was experiencing difficulties with its new 20 mm. cannon and was losing veteran pilots (one of whom had been the Squadron Commander) in daily skirmishes. The three replacement pilots were too green to be thrown into the battle without some training with the squadron (Johnson had not even fired his guns at Hawarden), but there was no time, and no one free to give it to them. In a few days the 19 Squadron adjutant called the three into his office. The squadron, he said, under prevailing conditions, couldn't give them the additional training they required; they were being immediately posted to 616 Squadron at Coltishall, an Auxiliary Air Force squadron which had been withdrawn from the battle for rest and reorganization, where they would get the much-needed training before being sent into combat.

And so Johnson departed for yet another training post—and began flying with 616 near Norwich. Fate continued to deny him a chance to participate fully in the Battle of Britain, for after getting off to a good start with 616 his right shoulder began paining him intensely; examination revealed that an old rugby break had not reset properly, the nerves being badly pinched. An operation was necessary and it was not until December, after the Battle of Britain was over, that Johnson was back on operations with 616.

At last, in January 1941, he got his first chance at an enemy aircraft, and he and another 616 pilot shared a claim of damaged after hitting and chasing a Do.17 bomber into the clouds. The year was an important one for him because it was in 1941 that he came under the watchful eye of Douglas Bader and learned the tactics and tricks of combat under one of the great R.A.F. leaders. Bader came to 616's home station at Tangmere as the new Wing Leader in March, and soon saw in Johnson the promise and ability which were to merge so strikingly later in the war. Bader selected him to fly in his leading section and thereafter, until Bader went down in France in August, Johnson was alongside Bader. He got his first kill in June and was promoted to Flight Commander. Flying regularly throughout the rest of 1941 (by the end of the summer he had 6½ victories) and into the summer of 1942, Johnson's flying and combat record were above average. He won the D.F.C. and was given command of 610 Squadron in July 1942. It was while leading 610, a squadron of mixed nationalities, that he emerged as one of the brightest stars in the R.A.F.

Though he engaged in combat from 1940 until May 1945, the great majority of his victories were to come in the summer of 1943 (nineteen in six months) and in 1944, escorting American heavy bombers on raids to France and the Low Countries. In this respect his record somewhat parallels that of Eric Hartmann, the top Luftwaffe ace, whose victory total only began to rise rapidly in 1943, the fourth year of the war. Johnson's last victory came in his last air battle, on 27 September 1944, during the ill-fated Arnhem operation. It was the only time in all his 515 sorties over enemy territory during the war that enemy fire found his fighter.

R.A.F. fighters lacked the range to participate fully in the then expanding daylight Battle of Germany—as Johnson himself points out in *Wing Leader* and *Full Circle*—but, based in Belgium, Johnson remained on combat operations until the end of the war.

He achieved his score neither in the Battle of Britain nor in the Battle of Germany but largely in the interval, when German fighters were, for periods, not numerous in the West. An impressive feature of his score is that all thirty-eight of his victories were against fighters.

What was the secret of Johnson's success? What qualitites did he possess in greater abundance than so many of his comrades? One was his unusual skill as a marksman; those who flew with him agree his shooting was superb. He was cool and clear-headed in battle, naturally gifted as a pilot, and had both courage and determination. These assets helped carry him unscathed through all his fighting to a victory total no other Allied fighter pilot in Europe equalled.

His closest brush with death came not on the September day in 1944 when his fighter was hit by enemy gunfire over Nijmegen—Arnhem—but over Dieppe, in the late summer of 1942. He was a relatively new squadron leader at the time, leading 610 Squadron on a patrol over the first Allied landing in occupied France. Based in Norfolk, 610 was ordered to fly south to West Malling to take part in the invasion—Operation 'Jubilee'.

Billed as a reconnaissance in force, and something of a dress rehearsal for the main Allied landings in Europe, Operation 'Jubilee' was carried out on 19 August 1942. It had been conceived and planned by the Planning Committee of Combined Operations Headquarters, and although Churchill called it a successful reconnaissance, it would not be unreasonable to suggest today that, from the tactical standpoint at least, Dieppe was a clear-cut German victory.

Unfortunately, the assault was postponed after troops had been loaded on transports in July and informed of their destination. Thus thousands of soldiers knew of the plan and it is likely that rumours, perhaps more than rumours, reached the Continent and German ears. It seems certain that the attack did not come as a complete surprise to the German defenders. Allied casualties totalled 3,829 (official records) and German casualties less than 600. Canadian casualties were heaviest, for Canadian troops made up the bulk of the assault force—3,369 (907 dead).

It would seem the Germans won this battle in the air also. The R.A.F. had agreed to commit up to sixty fighter squadrons and additional bomber squadrons: over 500 aircraft. German fighter strength in France was limited to two Geschwader, 2 and 26, which meant the Luftwaffe could put up between 200 and 300 fighters—perhaps half the number available to the Allies. The Germans, of course, had the advantage of defending, and shorter distances. In fierce all-day air battles which raged throughout the 19th the Luftwaffe claimed 112 aircraft destroyed. Actual R.A.F. losses were 108. R.A.F. claims were 91 kills and actual German losses appear to have been 35. It should be remembered that at this time the Luftwaffe's F.W.190 was probably the best fighter in the air and superior even to the Spitfire V.

With Russia urgently appealing for a diversionary action in the West, and German armies for the second successive summer driving deep into Russian territory, the Dieppe operation was a test of German nerves, and was not without some result.[1]

Troops who stormed ashore, or attempted to, at Dieppe—in the first test of the Atlantic Wall—were met with heavy defensive fire from the beginning. Though persevering courageously they were cut down in tragic numbers and finally withdrawn later in the day—with many of the tactical objectives of the operation unfulfilled.

The experience was dearly bought, but several benefits resulted. Allied commanders did not again underestimate the difficulties involved in amphibious assault. And the defensive victory, according to several German sources, gave Hitler an exaggerated idea of the strength of coast defences, a concept which partly motivated several unsound decisions in the crucial year of 1944.

At dawn on Wednesday, 19 August 1942, a clear summer morning, activity on the fighter field at West Malling was intense. From this station just west of Maidstone, squadrons were to be taking off at intervals all day long to support the first Allied landing in Occupied France. Riggers and fitters were checking aircraft, armourers were loading and checking guns and pilots were getting dressed or being roused from the safety of sleep.

In a ground-floor bedroom of West Malling's brick officers' mess a batman opened the door, respectfully announced: 'Five o'clock, sir,' and put a cup of tea on the bedside table of Squadron Leader J. E. Johnson. Johnson woke up immediately, thanked the batman and took a sip

[1] Liddell-Hart, *The Other Side Of The Hill* (Cassell, 1948), p. 313, quotes General Franz Halder, former Chief of Staff of the German Army, as saying that the Dieppe invasion caused Hitler anxiety. Speaking of the German offensive then in progress in the south of Russia, Halder says: 'The worst mistake of this kind happened in August, 1942 . . . Hitler then, on account of the landing at Dieppe, lost his nerve and gave the order that two of the best divisions, the S.S. Leibstandarte and the Grossdeutchland, were to be transferred to the West.'

of tea. After a few moments he washed his face in the basin and shaved, and called for another cup of tea. He dressed in R.A.F. blues, with a silk scarf (spotted with white foxes' heads) around his neck and tucked it into his open shirt. The scarf was a present from his mother—back home in the fox-hunting country of Leicestershire. He wore black three-quarter shoes, made especially for him by Len Leader of Melton Mowbray, and a pair of black cotton socks. Carrying a tie, which was compulsory wear at breakfast, he walked to the mess where pilots were already discussing the day's operation. Wing Commander Pat Jameson (a New Zealander) had briefed pilots the evening before, after a trip to Uxbridge to receive a headquarters briefing on a higher level. Pilots therefore knew that the day's sortie would take them to Dieppe, though the exact-take-off time was to be telephoned to squadrons at dispersal areas. Many expressed the feeling that security had not been what it should have, and the hope that the defending forces had not been alerted. They did not envy the 5,000 soldiers who were scheduled to take Dieppe and its airfield in a quick assault. In a short time breakfast of bacon and eggs, tea and toast was finished and Johnson of 610, Bill Newton of 411 (Canadian), and Grant of 485 (New Zealand), were on their way to squadron dispersal huts in vans. It was 7.00 a.m.

Jameson's instructions were that the three squadrons— and perhaps any others they might join—would fly one above the other at intervals of 2,000 feet. Johnson's 610 was to fly top cover at 10,000. The vans stopped and pilots hopped out and went into the hut to check their equipment or get another cup of tea. Then Johnson held a short informal briefing. His main theme was that 610 would spread into finger-four formation at his signal. Jameson preferred the old line astern formation and the three squadrons as a wing would fly to Dieppe in that formation. Having learned the finger-four with Bader at 616, and preferring it, Johnson explained to his eleven listeners that, at his signal, probably over Dieppe or near it, the squadron would take up this formation.

With that clear, Johnson puffed his usual Player's and enjoyed a cup of tea. Some pilots stretched out on the grass outside and others lounged somewhat nervously inside. The waiting was the worst of it; the minutes dragged by and everyone was eager to get started. In the corner of the thirty-by-fifteen-foot room on a small table was a black telephone. This was a direct line to Squadron Operations, and a clerk sat at the table to take messages and orders. At 7.30 the telephone rang. All eyes turned to the clerk. He listened a moment and then replaced the receiver and announced: 'Take-off at 7.40 for patrol over Dieppe.' The room emptied.

Johnson had only fifty yards to walk and was beside his grey-blue Spitfire VB before most of the pilots. He greeted fitter and rigger, climbed into the cockpit and went through the drill quickly, at the same time fastening his seat belt and shoulder straps with the help of a crewman. Trim in take-off, prop pitch fine. He looked across the field and located Grant and 485 Squadron; he would follow 485 out to take-off position. In a few moments it was 7.40. He saw the props of 485 begin to turn.

The crewman who had plugged in the accumulator sensed the moment: 'Ready for power?' he asked. Johnson nodded, checked to set mixture at fully rich, opened the throttle an inch, unscrewed the primer and primed the engine several strokes, checked the silver fuel lever, up, and then switched on the two magneto switches. 'All clear!' he shouted, which the crewman repeated and then: 'Contact!' When he heard the crewman's reply, Johnson pressed the two black buttons on the panel and the 1,300 horsepower Rolls-Merlin caught up with a blast of air and smoke and spun the prop out front into a blur. Tightening the primer, checking to be sure his radiator flaps were open, and looking over his temperature and oil gauges briefly (oil pressure had to reach 45 before take-off) Johnson waved to his comrades, and crewmen, and pushed the yellow throttle knob forward, releasing his brakes. The volume of wind increased with the heavier roar from the engine and the Spitfire began to roll.

Across the way the other two squadrons were lining up for take-off as he taxied 610 out, now strung out in line behind him. Soon 610 was at the edge of the field and Johnson checked his squadron's formation behind; it would take off in three sections of four. Grant was now following Jameson off and it was time for 610 to go. Johnson signalled with his right hand from the open cockpit, eased the throttle all the way to the stop and manœuvred the rudder pedals to keep the nose straight. The Spit lunged forward at full power, others behind followed, and soon the first four were rapidly gaining speed as they bumped and grew lighter racing over the grass. Airspeed climbed steadily. At about eighty or ninety came that weightless feeling for just a moment and then she lifted off. He held the stick back and began to bank slightly left.

Johnson pulls up the undercarriage lever and pushes it forward and the wheels begin to retract. He closes the canopy and flips the switch on the left of the panel to raise flaps. Jamie's voice comes in over the radio: 'Okay Johnnie?' 'Okay, Jamie, got you in sight,' Johnson answers. He banks 610 in a tighter circle than the two squadrons ahead, cutting them off, and begins to close into wing formation. Soon the squadrons are in wing formation, line astern, and set course at 170 degrees. A fourth squadron has also joined them and the 48 fighters streak almost due south, staying low—the rising eastern sun to the left. The wing passes over Hastings and the fighter's sky-blue bellies, the red, white and blue circles beneath the wings, are clearly visible to those on the ground. Their speed is 250 miles an hour, not exceptionally fast, but at this low altitude the landscape passes at a good clip.

Johnson switches on his gunsight and the electric light ring appears on the glass. He flicks on his guns. The wing roars across the coast and starts out over the water, still low, Jameson hoping to avoid radar detection. The airwaves are noisy. Johnson can hear many voices. As the wing approaches

Take-off at 7.40 a.m. and landing little over an hour later.

Johnson leads 610 off for early morning patrol over invasion at Dieppe

WEST MALLING

# FIGHTER

SPITFIRE

In desperate flying and manoeuvring Johnson escapes over Royal Navy warship and reaches West Malling safely

# FIGHTER SQUADRON

.610 SQUADRON

# FIGHTER STATION

WEST MALLING

# MISSION FLOWN BY

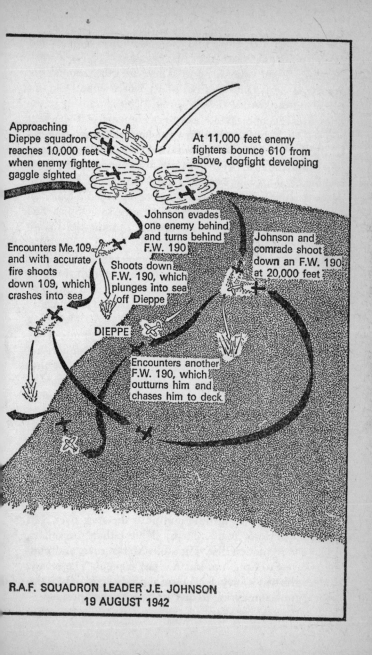

Approaching Dieppe squadron reaches 10,000 feet when enemy fighter gaggle sighted

At 11,000 feet enemy fighters bounce 610 from above, dogfight developing

Johnson evades one enemy behind and turns behind F.W. 190

Johnson and comrade shoot down an F.W. 190 at 20,000 feet

Encounters Me. 109 and with accurate fire shoots down 109, which crashes into sea

Shoots down F.W. 190, which plunges into sea off Dieppe

DIEPPE

Encounters another F.W. 190, which outturns him and chases him to deck

R.A.F. SQUADRON LEADER J.E. JOHNSON
19 AUGUST 1942

low over the water, closer and closer, the voices grow louder. He can make out some of the calls: 'Somebody's going down!' Another: 'Fight your way out.' There are other shouts over the earphones, obviously from pilots over Dieppe: 'Get out when you can!' And: 'Two Me.109s!' Heavy fighting in the skies over Dieppe! Jamie calmly comments to the wing: 'Looks like the boys are having a rough time.' Everyone tenses a little at the warning of desperate fighting ahead. Eyes strain and search the clear sky to the south. Johnson notices a fighter coming head-on, lower than the wing, then another. Friends. As he watches, he sees several more, and then a pair, all heading homewards. Most are Hurricanes, some Spits. The Hurricanes might have been strafing, but the Spits were obviously on the deck after a dogfight.

Dieppe is only ten miles away. Jameson points the nose of his Spit into the air and the wing begins to climb. Johnson applies a little more power than the wing leader, since he will fly top-cover. The Spits knife upwards into the blue . . . 5,000, 6,000, feet. Jameson calls over the radio: 'Throttling back and opening up.' Johnson continues to climb. They can all see Dieppe ahead clearly now, a smoke column rising over the port. Below is Grant's squadron and below that Jameson and his squadron. Now Johnson gives the signal to 610, waggling his wings. They ease out into a finger-four formation, still climbing. Dieppe is three miles ahead.

Something above, ahead, glinting in the sun! Fighters! A hard look . . . not Hurricanes, nor Spits. Enemy fighters . . . manœuvring to bounce the Spits, and with a height advantage. Johnson presses the mike button, calling Jameson: 'Jamie—large gaggle of Huns heading towards us, high!' Jamie replies: 'Right, Johnnie, keep your eye on 'em.' Johnson goes to full throttle and pulls the stick back. His squadron is closer to the enemy fighters than the others, is likely to see action first. The Rolls-Merlin roars and pulls the twelve 610 Spits up, but not fast enough. The enemy gaggle, thirty to forty F.W.190s and Me.109s, mixed together, are manœuvring to dive, to bounce the Spits.

Johnson reaches 11,000 feet, is jolted by the earphones: '*Break port!*' It's Crowley-Milling, and Johnson stamps on left rudder and moves the stick hard left. The Spit stands on a wing, as he turns into the attacking enemy. Some of the enemy dived before he knew it. The Spits evade most of the enemy fighters, but the squadron splits up in desperate manœuvring. More enemy fighters peel off and streak down for the Spits, which are now separating into sections and pairs, every pilot fighting for himself. Most of the enemy fighters have been F.W.190s. Johnson is still climbing; he racks around in a sharp turn to keep one from getting on his tail, and suddenly an enemy fighter rises up in view out ahead through the perspex. F.W.190! Johnson feels the tension, quickly moves stick and rudder to line him up. The 190 isn't aware that Johnson is behind. The Spit gains little. Yet the Focke-Wulf is squarely in his sight . . . but at maximum range 400 yards. Can he bring him down at that distance, or should he wait and try to draw closer? He will try a long shot.

He pulls the stick back to lift his guns a bit, allowing for the drop in the trajectory of his shells. Carefully he lines the wing-span up between the light bars . . . range slowly closing. He'll fire only the 20 mm. cannon, the range is too long for the smaller guns. Thumb down! The bigger guns roar, the Spit vibrates, and Johnson holds the button down four or five seconds, watching intently. At first nothing. Then he begins to see strikes and the starboard wing of the Focke-Wulf goes up. Johnson is easing up on him. The 190 banks to the left, hit and beginning to trail a thin smoke stream. Johnson lines it up in his sights for a deflection shot, left. Now the range is down to 200 yards, 150 yards. Fire! This time Johnson presses in the centre and the ·303s and the 20 mm. cannon spit fire at much closer range. The torrent of metal shatters the already damaged Focke-Wulf. The wheels drop and heavier smoke begins to pour out of the engine. A wing goes over! The grey-green enemy fighter dives towards the sea below in its last plunge.

Johnson is surprised to hear Crowley-Milling's voice:

'Good shooting, Johnnie!' Crowley-Milling, Smith, and his wing man, 'South' Creagh are still with him. Johnson takes a look down at the falling victim, but only a short one. There is too much action all around. His squadron is doing what it can to hold off the enemy but it's all they can do to avoid the constant diving passes from above, and more and more pilots are separating, as the diving, turning battle continues.

A German fighter dives and curves in behind him, but Johnson sees him in time, and pulls the Spit around in its tightest turn—thankful he can out-turn the enemy fighters. He sees others above diving into the attack and as he banks to stay out of their path his eyes suddenly catch sight of something to the east, a few miles inland. A good long look. Many dots. Big formation. He instinctively presses the mike button: 'Jamie, strong reinforcements coming in. About fifty plus, slightly inland!' Jameson acknowledges and calls in the report to 11 Group, which is controlling the battle. But he, like Johnson and all the other pilots, is busy with survival. Johnson still has two fighters with him (Creagh and Smith) and S-turns to keep his tail free of the enemy. The rest of the squadron is scattered. By now he is up to 16,000 feet . . . he has been climbing ever since first sighting the enemy.

As he banks out of one S-turn he turns almost directly in behind a lone fighter ahead. Can it be? Me.109! Separated from the pack. Full power. He gains and manœuvres to get the Messerschmitt in his sight. For the second time in minutes he has a dark wing-span widening in the sighting glass, his eyes fixed on the low-winged silhouette, a comrade on each side, slightly back. The Spits gain and the enemy's wing-span grows steadily wider in the glass. Johnson's thumb is on the silver button, as are those of both his two fellow pilots, right and left . . . the enemy is apprently still unaware of the danger from behind. The Rolls-Merlin roars at maximum revs and every second seems a long one. Finally in range. Johnson presses the button in the centre—both 20 mm. cannon and

·303 machine-guns spurt shell with a roar. Both Smith and Creagh also fire at the Messerschmitt, which takes heavy punishment. Johnson's aim is once again on the mark. White streaks mark the path of shells to the enemy and strikes begin to tear pieces off the small fighter. The enemy pilot is trapped before he can disengage. The Spits hold on behind, pouring fire into him. Suddenly a wing rises sharply, the fighter falls off, streaming glycol and smoke, and begins a vertical dive. It leaves a thin column behind as it plunges to the sea below.

Now, however, the enemy reinforcements arrive. The big gaggle above is diving on the Spits and Johnson breaks hard to avoid them. . . . The sky is full of the enemy. . . . Johnson estimates the number at over a hundred. He's constantly turning and jinking to avoid fighters and shells. Altitude is up to 20,000 feet, Johnson still climbing. As more enemy fighters bore in Johnson sees one alone, also at 20,000, across the sky to port. He leans into a sharp bank and pulls the stick back slightly. The enemy—a 190—flies on. The Spit comes around now and Johnson lowers his nose as he passes over the enemy's rear and zeros in for a pass from the starboard side. Most of the fighters are some distance away and he can concentrate on this one.

The lone enemy flies on, as Johnson roars in on the starboard beam. He lines up the blunt-nosed 190 in his glass and manœuvres stick and rudder to make the Spit a level gun platform. He has a good view of the enemy's starboard side as he streaks along, keeping the light circle ahead of his spinner just enough. Less and less as he comes closer. Now in range. Thumb down! The ·303s roar but not the cannon. They're empty! But the smaller shells strike home. The deflection shot was accurate. Pieces fly back from the cockpit area. A thin wisp of glycol streams backward. The range is fast closing . . . the 190 is fifty yards away in front, to port. Then, a shadow . . . Johnson turns his head . . . just yards away, left, coming from behind, another fighter, guns blinking! Smith! With a start, he banks hard right. Smith's fighter was almost into him. Smith is dead on the 190's tail, firing away. The enemy fighter can't stand up under the combined fire from both; now it wings over and begins a dive. It's the third victim Johnson has closed in on since arriving at Dieppe; now it plunges steadily down from the high altitude, leaving a fatal smoke trail.

Johnson has only a second or two to watch. There are too many aircraft about. Several enemy fighters curve in behind and he banks the Spit in its sharpest turn. Others close around him. The manœuvres are violent. A glance behind . . . he has lost Creagh, his wingman. Now he recognizes him, going down off to one side, white glycol vapours streaming from his engine. If he could only do something to help! But an enemy fighter is behind, he must turn. There's nothing he can do. Still enemy fighters come diving down, and Johnson stands the Spit on its wing and out-turns the enemy time and again to avoid their fire. Now an enemy fighter comes on from straight behind. Johnson breaks hard. This time his remaining 610 comrade breaks in the opposite direction! He successfully evades the enemy, but is alone. He glances around. 610 is completely scattered . . . it's every pilot for himself. Fighters are whirling and diving and turning, around him and below.

For the moment however, Johnson is not being bounced. His engine runs smoothly and he is directly above Dieppe at more than 20,000 feet. He can see Spits in twos and fours fighting in all directions; those which haven't gone down are doing their best to keep the Luftwaffe off the backs of invading forces below. As he turns and clears his tail he sees, ahead, a lone fighter. Spit or enemy? He will close. If it's a Spit he will join into a twosome, which will be safer than flying alone. If it's the enemy, he'll have a go. Checking behind, sometime yawing to throw off any unseen enemy's fire, Johnson banks towards the other aircraft. His eyes strain for identification . . . radial engine . . . enemy . . . F.W.190! Since the Focke-Wulf is superior to the Spitfire V, in speed, initial dive velocity and climb Johnson—without an altitude advantage—

must be careful. Still, he might take the enemy pilot by surprise. At that very moment, a sudden turn by the grey-green F.W. and Johnson knows he has been spotted. A frontal silhouette turns into Johnson and now the two fighters streak together over Dieppe at 500 miles an hour. It's head-on.

At about 800 yards Johnson sees blinks from the F.W.190's four cannon. But he doesn't return the fire. His advantage is that the Spit can out-turn the 190. As the two planes converge, Johnson leans into a tight turn to port. He will get behind the enemy. But the 190 also banks vertically left. Now it's a question of which gets on the tail of the other. Johnson, pulling the stick tightly into his stomach, standing on his port wing, which points straight down to Dieppe, looks across the circle as he sweeps through the turning arc . . . the enemy is there, turning with him, the blunt-nosed Focke-Wulf's white-trimmed crosses clearly visible. Johnson pulls the stick back to get in behind, to out-turn his opponent. To his dismay, the enemy fighter closes behind him, is out-turning him! He pulls the stick harder into his stomach until vision greys, blood drains from his head. He is turning so tightly that pre-stall shuddering shakes the airframe. He asks the aircrafts maximum.

A glance left, then behind. The worst. The 190 is still gaining! One or two more turns and Johnson will be in the line of fire. Instead of anticipating a victory, he feels growing apprehension! He is very nearly trapped. The 190 can out-dive him. His one advantage was supposedly a smaller turning radius! Now he has only seconds to make a move . . . behind him the cannon of the 190 are edging, degree by degree, into firing position. The Spit is shuddering, verging on a stall. Johnson must try to dive away, even though the Focke-Wulf can outdive him from an even start. Perhaps he can gain a second or more by a sudden dive . . . it's his only chance. Desperately, he throws the stick forward and left. Though tightly strapped in the seat his stomach feels the drop, the centrifugal force, and the Spit noses down at full throttle in a steep dive, gaining speed as she roars downwards. It's a dangerous gamble but Johnson is the hunted and close to becoming the victim. His sudden change of tactics seems to have caught the enemy pilot off guard, but only for an instant. The 190 dives straight after him, though Johnson has gained perhaps two precious seconds, lengthening the distance between the fighters by some hundred yards or more. The Spit whines downwards, flat out, the airspeed needle turning rapidly toward 500. Angle: sixty to seventy degrees. It's the maximum the airframe can stand. Dieppe is still several thousand feet below, the dive continues, Johnson looking behind. The Focke-Wulf is there! He plunges farther and farther.

Now the ground is fast rising up towards him. Johnson pulls the stick back, not harshly so that he'll keep his wings with him, and the blood drains from his head as he begins to level out. Hs kicks the rudder and goes into the steepest possible bank, still at speed, and looks behind. The Focke-Wulf is following. Lower and lower. Johnson is just over the roof-tops, standing on his wing, pulling the stick in tight. But the enemy pilot, in a masterly exhibition of flying, is only 200 or 300 yards behind, almost within firing range. Johnson must keep turning, weaving, to avoid his fire. As he roars over buildings and trees he catches glimpses of tanks, of the Dieppe promenade, of a white casino, a deserted beach . . . but he must continue banking. He sees a church steeple. He shoots past, to one side and below the top, and leans into his steepest turn. A glance backward: the F.W.190 is in position! He banks violently to port, trying to throw off his pursuer, to no avail. It's the longest dogfight Johnson has ever engaged in, and he's on the wrong end! Continuing to evade shells ready to be loosed at his first mistake, he knows the game can't go on indefinitely. He will have to make a break.

Now the Focke-Wulf pulls up several hundred feet, following from a height . . . waiting for the right chance, for Johnson to straighten out. But Johnson keeps the Spit banking hard one way and then the other, not offering a target, at the same time realizing he must make a move, an effort to escape. He must soon turn northwards, homewards. His fuel supply won't allow him to continue over Dieppe, nor can he for ever avoid the cunning adversary behind. How can he shake the 190 off and turn for home? Through his mind races the briefing . . . ships, friendly ships, off the docks . . . a short distance out is a destroyer, surrounded by other ships. All have their instructions to fire on any approaching aircraft below 4,000 feet. Johnson is on the deck . . . but perhaps he can get through the barrage . . . and perhaps his pursuer can't. It's a gamble, but the best he has.

Johnson must try it. With his left hand he rams the throttle knob forwards around the safety catch and through the copper wire to emergency power. The Rolls-Merlin roars with an extra burst of power and the Spit, banking steeply out to sea, lurches forward in its supreme effort. Johnson, with added speed of emergency boost and diving the last few feet to the tops of the white caps, sets a fast course straight for the cluster of ships. He notices the boost gauge— sixteen pounds! In seconds he is approaching them; the destroyer opens with flak bursts, now only a third of a mile distant. White 'golf balls' streak towards him from the ships' smaller guns. Above, slower white tracers pass overhead, going his way. The Focke-Wulf has opened fire behind! But the Spit is making her very best speed and the size of the on-coming destroyer is fast increasing. Johnson is ten feet above the water. He feels no hits, the engine still roars, but flak and tracer are all around him. Both friend and enemy are trying to shoot him down. He's on the destroyer . . not much time . . . he must pull up and over, exposing himself to both the 190 and the ships' guns as he flashes over the deck and away. He tugs the stick back just enough and the Spit's nose moves up . . . just high enough. He dumps it back again, rockets a few feet above deck and guns, then noses down to the sea and leans into the tightest bank he can pull, which pushes him down hard in the seat. For a moment everything seems still . . . he looks back and around . . . no more tracer. Even the ships' guns seem to have ceased firing. Did they recognize his wing markings? Did they shoot down the Focke-Wulf? He will never know. But the enemy pilot, who was quite a pilot, is no longer there.

Relieved, his tail clear for the first time in fifteen long minutes, Johnson reverses bank and sets course—still on top of the waves—350 degrees. The Rolls-Merlin roars a while longer at full power and he turns to check the sky behind . . . no enemy fighters. He eases back on the throttle. The tension begins to drain out; it has been an ordeal he is never to forget. He looks at his watch . . . approaching 8.30 . . . he's been airborne less than an hour . . . he wonders about the squadron, feels strange coming home alone. He thinks of Creagh, hopes he baled out or survived.

The Spit thunders over the waves, closer and closer to the English coast, and the closer he gets the more relieved he feels. He can see the cliffs! A wonderful sight this August morning.

Straight ahead, the white chalk cliffs loom higher and higher. He knifes up into the sky, hoping to avoid his own countrymen's anti-aircraft fire, and over the coast. No flak. West Malling is minutes ahead. He searches the landscape ahead for the field. In a few minutes, ahead, west of Maidstone, he sees it—West Malling. He slows to lower his gear . . . in seconds he is on the downwind leg, adds flaps, and turns into the approach. Speed down to 120, 110, 100, 90 . . . he is on the ground, rolling to the dispersal hut area.

Johnson is one of the last of 610 Squadron to land . . . crewmen are happy to see him, having had anxious thoughts as other pilots landed, reporting the hot fight over Dieppe. Johnson is worried about the squadron. How many got back? He cuts throttle, chats a moment about his experience (crewmen are always interested), and walks over to the dispersal hut. What is the news about Creagh? No word. The squadron? Not as bad as he feared. Four pilots presumed lost—of twelve. He had feared it might be more.

Claims? The Squadron gave as good as it received . . . three enemy aircraft destroyed and three damaged. Johnson shared two of his three victims with other pilots. And unknown to him at that moment, Creagh was to call later to say he was safe, having baled out six miles from Dieppe, where he was picked up by the Navy. That reduced 610's loss to three pilots.

But the morning flight was only the beginning. With enemy fighters continuing to appear over Dieppe and invasion forces up against heavy opposition, fighters were in constant demand. 610 Squadron was to fly to Dieppe three more times during the day on patrol and Johnson was to lead them each time. It was a long day . . . though none of the other battles were to be as desperate as the first that morning.

In recognition of his effort on the 19th, the Air Ministry awarded him a bar to the D.F.C. he had won in 1941 for fifty fighter sweeps over enemy-occupied territory.

Johnson's greatest success was to begin about six months later, in 1943. In March of that year he was promoted to Wing Leader of the Kenley Wing—127 Wing, where his main task was escorting American bombers on daylight attacks against targets on the Continent. It was a Canadian wing, and Johnson got on excellently with the pilots from the start. From April until September, leading the wing, he shot down nineteen enemy fighters, quadrupling his total to twenty-five. Fighter Command then withdrew him from combat operations for a six-months rest. In March 1944 he was given command of another Canadian wing—144. He achieved outstanding success with these Canadians also, and in the period March–September 1944 shot down thirteen enemy fighters—his last victory coming in September 1944, when for the only time in his wartime career his aircraft was hit. Before the end of the war, in April 1945, he was promoted to Group Captain.

At the end of the war he elected to stay in the R.A.F., and

was one of the English fighter pilots attached to the U.S. Air Force during the Korean War. He was sent to Korea to study and report on the lessons of air fighting there, and in appreciation of his work in Asia was awarded the U.S. Air Medal and the Legion of Merit. These were added to his C.B., C.B.E., D.S.O. and Two Bars, D.F.C. and Bar, D.F.C. (U.S.A.), and Order of Leopold, Croix de Guerre Belge.

Johnson has now retired as Air Vice-Marshal, twenty-five years after the events described in this chapter. He is recognized as one of the world's foremost authorities on air tactics and strategy and one of his books is widely accepted as the best historical outline of fighter tactics ever published.

Born a Leicestershire man, he is retiring to his home county with the satisfaction that comes from success in wartime, in his career and in marriage. This last began for him during the war, in November 1942, when he met a beautiful nineteen year-old who swept him off his feet. She didn't get a suitable engagement ring, however, until many years later. The man who was to become the top-scoring R.A.F. pilot of the Second World War, then flying and fighting for life and country almost daily, wasn't making enough to buy the ring!

Though Johnson wrote the foreword for the English edition of my first book, published in the fifties, and has been stationed in the United States, it was not until the preparation of this volume that I had the opportunity to discuss his experiences with him in detail—and his most memorable flight. On 8 May 1966, twenty-one years to the day after VE-Day in Europe, that opportunity came, after a drive north from London to Leicester on M.4. Two hours north, beyond Leicester and Melton Mowbray, by the tiny village of Saxby, lay Manor Farm, Johnson's home.

It is difficult to paint a word picture of Johnson for the reader. He is easy-going and relaxed, unpretentious and un-affected, and one finds it difficult to keep it in mind that this is the man who shot more German fighters out of the sky than any other Allied ace. In the good tradition, Johnson avoids any hint of boasting or bombastic talk, but despite such disarming modesty his record is a truly remarkable one and he is considered by many to have been the greatest ace on the Allied side in the Second World War.

# CHAPTER FIFTEEN

# THE BATTLE OF GERMANY

THE BATTLE OF GERMANY was the greatest air struggle of the war, and one of the two most critical decided by fighters. It was a battle fought by three air forces—the R.A.F., the U.S.A.A.F. and the Luftwaffe. The R.A.F. employed Bomber Command and both day and night fighters, the U.S.A.A.F. employed day bombers and fighters of its Eighth Air Force in England, the Ninth in France and the Fifteenth in Italy. To defend the homeland against these assaults, the Luftwaffe used conventional day fighters, night fighters, long-range fighters, the first rocket and jet fighters and other experimental weapons.

In terms of numbers of aircraft and personnel participating, the battles over Germany had never been equalled, and probably never will be again. The fighter conflict was all-important. On its outcome depended the continuance of the greatest strategic bomber offensive of the war. In the end the battle was decided by adding to the range of Allied fighters, and when they at last became capable of accompanying heavy bomber boxes all the way to German targets, the battle was won. Some of the Luftwaffe's leaders—and Hitler himself— had refused to believe that fighters could ever operate at such distances.[1]

One of the outstanding lessons learnt during the battle was that neither day nor night bombing could be carried out successfully against defending fighter forces unless bombers were escorted all the way. Both the R.A.F. and the Luftwaffe,

[1] Galland, p. 193, recalls that Hitler, relying upon assurances from Göring, refused to believe that the range of U.S. fighters could be extended sufficiently to enable them to escort heavy bombers deep into Germany.

of course, had abandoned daylight bomber offensives early in the war because of prohibitive losses at the hands of defending fighters. When the U.S.A.A.F. arrived in England, there was sharp disagreement between English and American planners on the feasibility of the proposed daylight bomber offensive. The Americans persisted, believing that their ten-gun Fortresses, massed in boxes, would prove up to the test. As it turned out, neither the British view nor the American was a correct aerial evaluation. Heavily armed American bombers proved more formidable than others which had been used, but not so much so that they could roam German skies without fighter escort. The American authorities never called off the offensive, but it became clear in late 1943 that the losses being inflicted by German fighters were too high to accept. The Eighth Air Force's heavy bombers suffered murderous losses in several battles to implant this lesson with a permanent root.[1]

The R.A.F. learned the same lesson in its night bombing campaign. When Bomber Command switched to night bombing (as the Germans did) losses were much less costly, but gradually the picture changed. The Luftwaffe began to concentrate on its night fighters, giving them production priority and allocating many of its best pilots to them. As a result of this, and also because of the perfection and use of German radar-finding devices, combined with ground control aids, the number of bombers shot down began to increase. Losses eventually reached a point where they became unbearable (on some deep night penetrations

[1] See my *American Aces*, pp. 202–3. In the first American heavy bomber raid on Schweinfurt and Regensburg, in the summer of 1943, before fighter escorts could fly all the way to the target with the bombers, even the heavily armed B.17s suffered disastrous losses. Of 315 heavies which reached the target, 60 were shot down (600 men) and 138 damaged. The Luftwaffe lost 25 fighters. The Eighth Air Force tried again, in October, again without long-range fighter escort, and the result was even worse. Of the smaller force dispatched (291 took off and 229 reached the target), 60 were shot down and 140 damaged. This time 35 German fighters were destroyed. In effect, Germany won the battle against the Eighth U.S.A.A.F in 1943 in deep penetration attacks.

eighty or ninety bombers and their crews were lost, and many others damaged),[1] and targets were limited to nearer, fringe areas of Germany.

Thus it can be seen that in both daylight and night bombing offensives German fighters almost turned the tide, and only the use of Allied fighters saved the situation. One could say, therefore, that R.A.F. theorists were right in pointing to the danger of defensive fighters in daylight, but that the night raids soon became comparably dangerous. What some failed to see at the beginning of the strategic offensives was that only long-distance fighter protection would enable them to continue. America's production of a long-range fighter force and her use of it to ensure the success of the daylight bombing offensive are tributes to U.S. industry, and to the determination of U.S.A.A.F. leaders. The British did, to a large degree, the same thing to provide night protection for their bombers, though relying primarily on twin-engined aircraft.

What is not often realized is that it was only because of German planning lapses and organizational failures that the Luftwaffe was unable to do better. German fighter production was one of the surprising inadequacies of the German war effort. It did not become adequate, as we have already seen, until 1944,[2] the last full year of the war, when first-class

[1] Johnson in *Full Circle*, pp. 224–5, credits German night fighters with winning this round in the battle for Germany, forcing Bomber Command to discontinue deep penetration attacks because of heavy losses until night-fighter escort was available. Johnson lists Heinz Schaufer as the top Luftwaffe night ace, with 121 victories. Bekker, *Angriffshöhe* 4000 (Gerhard Stalling Verlag, Munich 1964), p. 444, says that on the night of 30—1 March 1944, Bomber Command lost 95 heavies, another 71 being heavily damaged, of which 12 were total losses in crash-landings. One German night-fighter pilot shot down seven bombers during this raid (Oberleut-nant Martin Becker, Staffelkapitän). Galland, pp. 263–4, gives the same figures for British losses.

[2] Tedder, p. 506, reports the opinion of A. C. M. Leigh-Mallory that the air assault against German industry had, by early 1944, succeeded in holding German fighter production to 600 units per month rather than planned production figure of 1,000 to 1,500. Nevertheless, German

pilots were not available in sufficient numbers and when Allied fighters had achieved at least technical equality, and probably slight superiority. Had the defenders of Germany possessed a year or two earlier the number of fighters which could have been produced—and were produced, too late— the bombing offensive against Germany could have been severely punished, if not repulsed. And had Me.262 production been pushed in 1941 and 1942 (also possible, see p. 141) it is doubtful whether the bombing offensive could have been continued at reasonable cost.

The Battle of Germany involved greater and greater numbers as it progressed. Towards the end of the campaign, it was not unusual for Germany to be attacked by day by some 1,200 to 1,500 heavy bombers, protected by 600 to 700 fighters, and then to be visited that night by a comparable R.A.F. force, dropping an even heavier bomb load[1] and also protected by fighters. Against such a massive assault the defence broke down, but only, as we have seen, after a determined resistance. Luftwaffe fighters, which had been exacting a heavy toll of bombers, became the hunted when Allied fighters began to accompany the bombers all the way. They were forced to become occupied with their own defence, at least to a degree, and thus the force of their attack on the bomber squadrons was dissipated.

The bombers which ranged over Germany (and over occupied countries) inevitably killed numbers of innocent civilians. At first military installations were the targets, but later whole cities were attacked. Whether such civilian slaughter was justified by military results is still debated. Allied countries, such as France, also received heavy bombings. This question nagged Churchill and others for

---

aircraft production soared in 1944, the biggest year of the strategic bombing offensive.

[1] The tonnage of bombs dropped on the enemy by Bomber Command exceeded that of the Eighth Air Force in England in every year of the war, and in the months of 1945, until the surrender. *History Of The Second World War*, The Strategic Air Offensive Against Germany, Vol. 4, p. 456.

months.[1] Escort fighter pilots didn't carry bombs, though after they had carried bombers out as far as the Rhine they often returned and strafed selected targets. Civilians no doubt suffered losses from some of these attacks, which were, however, primarily against military targets. One sympathizes with German lamentations over the raid on Dresden, in the closing days of the war, a raid which would seem at this date to have been unnecessary. On the other hand, there were many unnecessary raids throughout the war. The Luftwaffe, in Poland, in Holland and elsewhere, attacked cities in the earliest days, to establish the grim tone of the struggle in the air.

Losses in the Battle of Germany are not easily determined beyond a certain point, for the battle affected fighters and bombers from a number of countries, operating in both daylight and in darkness, and loss breakdowns have not been released. But an American postwar study indicated that the American Army Air Forces lost 11,687 aircraft in Northern Europe and 6,731 in the Mediterranean area, for a grand total of 18,418 plus almost 80,000 airmen,[2] and most of this loss can probably be attributed to the Battle of Germany. Bomber Command lost 10,688 bombers, the majority presumably in the battle. Only a small percentage of Fighter Command's losses, which are listed as 4,760, and tactical fighter force losses, which were 2,822, could be attributed to this phase of the conflict.

A reasonable estimate might be that between 10,000 and 15,000 Allied aircraft were lost in the battle. Not all of these

[1] Tedder, pp. 527–32, tells of long discussions on the question of French bombing casualties, how Churchill expressed reservations and how the issue was finally settled when the War Cabinet decided to put the issue to Washington and President Roosevelt.

[2] American aircraft losses, Craven and Tate, *The Army Air Forces in World War II* (C.U.P., 1948–52), Vol. 6; British losses, Macmillan, appendix. Galland, p. 256, says U.S. Commission under General Anderson concluded U.S. bombers dropped 2.7 million tons of bombs on Germany, flying 1,440,000 bomber missions and 2,680,000 fighter missions. Galland estimates U.S. losses in the Battle of Germany at 18,000 aircraft.

losses were the result of enemy aerial interception as any former 'flak-happy' bomber crewman can testify, of course. But German fighters certainly accounted for a very high percentage.

What were German losses? In this battle, even German figures are not entirely clear. Figures published in 1966 estimate the Luftwaffe lost at about 20,000 fighters and destroyers during the war due to enemy action—on all fronts.[1] More than half this number were lost in the last two years, and losses in these years were heavier on the Western Front than on the Eastern. This would apparently mean 6,000 or 7,000 fighters might be a reasonable estimate for the battle. In addition, another 4,000 estimated fighters and destroyers were damaged due to enemy action, in the last two years—most of these in the West. We approach a figure of 9,000, perhaps 10,000, which Allied pilots might have claimed, as a very rough calculation.

If these figures seem low—for Luftwaffe losses—it should be remembered that German losses not due to enemy activity were abnormally high under the conditions which prevailed in the last two years of the war. This can be seen from the estimate that almost as many German fighters and destroyers were lost during the war (largely in the last two years) from other causes as from enemy action.[2]

The interesting part of these general measurements of the battle is that they show that American fighters won a significant victory. One source has estimated U.S. Eighth Air Force fighter losses at 2,206.[3] If that figure is accurate, and we know R.A.F. fighter losses were lower, it indicates that perhaps 3,000 or more Allied fighters were lost, thus leaving a figure of between 8,000 and 12,000 bombers as our rough loss estimate. One can see, from Allied fighter loss figures, why fighter pilots saw the Battle of Germany as a victorious one. Eighth Air Force fighter pilots received confirmations for

[1] Obermaier, Appendix.
[2] Estimate of Hans Ring.
[3] Gurney, *Five Down and Glory* (Putnam, 1959), appendix.

over 5,000 combat victories. While these figures would seem somewhat high, as can be expected, nevertheless, against losses of 2,206, it seems obvious that American fighters scored more kills than were scored against them, by a good margin. Since one German source[1] reports Luftwaffe fighter losses in the first four months of 1944 (Western Front and Germany) running at an average of just under 400, from enemy action, it may be that Luftwaffe fighter losses in the West in the last two years were a bit higher than we have estimated.

In the early stages of the battle German fighter losses were usually not as high as Allied bomber losses, but later, when escort fighters sometimes shattered the green Luftwaffe fighter formations with better performing fighters, and strafed others on the ground, the tide was turned. The loss discrepancy in the battle which might shock some is that concerning airmen. The Allies lost perhaps 100,000 airmen. Allied bombers carried as many as ten crewmen, and when 50 of these aircraft went down, the equivalent of half an army battalion (500 men) had been lost. Thus it seems likely that, numerically the Luftwaffe lost perhaps one airman to every ten lost by the Allies, or even less.

This does not necessarily indicate that the offensive was a failure because the effect of the bombs is not considered, nor are we seeking to evaluate strategic bombing. It does show however, the high cost of the bombing attack, most of which was exacted by the Luftwaffe's fighter arm, itself suffering relatively acceptable losses until well into 1944. And it shows that Allied long-distance fighters, which appeared in 1944 were decisive in winning the battle. The R.A.F. operated some of these (P.51s)[2], though it was the American Eighth

[1] Original source, staff records of the General of the Luftwaffe Fighter Arm. Bekker, p. 447, says the Luftwaffe lost 70,000 airmen in the war, and (p. 465) puts total German fighter production at 53,728. Ring's estimate of the total number of Luftwaffe fighters lost with operational units is 25,000.

[2] The P.51 became standard equipment with R.A.F. Squadrons 19, 64, 112, 118, 122, 154, 213, 249, 250, 303, 306, 442 and 611. Other squadrons which received P.51s were 26, 237 and 442. Still others received later model Mustangs.

Air Force which provided most of the long-range fighter escort for daylight bombing.

In summary, we see that in aircraft losses (not taking into account the considerable effect of bombs), the Luftwaffe did not do badly in the Battle of Germany until the last of the war, when Allied fighters shot up airfields and aircraft almost at will. The only way the Luftwaffe could have won was to have inflicted such high losses that the offensive would have been called off. This German fighter pilots were unable to do, and thus they lost the battle.

# CHAPTER SIXTEEN

# THE U.S.A.A.F.

THE OTHER fighter force with which we are concerned, and which played a major role on the European scene, was the combined strength of several United States Army Air Forces. American air power experienced a baptism of fire in Europe in 1918. American industry was not able to meet the technological demands of the day before the armistice, and engines and other equipment had to be obtained from Allies.

Nevertheless, the U.S. Army Air Corps developed its organizational structure and gained valuable experience. Unlike England, America was to take a long time to separate her aerial troops from the Army and Navy, and the United States fought in the Second World War without a separate air service. Between the wars Billy Mitchell tried to convince the nation that air power could do much of what it eventually did in the war, but only partly succeeded.

When the war began in 1939, the Army fighter arm was technically behind the best in Germany and England, as had been the case in 1914–18; but not far behind. The Army Air Force, as it became, had stressed the long-range heavy bomber. In this field it was not behind any air force in the world. Plans to bomb small targets, such as ships, with high-flying B.17s were somewhat optimistic—as the war with Japan proved, despite claims by bomber crews. But the U.S. Army's heavy-bomber arm was then both advanced and effective, perhaps the best in the world.

The U.S. Navy pioneered the dive-bomber, a development Germany watched from a distance with interest. It proved highly successful in the Pacific early in the war, as did the Stuka, which had been influenced by it. (The dive-bomber won the battle of Midway, the turning point of war in the Pacific.)

Fighters of the Eighth (England), Ninth (France), Fifteenth (Italy) Air Forces fought the war in Europe the Luftwaffe. Those of the Eighth, primarily, took on the enemy's fighters over the heart of Germany in 1944–5.

A financial boost, important to both technical advancement and production, which did much to enable American industry to produce superior fighters in 1943–4, came from British war orders. The British, for example, were first to order the P.51.

America began the war with the Curtis P.40 and the Bell P.39. Both were good fighters in their day but that day had largely passed. The Russians used many of each, while American pilots flew the P.40 in China and both types in the early days in the Pacific, and in Africa, among other places. The P.40s enjoyed some success, but were no match for the Me.109s they met in Africa, or for the Zero.

The next development was a two-engined experiment, the Lockheed P.38 (Lightning), which shared to some degree the fate of the German Me.110. While pilots who became accustomed to the Lightning swore by it, German pilots soon felt they could take its measure and, in any event, its range was not sufficient for the long-range escort duty required in 1944–5.

After the P.38 came the Republic P.47 (Thunderbolt), the biggest single-engined fighter of the war. Sitting in the cockpit of the Thunderbolt one felt as if one were looking out over the cowling of a locomotive—the big radial power plant had to lift seven tons. But it was the first American fighter which could excel the enemy's best. It was fast, had good range and could fly in the tops of big trees and through small ones and come home undamaged. Bullets and small shells often pierced the engine; it flew on.

The best conventional fighter, used by the Army at least, was the North American P.51 (Mustang). It had the greatest range, the greatest speed (the P.51D did 437 m.p.h. at

‚‚000 feet and later models were even faster), and handled nicely in combat. It was more than a match for the Me.109 and F.W.190, because it was faster, more strongly built and could fly farther. The P.47 and P.51 were the long-range escort fighters which did so much to crush the German fighter arm in 1944-5. Often in these years American squadrons scored one-sided victories deep over Germany against green Luftwaffe formations in their 109s or 190s.

The U.S.A.A.F. flight formations were different from those of the R.A.F. and the Luftwaffe. An 'element' consisted of two fighters. Two elements made up a flight; four flights a squadron; three squadrons a group. Thus a U.S. Army Group (usually the complement at a fighter station) comprised 48 aircraft in flight, or 50 (two spares). A group was similar to an R.A.F. Wing, but not identical, because when an R.A.F. Wing was made up of three squadrons, its strength was only 36 fighters. And an R.A.F. wing might contain more than three squadrons.

Several groups formed a wing. For example, Fighter Command of the Eighth Air Force contained three wings, the 65th, 66th and 67th, each of five groups.

The U.S. army pilot-training system allowed West Pointers to integrate into the flying service and receive flying training after graduation, and there was a cadet programme which was greatly expanded during the war. College training detachments were established, as they had been in Britain. In fact, pilots were recruited to a greater extent from colleges and universities in the United States than elsewhere, and one or two years at a college or university was a requirement for entry into the service as a cadet. The cadet in the Army Air Corps won his wings and a commission—for Army Air Corps pilots were officers. (Towards the end of the war the system was slightly altered so that some graduates were made warrant officers.)

The emphasis placed on college or university training was one reason for a high average ability among American fighter pilots. Combined with excellent flying training and equipment, such pilot qualifications helped make the American fighter force in Europe a very effective one by mid-1944. On a new continent, over strange territory and in different weather, the pilots acclimatized themselves surprisingly quickly.

The American training programme, of course, benefited from visits by successful R.A.F. pilots, like Stanford Tuck, 'Sailor' Malan, and others. They flew with training squadrons, and informed instructors of the weaknesses in the training schedule, with a view to what lay ahead in Europe.

Morale was high in both Army and Navy air forces. The aggressive spirit among squadron and group leaders was probably unsurpassed. Perhaps the high-command team of General Carl Spaatz, commanding the U.S.A.A.F. in Europe, General James Doolittle (of Tokyo raid fame), commanding the Eighth Air Force, and General William Kepner, commanding Eighth Air Force's Fighter Command, was the outstanding American air leadership combination in the war. The Eighth, of course, was at the time the biggest, produced more of the top fighter aces than any other, and met the strongest fighter opposition. (The most accurate description of the wartime life of an American fighter group in Europe can be found in Grover C. Hall's hilarious *1,000 Destroyed*, the story of the 4th Fighter Group.)

When added to the Allied effort, the U.S. Army Air Force made a heavy impact on the European scene, flying first from English airfields, then from African, Sicilian, Italian, French and other continental bases. The situation had changed since 1918: its aircraft were now among the best, pilots well-trained before they arrived, and organization efficient. Morale within fighter groups of the U.S.A.A.F. was high throughout the war in all theatres, perhaps especially in Europe. Commissioned flying ranks in the U.S.A.A.F. (the same as ground ranks), from lowest to highest, were as follows:

2nd Lieutenant
1st Lieutenant

Captain
Major
Lieutenant-Colonel
Colonel
Brigadier-General
Major-General
Lieutenant-General
General

The Eighth Air Force, whose fighters did the lion's share in winning the Battle of Germany, was composed of the following Groups, with the indicated number of confirmed aerial victories:[1] 4th Group—550; 20th Group—205; 55th Group —305½; 56th Group—679½; 78th Group—330; 339th Group—234; 352nd Group—493½; 353rd Group—340; 355th Group—356; 356th Group—193; 357th Group— 586½; 359th Group—247½; 361st Group—219½; 364th Group—261; 479th Group—155.

[1] Hall, appendix. Some of these figures are subject to slight adjustments.

# CHAPTER SEVENTEEN

# ESCORT TO BERLIN

*6 March 1944—Lieutenant R. S. Johnson, U.S.A.A.F.*

UNITED STATES heavy bombers made their first daylight raid on Germany on 27 January 1943, and although the bombing of Wilhelmshaven was not one of the great aerial attacks of the war, the mission was significant because it was the opening of the daylight bomber offensive against Germany itself.

Since 1942, the Eighth U.S. Army Air Force had been challenging the theory, accepted in both the R.A.F. and the Luftwaffe, that defending fighters inevitably win a contest with bombers attacking in daylight. The Germans had learned the lesson in 1940 when they had attempted to subdue England with daylight bomber attacks. Losses became so heavy that the offensive was called off.

The R.A.F. had come to the same conclusion and was bombing Germany at night, and from the beginning urged the Americans to do likewise.

In anticipation of the American attacks, Reichsmarschall Göring stationed two newly-formed fighter wings in the two major approaches to Germany: Holland, and the German Bight. He was confident that American daylight attacks would not succeed.

Adolf Galland, General of the Luftwaffe Fighter Arm, disagreed with Göring's theory that German fighters could easily defeat the big American bombers in daylight, but, given adequate forces, Galland also felt he could turn back the daylight assault.

While the R.A.F. had been bombing the enemy since 1939, the Germans regarded their night attack on the Renault works in Paris, on 3 March 1942, as the first attack strong enough to be classified as strategic bombing.

In the first phase of American daylight participation, American bombers were often protected by Spitfires or Thunderbolts (P.47s) up to the borders of Germany, and by P.38 Lightnings over Germany. On the longer missions, however, there was sometimes no fighter support at the point of deepest penetration, the target vicinity itself. When Luftwaffe fighters caught the bombers without escort, maximum defensive results were most often achieved by Me.109s, F.W.190s, and long-range fighter units (destroyers) with rockets.

On some occasions when this occurred, results seemed to vindicate Göring's judgement. And since, as General Omar Bradley notes in *A Soldier's Story*, the Germans finally awoke to the fact that the crucial task facing them, from 1943 onwards, was the expansion of their fighter force, the prospect of reducing bomber losses was directly related to the strength and effectiveness of long-range American fighter escorts.

After the Wilhelmshaven attack, American bombers steadily increased the strength and range of their operations. By the latter half of 1943 Allied bombers were heavily assaulting Germany. The Luftwaffe's fighters aimed for a victory similar to that of the R.A.F. in 1940, and in the summer of 1943 German fighter strength was increased and resistance stiffened considerably. When a large, four-engined force of American bombers attacked the Messerschmitt works at Regensburg and Schweinfurt, the Luftwaffe threw approximately 300 interceptors against the bombers, shot down 60 and damaged 138, with a loss of only 25 fighters. Over 600 American airmen were killed or captured.

The Eighth Air Force attacked Schweinfurt again on 14 October. Although fewer bombers were dispatched, and a tighter defence formation attempted, German fighter strength had increased, and 60 bombers were shot down and 140 damaged—out of a raiding force of 229! (Although 291 bombers took off for Schweinfurt, only 229 actually attacked.)

A mere 35 German fighters were destroyed. It was another shattering defeat.

The Luftwaffe was rapidly increasing the strength of its day fighter force to counter the American threat, and this was responsible for increasing American losses. In the six months from April to October 1943, for example, day fighter strength in Germany rose from approximately 152 to 765, and in France from approximately 307 to 505.

The challenge was countered in several ways. The Eighth Air Force had already requested long-range fighters, so that the bombers could be escorted all the way to distant targets. The need had now obviously become urgent.

An immediate relief for the bomber crews was a switch from deep penetration raids to shorter ones and from precision bombing to area bombing, as practised by the British. The weather actually made area bombing a logical step as it worsened in the autumn of 1943. In November, flying conditions were the worst in years.

Long-range American fighters began arriving in England late in 1943, and by early 1944 heavy bombers of the U.S.A.A.F. were being provided with fighter escort all the way to deep-penetration targets and out again. This proved decisive in the Battle of Germany, and answered the challenge of defending German fighters. But victory was not certain in the early months of 1944, and the early strikes at Berlin produced bitter battles which cost American and R.A.F. forces heavily.

Fifteen months after the first U.S.A.A.F. bombing of Germany and four months after the first large-scale R.A.F. raid on Berlin (November 1943), a small force of thirty B.17s bombed Berlin. Two days later, on 6 March 1944, the first large-scale American attack on the Nazi capital was carried out. On this day 660 heavy bombers dropped 1,600 tons of bombs on Berlin in broad daylight, protected by long-range fighters, which now made the bombing of Berlin feasible.

The Luftwaffe's reaction to the assault on Berlin was naturally vigorous. The threat of extermination had become a grim reality to Germans in 1944 as the R.A.F. struck at night, to be followed by the U.S.A.A.F. next day, even as Berlin attempted to dig out and put out the fires caused by the raid the night before. A year after the first American raid on Berlin, in March of 1945, notwithstanding record German fighter production in 1944, the 'round-the-clock' offensive against the German capital reached its peak. In this fiery climax the Eighth Air Force dispatched more than 1,200 heavy bombers on its Berlin missions—and, worst of all for the Germans, this great onslaught of bombers was escorted all the way to the target and back by more than 800 long-range fighters.

From the night of 18–19 November 1943, then until 10 April 1945—when the last American daylight raid on Berlin was carried out—the 'Battle of Berlin' was waged with ferocity and persistence. On some of the raids the Americans lost hundreds of airmen in the space of a few hours to determined German fighters. The most costly year, in overall losses, was of course 1944, and the worst part of 1944 the early months, when Allied fighter strength available for these long Berlin raids was not what it came to be in the last six months of the war.

Losses on the first large-scale American attack on Berlin were very heavy, as will be seen later in this chapter. But the U.S.A.A.F. was only beginning. The German capital was bombed five times in the opening week of the American offensive. Two days after the first heavy attack, on 8 March 1944, another massive raid was carried out by the Eighth Air Force. On this raid 54 aircraft and 396 airmen were lost, an indication of the bitterness of the Battle of Berlin in its early days. But losses would have been higher had not long-range fighters provided escort all the way.

As the campaign wore on, the Fifteenth Air Force in Italy participated in the bombing of Berlin and relative losses decreased as American fighter forces became stronger and more and more fighters became long-range types. The R.A.F. also increased the tempo of its assault, and losses in its early large-scale attacks are a grim indication of the savage fight which raged in German skies on the route to Berlin at night. For example, on the night of 24 March 1944, the R.A.F. admitted the loss of 73 aircraft on a Berlin raid—a loss comparable to the destruction of a battalion of troops in a few hours. (On another night the R.A.F. lost over 90 bombers.)

The Battle of Berlin, then, was one of the greatest aerial battles of the war, extending over a period of eighteen months, at a cost of thousands of American, German, and British airmen, and scores of thousands of German civilians on the ground below. Pilots and crews who went on raids to Berlin flew death-laden skies, withstood the ordeal of heavy flak, cannon, rocket, and machine-gun fire from Luftwaffe fighters, which streaked in from all sides, and the sometimes grim task of limping home over long stretches of hostile territory and the dark wastes of the North Sea.

In 1928, at one of the early shows at Post Field, Oklahoma, eight-year-old Robert S. Johnson watched spellbound as three Army pilots—the Three Musketeers of the First World War—did their stuff. Then and there Bob Johnson set his heart on becoming a fighter pilot. Sixteen years later, on 6 March 1944, Johnson was leading a Group of U.S.A.A.F. fighters on the first heavy American bombing of Berlin. In the meantime he had grown up, joined the Army as a cadet, won his wings, reported to a combat area and become a leading fighter ace. The Three Musketeers had done a good job.

Bob Johnson was the first American pilot in Europe to equal the aerial combat record of Captain Eddie Rickenbacker of the First World War. In the Pacific, Major Richard I. Bong beat Johnson by a nose to the distinction of being the first American pilot in the Second World War to surpass Captain Eddie's record. The 'ace of aces' for his country, Bong was credited with forty kills at the end of the war. But he was not to live long afterwards. In the year following Japan's surrender he died in a jet fighter in California. Johnson, however, finished his combat before the Allies invaded France, returning to the United States, and is still in flying—with Republic, at Farmingdale, New York.

Bob Johnson scored twenty-eight kills, all in the air, between 13 June 1943 and 8 May 1944—less than a year. He was the fourth-ranking of all American aces in aerial combat, and the second highest scorer in the air in the European theatre. His feat in shooting down twenty-eight German aircraft in less than eleven months stands alone in the history of American air operations in Europe.

Curiously, Johnson's aggressiveness in combat involved him in deep trouble on the day of his first kill, and probably prevented his victory total from being higher than it was. The incident which was to affect his career occurred during a mission on 13 June 1943. Flying with the 61st Squadron of the famous 56th Fighter Group, Johnson spotted twelve 190s below his squadron. When the squadron didn't go after the enemy fighters, Johnson bade the others a hasty farewell and dived on the unsuspecting bandits, shooting one down in an audacious surprise attack. The legendary leader of the Wolfpack (56th Group), Colonel Hubert Zemke, adopted the same tactics and shot down two of the enemy fighters.

Johnson was reprimanded for leaving his squadron when he returned to base after the mission. He was so sternly chastised that he dared not venture out of formation for a long time thereafter, although he disagreed violently with the strategy being followed at that time by most squadrons—in general, one of waiting to be attacked. Some time after his initial kill, having missed several golden opportunities to attack, Johnson was caught from behind maintaining formation and almost shot down.

Finally, tactics were changed, though in the face of objections from some high-ranking air officers in the theatre. Major-General O. A. Anderson at last won approval for his proposal of more aggressive escort tactics for the Eighth Air Force. Thereafter, Johnson would never again sit still waiting to be attacked. And, realizing that Johnson's philosophy of battle had been a good one, his comrades who had dubbed him, tentatively, as an over-enthusiastic and unpredictable pilot began to extend their friendship. Henceforth the squadron went after Germans with gusto, and with more victories.

Ironically, Johnson could never qualify for fighters in gunnery—in which he so obviously excelled in combat. Beginning Texas A. & M. in the autumn of 1941, he thought better of it and joined the Army as an aviation cadet on 11 November of that year—twenty-three years to the day after Rickenbacker and other American pilots in France had celebrated the end of the war in Europe by shooting off rockets and burning fuel on their field behind the front lines in France.

He completed flying training successfully, except in gunnery, which necessited his designation as a bomber pilot and final training in twin-engined aircraft.

Six months after Pearl Harbor, however, he managed to be assigned to 56th Fighter Group—no one was worrying about his gunnery then—and in less than a year's time found himself in England, preparing for combat with the formidable Luftwaffe.

He arrived in England with the 56th Group on 13 January 1943. Technically, the group began operations that winter, but because the 56th had to await the arrival of a full complement of aircraft, most 56th pilots had to wait until spring to begin operations.

In April, having requested the forty-eighth position in the group (tail-end Charlie of the last of the three squadrons), Johnson flew his first combat mission. Six months later he was unofficially an ace. By 6 March 1944—the date of the first heavy American daylight bombing of Berlin—Johnson was one of the war's foremost aces, leading the 61st Squadron of Colonel Zemke's celebrated Wolfpack, which was protecting the first three boxes of heavy bombers on that historic attack.

Every American pilot in the Eighth Air Force knew that

sooner or later it would join in the attack on Germany's capital. Therefore, after fourteen months of raids on other targets inside Germany, when American bombers and fighters were ordered to fly to Berlin on 3 March 1944, pilots had been anticipating the event. On that day, however, the bombers were forced to turn back because of the weather.

A small force of bombers blazed the way the very next day, 4 March, without encountering unusual difficulties. Late on 5 March orders were prepared directing 800 heavy bombers to attack Berlin the next day. Naturally, receipt of the orders at bomber and fighter bases around England caused a ripple of excitement and anticipation. The United States had been at war with Hitler's Germany for two years and three months. The Eighth had been operating from England for more than a year and a half. It was time Hitler's capital felt the weight of the Eighth's bombs, and looked up at the awesome sight of four-engined American bombers unloading lethal cargoes over Germany's greatest city in broad daylight —the city Hermann Göring had said would never suffer such an ordeal.

But in March 1944 the task of providing fighter escort for heavy bombers on such a long raid was formidable. Not many of the new long-range fighters, which made the Berlin attacks possible, were yet availabe. There were P.38s and P.47s, for the most part, which were not able to fly in and out all the way and do battle with the enemy also. Thus a schedule had to be worked out for some of the fighters to escort the bombers a certain distance and then be relieved by other fighters, a partial relay process.

The 56th Group, which emerged from the war as the second highest-scoring unit in the Eighth Air Force, flew P.47s throughout the war, and was therefore equipped with Thunderbolts in March 1944. The 4th Group—56th's greatest rival, which finally came out with top honours by a hair (in the victories race)—had just been equipped with P.51s. Both 56th and 4th were among the many fighter groups assigned escort duties for the Berlin attack. The Thunderbolts of 56th would split into two under-strength groups for the raid, thirty-five fighters making up each group. The groups would rendezvous with the bombers as they approached Germany and provide penetration support.

At this time the Germans occupied the Low Countries and France. Every pilot knew, when he took off on escort duty and crossed into enemy-occupied territory, that an hour or two later he would have to fly back across the North Sea to England. If he was forced down in France, Holland, or Belgium, short on fuel, it meant capture by the Germans. The enemy, then, was not the only worry of fighter pilots. Each sweated out his fuel supply on the longer raids, especially pilots in P.38s and P.47s.

On the night of 5 March pilots of the 56th were alerted and told that a major operation would be mounted the next morning. Since the number of pilots in the group was not what it was later in the war, 56th fliers knew most of them would participate. With that knowledge, and the forecast that tomorrow's weather would be good, the group's fighter pilots went to bed early at Halesworth. Unlike bomber crews, and crewmen, many did not learn they were going to Berlin until next day.

At 4.30 a.m. next morning, the drone of heavy bombers in the winter darkness above roused Lieutenant Bob Johnson from his slumber. Dressing in O.D. pants and shirt, silk scarf and leather jacket, and carefully checking the knife he carried in his right boot, Johnson made off into the blackness for a Nissen-hut mess hall. There he grabbed a few slices of bread, toasted them against the side of the iron stove in the centre of the hut, and drank his coffee. In a few minutes he departed for the operations room of 61st Squadron, where pilots checked the position they would fly, and also their flying equipment. They still did not know their destination for the day.

A jeep carried 61st Squadron to group briefing—where a lot of their questions would be answered. A curtain hid the big wall map from view. After pilots from all three squadrons had taken their seats, the Group Intelligence Officer stepped up on the platform at the front of the room and pulled the curtain string.

The ribbon marking the route stretched from England to . . . Berlin! Amid whispers and excitement, the I.O. briefed the group on flak, expected enemy resistance, and escape procedures. The Weather Officer followed—explaining the conditions pilots would encounter on the way into Germany and back.

The three squadrons of the 56th were 61st, 62nd, and 63rd. The Commanding Officer of the 61st, Johnson's squadron, was one of the war's great fighter pilots, Francis S. Gabreski. Johnson was one of 61st's flight leaders, destined to emerge from the war in Europe second only to Gabreski in the number of confirmed aerial victories. The 61st, then, was an outstanding squadron.

The Group Commander, Zemke, completed the briefing. He announced that 56th would divide into two groups. He would lead A Group and Johnson would lead B. The group's Executive Officer, Lieutenant-Colonel Dave Schilling—who was to become the fourth-ranking American ace in Europe—was not scheduled to fly, nor was Gabreski.

Johnson, then, was to have charge of thirty-five P.47s, half the group's total effort. Take-off was set for 10.32 a.m. If the group encountered no opposition from the Luftwaffe during escort duty, it was to descend to low altitude on the way home and strafe targets as the opportunity arose. After a few last words from Zemke, gripes that the trip was either too short or too long, and exclamations—as pilots eyed the long route-marker ribbon stretching to Berlin and back—group briefing ended. Pilots and officers of the 61st climbed on their jeep and headed back to the squadron building.

At squadron briefing Johnson kept his talk short. He merely confirmed the order of flight, outlined a few general rules for close-in and combat formation, and warned his men to be on the alert. Pilots then went to their lockers and pulled out parachutes, Mae West and helmets. Johnson took with him one glove—for his left hand, which would rest on the metal throttle handle much of the time in flight. In March over England and Germany temperatures above 20,000 feet were below zero, and while the cockpit was partially heated, it nevertheless became quite cold at higher altitudes.

Pilots lounged around and the morning wore on. It was a few minutes after ten. Johnson wished his men luck and they walked out to their aircraft. In a couple of minutes he stepped up on the wing of a blunt, red-nosed Thunderbolt, the words 'All Hell' painted on its side. Before the day was over Keyworth Red Leader—that was Johnson's code identification—and 'All Hell' would weather an experience to justify the aircraft's name.

The fat fighter kicked over a few minutes before 10.32, and after Johnson had listened to a few words of encouragement from his crew chief, the radial-engined Thunderbolt, a 150-gallon extra tank slung beneath its belly, rolled away towards the end of a black-surfaced runway on which 61st would take off. Without a hitch, the other fighters of B Group fell in behind Keyworth Red Leader and followed him towards the runway.

Half the fighters lined up on the end of one of Halesworth's two runways and half on the other. At 10.32 a.m. Keyworth Red Leader and his wingman roared off towards the far end of one runway. As soon as they passed the intersection where the runways crossed, two fighters on the other runway began to roll. In a few minutes the thirty-five P.47s were all safely off, turning in a wide left turn, and rolling out on course, almost due east. Colonel Zemke's thirty-five fighters—the rest of 56th—were only a short distance away.

The few clouds which covered England were easily topped in a shallow climb. To conserve fuel, power was set at 1,800 r.p.m. and 29 inches of mercury. Johnson looked behind and around; his P.47s were in perfect formation, closed in properly behind. He was leading three under-strength squadrons, totalling thirty-five fighters in all. Normally, a

Take-off at 10.32 a.m. and landing at 1.51 p.m.

Halesworth

Berlin

Mission to Be[r]
escorting heav[y]
bombers

HALESWORTH

Johnson and wingma[n]
escorted bomber saf[e]
to mid-channel

### FIGHTER

P. 47 THUNDERBOLT

### FIGHTER SQUADRON

61 SQUADRON

### FIGHTER STATION

HALESWORTH

**MISSION FLOWN B[Y]**

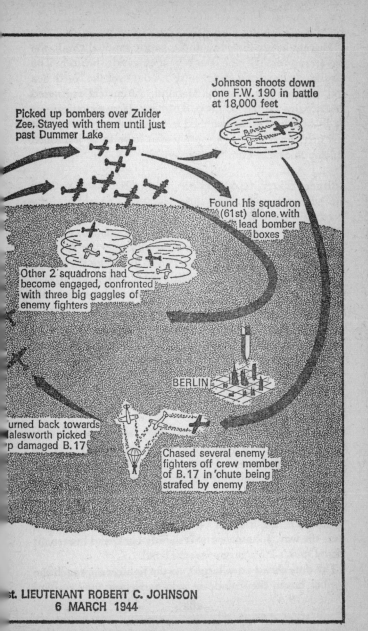

Picked up bombers over Zuider Zee. Stayed with them until just past Dummer Lake

Johnson shoots down one F.W. 190 in battle at 18,000 feet

Found his squadron (61st) alone, with lead bomber boxes

Other 2 squadrons had become engaged, confronted with three big gaggles of enemy fighters

BERLIN

urned back towards alesworth picked p damaged B.17

Chased several enemy fighters off crew member of B.17 in 'chute being strafed by enemy

st. LIEUTENANT ROBERT C. JOHNSON
6 MARCH 1944

squadron sent out sixteen planes on a mission.

Making better than 154 m.p.h. in the gradual climb, the group rapidly left the English countryside behind. The Thunderbolts roared on upwards . . . out over the North Sea and towards the coast of Holland. Altimeters registered steady gains . . . 6,000, 7,000, 8,000 feet. Now superchargers were cut in and pilots switched to belly tanks, to use up that fuel first, since the extra tanks would have to be jettisoned quickly in case of imminent action.

Altitude registers 10,000, 11,000, 12,000 feet. Below nothing can be seen but a vast expanse of water. The width of the North Sea at this latitude is over a hundred miles. It is a cold dip for the pilot who is forced down, either going or coming. The blunt-nosed fighters slice upwards into the sky . . . pilots check their gun switches . . . begin to look for the outline of the Dutch coast ahead. The altimeter needle reads 15,000, 16,000, 17,000 feet. The coast of Holland can't be far away. Johnson orders the three squadrons to spread out into combat formation.

The Thunderbolts wing out wide, come into almost line-abreast formation, continue slanting. Altitude reaches 23,000, 24,000, 25,000 feet. Now the coast of Holland is visible ahead. Each pilots flips on his gunsight switch. The yellow circle on the sighting glass appears. Altitude 27,000 feet.

The group crosses the coast. The landscape below is blurred by a general haze, but the sky is cloudless. The group passes over Walcheren Island . . . and then in above the Zuider Zee. Up ahead the lead boxes of bombers come into view, clusters of small outlines, more than thirty bombers to a box—B.17 Flying Fortresses. Johnson points the group towards the 'big friends'. Of the three squadrons, the 63rd leads the way. Johnson's 61st is slightly back, and lieutenant Mike Quirk's P.47s are next—the 62nd.

The dots ahead grow larger. As the fighters approach the bomber boxes, the squadrons split and curve into position around the heavies. One squadron leader takes his P.47s directly above the bombers, Johnson banks left and eases up on that side, and Quirk guards the right flank. They stay several thousand feet out from their big friends—begin to S-turn, to keep from running away from the slower bombers.

The spearhead of the aerial armada streaks on through the Dutch sky at 25,000 feet—one squadron of fighters above. For a short time the procession drones on inland. Then it reaches the vicinity of Zwolle. Heavy flak bursts dot the sky. The fighters manœuvre radically to be on the safe side—but the guns below are aiming at the bombers, where the bomb load, on its way to Berlin is carried.

A group of unidentified specks ahead . . . pilots tense. The bogies are small fighters. The 56th prepares for a fight. On come the bogies . . . at the 56th's altitude. As they approach, Johnson leans into a slight left turn to meet them head on. They come closer and closer . . . now their blunt noses are identifiable . . . they are coming right through the 56th's formation! At the last moment, with pilots' fingers itching near trigger buttons, someone calls in identification—the bogies are P.47s. They fly right through the 56th. It's a new group. It is a dangerous situation . . . but the inexperienced pilots get away with it . . . they flash on by and back . . . no one slips and fires at his comrades. For a few minutes the flight continues uneventfully . . . then bogies are spotted off to one side. Once again the escorting fighter pilots tighten up . . . the bogies come on, closer . . .

Blunt noses! F.W.190s or P.47s? On and on come the fighters . . . now they are almost on 56th. 'Those same boys,' someone yells over the radio . . . and once again the Wolfpack holds its fire, and curses. The orderly flight continues. The sky is clear. The bombers leave no vapour trails.

Then, ahead, lies the German border. At this moment Lieutenant Quirk's P.47s break sharply. They go into a dive . . . Johnson looks hard but can see nothing. He maintains position. Quirk's fighters rapidly disappear below. Then, on the radio, Johnson hears shouts from Quirk's men . . . they are in a fight! They spotted a gaggle of Me.190s climbing up for an attack. They háve jumped the enemy fighters and are having a quick battle. Quirk estimates the gaggle at about thirty fighters.

Johnson calls and asks the location of the dogfight. No answer. He calls again, hoping to get into the fight. Quirk is too busy . . . and maybe 62nd want the bandits for themselves. Pilots in the two squadrons with the bombers envy 62nd. Johnson pulls to the left, to search a little wider. The other squadron curves right—to the south—for the same purpose. But neither finds the enemy fighters. Johnson curves back in towards the bombers as the stream is approaching the Dümmersee—an unmistakable landmark on the route to Berlin. The other squadron is still to the south, so Johnson comes in close to the bombers and flies over the boxes. As he reaches the front box, he leans into a left turn. The three boxes of bombers 56th is protecting fly silently and majestically on—dozens of Forts in each closely packed box.

The blunt nose of 'All Hell' heels around towards the north . . . and up ahead Johnson spots suspicious specks. It's 11.40 a.m. They're closing on a southerly course. Johnson watches as they come closer. They must be the same P.47s that have already flown through the 56th twice. He speaks over the radio to seven 47s behind him: 'Watch those monkeys ahead.' At the same time he realizes the oncoming fighters aren't P.47s. Bandits! Into the mike he yells: 'Hell, they're Focke-Wulfs!' Thunderbolts drop tanks, spread out farther and wheel out into position to turn in on the enemy fighters as they come through. The Germans are heading for the leading box of bombers. Johnson is so close to the bombers there's no chance to stop the enemy fighters before they reach their objective.

The gaggle is now fast approaching—F.W.190s and Me.109s, clearly identifiable. Johnson times his manœuvre to the second. As the Germans reach his vicinity he swings into a sharp right turn to pull in behind . . . throttle wide open. The fighters flash together at 600 m.p.h. In a second the

German fighters are past the Thunderbolts and boring in on the leading box of bombers. Johnson pulls into a steep turn and is on the tail of the bandits almost immediately, who ignore the American fighters and go for the bombers. Now the big friends get set for the shock of attack . . . the guns of each Fortress train on the German fighters as the radio hums with cries of warning and the excitement of combat.

There is so little distance between the German and American fighters that it's impossible for the Fortress gunners to distinguish between friend and foe. Johnson watches the enemy ahead draw into range . . . he's overtaking them. To his left he catches sight of another gaggle, slightly east. In a split second, his eyes pick out a third gaggle above. Each enemy formation contains thirty to forty fighters!

Johnson's Thunderbolts, all that are available at the moment to protect the bombers, close the range behind the gaggle in front. But the Germans are already on the bombers. The sky lights up. Enemy 20 mm. shells throw white bursts into the bomber formation. Rockets leave a zigzag smoke trail as they streak into the heavies. The B.17s, ten 50 mm. cannon to a bomber, open up with all guns. The Germans fly right in. The Thunderbolts follow . . . too late to turn away now. The bombers shoot at friend and foe. The P.47s open up on the Germans ahead and German 20 mm. machine-guns and cannon and rockets clutter up the air. The fighters flash through the formation, under and over and by the sides of the bombers.

Parachutes begin to dot the sky. The action is so fast, so deadly, it's hard to comprehend. The other two gaggles of German fighters have picked the second and third boxes of bombers, and now they bore in . . . splashing fire and shell through the formations, unhindered by defending fighters. The 61st Squadron, right behind the enemy gaggle, passes through and by the leading bomber box and down and out, hanging on and firing away. Johnson sees scores of parachutes. One B.17 is cut in half . . . the tail assembly glides off in one direction, the rest of the fuselage and wing in another.

Ten men were safe and sound in the Fortress seconds ago. Other B.17s drop back out of the lead box, trailing smoke, crippled. Several plunge earthwards, trailing a black column of smoke. Now a hundred parachutes fill the sky!

Several enemy fighters smash into the big bombers. A huge flash of fire follows and both planes go down. It is a savage encounter. A number of enemy fighters are burning. Johnson closes four F.W.190s at about 18,000 feet. He slams his throttle the rest of the way forwards, approaching from five o'clock. So far he hasn't scored a kill and planes are falling all around him.

The F.W.190s draw closer into range, Johnson at full throttle. He watches the four 190s closely—they're making good speed, in two elements—ahead and slightly left. He looks through his sight ring—one of the bandits is now almost filling it.

Just as 'All Hell' flashes into range behind, the Germans see the danger to their rear. The four F.W.190s break sharply up, in pairs. But Johnson is opening fire. The Thunderbolt roars and shakes . . . and the 190 directly ahead takes hits.

Johnson pulls stick back and hangs on behind the climbing enemy. 'All Hell' spits tracers and shells, which converge on the grey-black, radial-engined fighter. Johnson's fire is accurate and inflicts fatal damage.

The enemy's engine is hit . . . his propeller seems to spin slower. Pieces fly backwards. Something moves on top . . . suddenly the enemy pilot leaves the cockpit. He jumps at good speed and falls rapidly. Then a 'chute opens below. The F.W.190 plunges earthwards.

Enemy fighters are scattered all over the area, in singles, in pairs and larger groups. Johnson, flushed with victory, spots a lone bandit and banks sharply to come in on his tail. He looks back to check his wingman—a new pilot—and is shocked to see a German squarely on his tail. He racks around and turns into the enemy as fast as he can, breaking up the attack. Now some thirty falling planes fill the sky.

Again he sees a target ahead. He manœuvres for position,

but remembers to check his wing man. Behind him is another German fighter. For the second time Johnson breaks off his attack and turns sharply to make a pass at the enemy. In all his combat he has never lost a wingman. The bandit breaks away as Johnson threatens to close his tail.

The scene above is bedlam. Burning aircraft and hundreds of parachutes dot every corner of the sky. Johnson notices another fighter curving in behind his wingman, and, almost by force of habit now, he stands on a wing and turns into the enemy. He succeeds, for the third time, in driving him off. It's a strange battle. By now he could have scored several victories had he not bothered about protecting his wingman.

Up above Johnson sees two F.W.190s firing away. He yanks the stick back and 'All Hell' climbs at a sharp angle, towards the enemy fighters. Johnson—at extreme range—opens fire. The tracers catch the attention of the enemy planes . . . they drop their noses down towards the climbing P.47s. Only Johnson and his wingman are left together. The other P.47s of 61st Squadron are scattered in every direction.

The two enemy fighters grow larger and larger as they approach at great speed. Johnson sees the light flashes from their wing guns. He, too, opens fire, but observes no hits. As they close, the Germans break to Johnson's right and continue to dive. Johnson shoves his stick forwards, hits right rudder and plunges after them. For a moment the Germans, with their greater diving speed, pull away, but then the two heavier P.47s come on strong and Johnson can see the F.W.190s are no longer gaining.

By now all four fighters are just a few thousand feet above the ground. They continue their steep dive . . . in the direction of Hanover, not far away. The distance begins to close. Airspeed climbs at a rapid clip . . . 325, 350, 375, 400, 450. The two Thunderbolts are gaining. The German pilots realize they're being caught from behind. Without warning, they suddenly part . . . the enemy leader's wingman turns sharply to the right. Two targets. Johnson must choose. He and his wingman stay with the enemy leader, the other

German fighter gets away.

The distance is closing . . . and Johnson is almost in range. The F.W.190, now levelling out, tries an old trick. Suddenly the thin dark exhaust smoke from his stack disappears. Johnson's left hand races for the throttle, jerks it back. The enemy is cutting his engine to make the Thunderbolts overshoot, and zoom out in front of his guns. 'All Hell' slows up . . . but still eases up on the German fighter . . . just about right. Now the 190 pilot stands on his port wing in a vertical turn. Jonhson cuts tight behind him, cutting him off in turn, not going too fast to stay in there on the enemy's tail, as the German pilot had planned. The cut-off turn brings Johnson into range. He presses the firing button. Eight fifties roar and shake 'All Hell'. Tracers mark an aerial path to the German fighter. Johnson pulls the stick into his stomach and sees the silhouette of the low-winged enemy fighter pass through his gunsight ring from tail to nose . . . proof he's out-turning his foe. His shells rake over the top of the enemy fighter, from tail to engine nacelle. For a second or two he spits shells at the German at close range. Johnson is on top of his victim now and banks to the right, pulls up to come around for another pass. As soon as he gets another glance at his foe, turning to come in from behind again, Johnson notices the enemy fighter is diving. Already close to the ground after the first long dive, Johnson pushes stick forward and 'All Hell' streaks after the fleeing German. This time the chase is short. The crippled enemy fighter can't make top speed. The Thunderbolt walks right up on him in the dive, easing up through the smoke stream and into point-blank range. The enemy fighter's wing-span fills the orange sight circle and Johnson fires again. Shells reach out and smash into the German fighter. The 190 noses down, heavily hit. Now the earth is racing up, below. The enemy fighter plummets straight downwards.

Suddenly Johnson sees an F.W.190 on his wingman's tail. He hauls the stick back and breaks off the chase, turns into the enemy fighter, drives him off.

Johnson is too low for comfort, and begins the long climb back to high altitude. His wingman is in position. He wonders if the 190 went straight in. In protecting his comrade, again, he lost sight of his foe at the critical moment. He can only claim a probable!

The two Thunderbolts slice upwards through the clear sky and Johnson looks up in search of the bombers and whatever action might be in progress. He sees nothing. The altimeter registers steady gains and the fighters soon find themselves back at high altitude . . . 15,000, 16,000, 17,000 feet. Still climbing, he makes out bandits at two o'clock high. About six of them. F.W.190s and Me.109s, are firing on a lone B.17. Johnson gives 'All Hell' right stick and rudder and continues his climb . . . straight into the German fighters. His wingman sticks in position. Full throttle.

The distance closes rapidly and Johnson gets ready to open fire, coming up on their rear. The approaching fighters are now almost at the same altitude and Johnson puts his finger on the trigger. He lines up one of the bandits in his sight. Fire! His guns spit and the aircraft shudders from the vibration. The Germans now break sharply left and go into a dive. Johnson rolls over to his right and starts down again, in another vertical chase following two 109s.

The 109s are initially faster than the two P.47s, and pull away. Johnson's two Thunderbolts keep them in sight and at full throttle rapidly increase speed. But Johnson knows he can't stay over Germany much longer at full throttle, with fuel burning at a terrific rate. He has been taking on German fighters for a long time now, and his fuel supply is running low.

Still, he begins to gain gradually on the 109 directly ahead and decides to hang on a while longer. Slowly the enemy plane grows larger in his sight . . . speed building up in the roaring dive. Down and down they go, close to the deck again . . . and Johnson begins to approach firing range. Now, almost ready to close the enemy, he spots two other bandits approaching, just as he begins to slacken the angle of dive, following the nearest bandit ahead.

The distance to the target is great, but Johnson is in a hurry. He opens with his eight wing guns. Shells streak out, marked by the flight of tracers. The Thunderbolt shudders. But he must break off the encounter. The enemy fighters coming to the rescue are almost on him, and Johnson turns in their direction. They flash by, as the great speed of each pair of fighters brings them together in seconds. Johnson doesn't turn to go after them. Never can he remember having started so many attacks in one day, only to have to break off before attaining victory. Today the sky is full of Germans. He must start home without delay.

A glance at the enemy fighters shows they are pulling away to the east . . . they choose to fight again another day. Johnson is relieved. His ammunition is low, but fuel supply is his main problem. The North Sea ahead seems very wide when it must be crossed with limited fuel. Climbing once again, Johnson spots a flight of four P.47s not far away, heading west. He calls on the radio and identifies their marking: they're Keyworth Red Leader's second flight. They, too have seen plenty of action. All six of the P.47s join up and head for England. Johnson orders each pilot to throttle back and use as little fuel as possible.

One of the P.47s of the squadrons is badly damaged. As they head west the pilot radios that he can't make it. His engine has been hit and has packed up. Johnson tells him to bale out at 18,000 feet. But the pilot, Lieutenant Andrew B. Strauss, replies it's too cold at that altitude. He will go down to 5,000. The other pilots watch in sympathy, escort him down. He points his P.47's nose towards the deck for the last time, loses altitude rapidly. Then they hear him call—at 6,000 feet: 'So long, you guys. I'm cutting off my radio, rolling over and dropping out.' And he does.

Strauss's 'chute billows open and the stricken fighter spirals crazily down. His body swings back and forth, like a pendulum. Strauss can't arrest the motion. He drops closer and closer to the ground, still swinging back and forth, strikes the earth on the back of his neck and head. His comrades above circle and watch, hoping he will get up. He stands up, rubs his head and looks up. He sees his friends, up where he was a minute before, who will soon be back at Halesworth. Then he puts his hands in his pockets and slowly walks away from the spot where he landed.

The rest of the 61st has to resume the flight home at once. Johnson points his growling fighter towards England. The others follow. The sky is now largely clear of German fighters. Johnson's Thunderbolts climb back to safe altitude and cross into Holland. Ahead they see a lone crippled Fortress, and provide an appreciated escort. Johnson wonders how many others won't come back this far. Soon they are out over the North Sea.

Watching the fuel gauges constantly during the last part of the flight, the 61st makes it across the North Sea, flashes in over England. In another fifteen minutes the big fighters are landing at Halesworth. As they lose altitude and come down for a landing, Johnson notices the clock on his instrument panel. It is 1.51 p.m., still early in the day—and the Wolfpack has been deep inside Germany, run into four big gaggles of enemy aircraft, and returned home.

Shortly after touching down, and taxi-ing to the parking area, Johnson and the other pilots were answering questions for the Intelligence Officer. Pilots agreed that the Luftwaffe threw the works at the first three boxes of bombers—more German fighters than most of them had seen in a long time, more than many had ever seen! American losses, as a result, had been heavy.

Though Berlin was bombed successfully, the Eighth lost 69 bombers (690 men), not counting fighter losses, which were light (11 aircraft), in its first major daylight bombing of Berlin. The 56th happened to be escorting the boxes singled out by the enemy as targets for their attacks. Some of the other boxes were almost untouched, and some of the other fighter groups missed most of the fighting action.

Johnson had had little to be worried about, or envious over, when Mike Quirk spotted a gaggle of Me.109s and dived on them, though at the time he feared Quirk would get in all the fighting for the day. That had been only minutes before Johnson's squadron spotted the three large enemy gaggles queuing up for a strike at the three lead B.17 boxes and that battle had far eclipsed Quirk's dogfight.

Johnson and the Eighth Air Force profited from the experience of the grim battle, in which so many Americans in the leading boxes were killed—in minutes. The inevitable conclusion was reached—American fighters must get farther out and away from the bombers, to be in position to head off enemy gaggles preparing to attack. Johnson suggested that 56th should try such defensive tactics in the future. (Eventually Fighter Command ordered such tactics for all fighter groups.)

On 15 March, on another major bombing sweep, the new tactics were put to the test. Escorting fighters stayed well out ahead and to the side of the bombers. Success crowned the effort. Although not every attack was broken up, losses were relatively light and pilots agreed that the system paid dividends. The German fighters were intercepted by the Americans on several occasions before they could get their mass attacks organized, and many of their fighters were scattered before they were able to make the first pass at the bombers.

So the first great daylight raid on the enemy capital, which was one of the bitterest battles ever fought in the skies over Germany, was significant in several ways. For Johnson, it was one of his last trips. On 8 May he completed a second extension of his combat tour and was sent back home shortly afterwards, leaving for the States on the very day that the Allies landed in Normandy. Back in the U.S.A. he went on tour and helped sell Government bonds—travelling over the country in a P.47. He had another great fighter pilot with him on the tour, a P.38 pilot from the Pacific, credited with twenty-seven victories at the time, Richard I. Bong.

After touring the States with Johnson, Bong managed to

get back into combat, and destroyed another thirteen enemy planes before the end of the war. That gave him forty aerial kills, the all-time victories record for an American fighter pilot. At the time of his bond-selling tour with Bong, Johnson was the highest-ranking aerial combat ace from the European Theatre of Operations, with his twenty-eight confirmed aerial kills.

For his gallant attempt to break up the enemy's fighter attack on the bombers, while heavily outnumbered, on 6 March 1944, and for the destruction of one enemy fighter (possibly two), and aggressive leadership and daring in combat, Johnson was awarded the Distinguished Service Cross. His group had destroyed seven German fighters on the raid, while losing only one. When he had completed combat, he wore, in addition to British and French decorations, the D.S.C., the Distinguished Flying Cross with eight clusters, the Silver Star, the Purple Heart, the Air Medal with four clusters and other medals. His unit had been awarded the Presidential unit citation.

These honours for the youngster they had said was deficient in gunnery, who was sent to twin-engined school because he couldn't pass a gunnery course! This for the boy who, at the age of eight, thrilled to the bravado and daring of the Three Musketeers and who decided then to become an Army fighter pilot—and did.

# APPENDIX I

Aerial Victories of R.A.F. Fighter Pilots in the Second World War
(20 or more victories)[1]

| Name | Nationality | Victories | Theatre |
|---|---|---|---|
| Sqn. Ldr. M. T. St. J. Pattle[2] | S. African | 41 | Desert-Greece |
| Gp.-C. J. E. Johnson | British | 38 | Europe |
| Gp.-C. A. G. Malan[2] | S. African | 35 | Europe |
| Sqn. Ldr. P. H. Clostermann | French | 33 | Europe |
| Wg. Comdr. B. Finucane[2] | Irish | 32 | Europe |
| F.-L. G. F. Beurling[2] | Canadian | 31⅓ | Malta–Europe |
| Wg. Comdr. J. R. D. Braham | British | 29 | Europe–night-fighter |
| Wg. Comdr. R. R. S. Tuck | British | 29 | Europe |
| Sqn. Ldr. N. F. Duke | British | 28.83 | Med.–Europe |
| Gp.-C. C. R. Caldwell | Australian | 28½ | Med.–Australia |
| Wg. Comdr. C. R. Carey | British | 28 | Europe-Burma |
| Sqn. Ldr. J. H. Lacey | British | 28 | Europe-Burma |
| Wg. Comdr. C. F. Gray | N. Zealander | 27½ | Europe–Med. |
| F.-L. E. S. Lock[2] | British | 26 | Europe |
| Wg. Comdr. L. C. Wade[2] | American | 25 | Med. |
| Wg. Comdr. B. Drake | British | 24½ | Med.–Europe |
| Sqn. Ldr. W. Vale | British | 24 | Greece |
| F.-L. G. Allard[2] | British | 23.83 | Europe |
| Sqn. Ldr. J. J. Le Roux[2] | S. African | 23½ | Europe–Med. |
| Wg.Comdr. D. R. S. Bader | British | 23 | Europe |
| Wg. Cdr. R. F. Boyd | British | 22½ | Europe |
| Wg. Comdr. D. E. Kingaby | British | 22½ | Europe |
| Wg. Comdr. H. M. Stephen | British | 22½ | Europe |
| Wg. Comdr. M. N. Crossley | British | 22 | Europe |
| Wg. Comdr. T. F. Dalton-Morgan | British | 22 | Europe |
| Wg. Comdr. A. C. Deere | N. Zealander | 22 | Europe |
| Wg. Comdr. P. H. Hugo | S. African | 22 | Europe–Med. |

| Name | Victories | | Theatre |
|------|-----------|---|---------|
| Wg. Comdr. E. D. Mackie | N. Zealander | 22 | Europe–Med. |
| Wg. Comdr. M. M. Stephens | British | 22 | Europe–Med. |
| Sqn. Ldr. V. C. Woodward | Canadian | 21.83 | Desert–Greece |
| Wg. Comdr. W. V. Crawford-Compton | N. Zealander | 21½ | Europe |
| F.-L. R. B. Hesselyn[2] | N. Zealander | 21½ | Malta–Europe |
| Wg. Comdr. H. J. L. Hallowes | British | 21⅛ | Europe |
| Wg. Comdr. B. A. Burbridge | British | 21 | Europe–night-fighter |
| Wg. Comdr. J. E. F. Demozay[2] | French | 21 | Europe |
| Gp.-C. G. K. Gilroy | British | 21 | Europe–Med. |
| Sqn. Ldr. E. W. F. Hewett | British | 21 | Med. |
| Sqn. Ldr. A. A. McKellar[2] | British | 21 | Europe |
| Sqn. Ldr. H. W. McLeod[2] | Canadian | 21 | Malta–Europe |
| Gp-C. J. E. Rankin | British | 21 | Europe |
| Wg. Comdr. R. H. Harries[2] | British | 20¼ | Europe |
| Gp.-C. J. Cunningham | British | 20 | Europe–night-fighter |
| Gp-C. W. D. David | British | 20 | Europe |

Also Wg. Comdr. W. Urbanowicz, Polish: 20 (17 with R.A.F. Europe, 3 with U.S.A.A.F.) and Sgt. J. Frantisek,[2] Czech: 28 (11 in Poland and France, 17 in Europe with R.A.F.).

[1] Based on R. A. F. releases and the semi-official compilation of *Aces High*.
[2] Deceased

# APPENDIX II

Aerial Victories[1] of U.S.A.A.F. Fighter Pilots[2] in the
Second World War (20 or more victories)[3]

| Name | Victories | Theatre |
| --- | --- | --- |
| Major Richard I. Bong[4] | 40 | Far East |
| Major Thomas B. McGuire[4] | 38 | Far East |
| Col. Francis S. Gabreski | 31 | Europe |
| Lt. Col. Robert S. Johnson | 28 | Europe |
| Col. Charles H. MacDonald | 27 | Far East |
| Major George E. Preddy[4] | 26 | Europe |
| Col. John C. Meyer | 24 | Europe |
| Capt. Ray S. Whetmore | 22½ | Europe |
| Col. David C. Schilling[4] | 22½ | Europe |
| Lt. Col. Gerald R. Johnson[4] | 22 | Far East |
| Major Neel E. Kearby[4] | 22 | Far East |
| Lt. Col. Jay T. Robbins | 22 | Far East |
| Capt. Fred J. Christensen | 21½ | Europe |
| Col. John C. Herbst[4] | 21[5] | China–Burma–India |
| Major John J. Voll | 21 | Mediterranean |
| Lt. Col. Walker M. Mahurin | 21 | Europe |
| Lt. Col. Thomas J. Lynch | 20 | Far East |
| Lt. Col. Robert B. Westbrook | 20 | Far East |
| Capt. Donald S. Gentile[4] | 20 | Europe |

Aerial Victories of U. S. N. Fighter Pilots in the
Second World War (20 or more victories)

| | | |
| --- | --- | --- |
| Capt. David McCampbell | 34 | Far East |
| Lt. Cecil E. Harris | 24 | Far East |
| Cdr. Eugeane A. Valencia | 23 | Far East |

## Aerial Victories of U.S.M.C. Fighter Pilots in the Second World War (20 or more victories)

| Name | Victories | Theatre |
|------|-----------|---------|
| Major Joseph J. Foss | 26 | Far East |
| 1st Lt. Rovert M. Hanson[4] | 25 | Far East |
| Lt. Col. Gregory Boyington[6] | 22 | Far East |
| Major Kenneth A. Walsh | 21 | Far East |
| Capt. Donald M. Aldrich[4] | 20 | Far East |

[1] The list is not actually historically complete because the Eighth Army Air Force in England in the Second World War credited pilots with both ground and air victories. Post-war scoring theories cannot change historical fact; however, since ground victories were not credited to R.A.F. and Luftwaffe pilots, in this book only aerial victories are listed.

[2] One American pilot serving with the R.A.F. shot down more than 20 aircraft. He is listed in the service in which he served.

[3] To the nearest half-aircraft.

[4] Deceased.

[5] Air Force officials originally listed Herbst with 21 confirmed claims; in some later retabulations some of the 21 are not confirmed.

[6] Also credited with 6 kills flying for Chiang Kai-shek's 'Flying Tigers'.

# APPENDIX III

Aerial Victories of Luftwaffe Fighter Pilots in the
Second World War (150 or more victories)

| Name | Victories | Theatre[1] |
|---|---|---|
| Major Erich Hartmann | 352 | East |
| Major Gerhard Barkhorn | 301 | East |
| Major Günther Rall | 275 | East |
| Oblt. Otto Kittel[2] | 267 | East |
| Major Walther Nowotny[2] | 255 | East |
| Major Wilhelm Batz | 237 | East |
| Major Erich Rudorffer | 222 | East (West, 86) |
| Obstlt. Heinrich Bär[2] | 220 | West (East, 96) |
| Oberst Hermann Graf | 211 | East |
| Major Theodor Weissenberger[2] | 208 | East |
| Obstlt. Hans Philipp[2] | 206 | East (West, 25) |
| Oblt. Walther Schuck | 206 | East–West |
| Major Heinrich Ehrler[2] | 204 | East |
| Oblt. Anton Hafner[2] | 204 | East |
| Haupt. Helmut Lipfert | 203 | East |
| Major Walther Krupinski | 197 | East |
| Major Anton Hackl | 190 | East |
| Haupt. Joachim Brendel | 189 | East |
| Haupt. Max Stotz[2] | 189 | East |
| Haupt. Joachim Kirschner[2] | 188 | East |
| Major Kurt Brändle[2] | 180 | East |
| Oblt. Günther Josten | 178 | East |
| Oberst Johannes Steinhoff | 176 | East–West |
| Oblt. Ernst-Wilhelm Reinert | 174 | East |
| Haupt. Günther Schack | 174 | East |
| Haupt. Emil Lang[2] | 173 | East |
| Haupt. Heinz Schmidt[2] | 173 | East |
| Major Horst Adameit[2] | 166 | East |
| Oberst Wolf-Dietrich Wilcke[2] | 162 | East |

| Name | Victories | Theatre |
|---|---|---|
| Haupt. Hans-Joachim Marseille[2] | 158 | West (Africa) |
| Haupt. Heinrich Sturm[2] | 158 | East |
| Oblt. Gerhard Thyben | 157 | East |
| Oblt. Hans Beisswenger[2] | 152 | East |
| Lt. Peter Düttman | 152 | East |
| Oberst Gordon Gollob | 150 | East |

[1] The theatre designated is that in which the pilot scored the great majority of his victories, though some of the pilots above scored some of their kills in theatres other than that designated.

[2] Deceased.

# APPENDIX IV

Aerial Victories of Luftwaffe Fighter Pilots
who Scored 100 or More Victories
against the West[1]

| Name | Victories | Geschwader |
|------|-----------|------------|
| Haupt. Hans-Joachim Marseille[5] | 158 | J.G. 27 |
| Obstlt. Heinrich Bär[5] | 124[2] | J.G. 51,77,1,3 |
| Obstlt. Kurt Buehligen | 112 | J.G. 2 |
| Gen. Lt. Adolf Galland | 103 | J.G. 26 |
| Major Joachim Müncheberg[5] | 102[3] | J.G. 26,51,77 |
| Major Werner Schroer | 102[4] | J.G. 27,54,3 |
| Obstlt. Egon Mayer[5] | 102 | J.G. 2 |
| Oberst Josef Priller[5] | 101 | J.G. 51,26 |

[1] Includes Africa; Marseille and Schroer scored most of their victories in Africa (J.G.27). Thus six Luftwaffe pilots were credited with 100 victories against the Western air forces in Europe.

[2] Scored 220 victories, all fronts.

[3] Scored 135 victories, all fronts.

[4] Scored 114 victories, all fronts.

[5] Deceased.

# BIBLIOGRAPHY

*Aces High*, Christopher Shores (Spearman, 1966)

*Air Power: Key to Survival*, A. P. De Seversky (Jenkins, 1952)

*Angriffshöhe 4000*, Cajus Bekker (Gerhard Stalling Verlag, Munich, 1964)

*The Battle of Britain*, E. Bishop (Allen & Unwin, 1960)

*The Battle of Britain*, B. Collier (Batsford, 1962)

*Barbarossa*, Alan Clark (Hutchinson, 1963)

*Battles Lost and Won*, Hanson Baldwin (Harper Bros., New York, 1966)

*Bomber Offensive*, Sir Arthur Harris (Macmillan, 1947)

*British War Production* (H.M.S.O., 1952)

*The Central Blue*, Sir John Slessor (Cassell, 1956)

*Chief of Intelligence*, I. Colvin (Gollancz, 1951)

*Commando Extraordinary*, Charles Foley (Pan Books, 1956)

*Defeat in the West*, Milton Schulman (Secker & Warburg, 1947)

*The Desert Air Force*, Roderic Owen (Hutchinson, 1948)

*The Desert Generals*, C. Barnett (Kimber, 1962)

*Diary*, Count Ciano, ed. Muggeridge (Heinemann, 1947)

*Evidence in Camera*, Constance Babington Smith (Chatto & Windus, 1958)

*The Fatal Decisions*, K. von Zeitler and others (Michael Joseph, 1956)

*Fighter Aces*, R. Toliver and T. Constable (Macmillan, New York, 1965)

*The Fighter Aces of the R.A.F., 1939–45*, E. C. R. Baker (Kimber, 1962)

*Fighter Command*, P. Wykeham (Putnam, 1960)

*Fighters Up*, E. Friedheim (Nicholson & Watson, 1944)

*The First and the Last*, Adolf Galland (Methuen, 1955)

*Flames in the Sky*, Pierre Clostermann (Chatto & Windus, 1952)

*Fly for your Life*, L. Forrester (Muller, 1956)

*Full Circle*, J. E. Johnson (Chatto & Windus, 1964)

*Great Air Battles*, Gene Gurney (Sloan Assoc., New York, 1956)

*Ginger Lacey—Fighter Pilot*, R. T. Bickers (Hale, 1962)

*History of the Second World War*, The Strategic Air Offensive against Germany, 1939–45 (H.M.S.O., 1961)

*Hitler—A Study in Tyranny*, Alan Bullock (Odhams, 1952)

*Hitler's Table Talk*, ed. Trevor Roper (Weidenfeld & Nicolson, 1953)

*I Flew for the Führer*, H. Knoke (Evans, 1953)

*Invasion 1940*, P. Fleming (Hart-Davis, 1957)

*The Last Days of Hitler*, Prof. H. Trevor-Roper (Macmillan, 1947)

*Lost Victories*, E. von Manstein (Methuen, 1958)

*Mein Freund Marseille*, Fritz Dettmann (Verlag Die Heimbücherei John Jahr, Berlin, 1944)

Memoirs, A. Kesselring (Kimber, 1953)

Memoirs, Lord Montgomery (Collins, 1958)

Memoirs, W. Schellenberg (Deutsch, 1956)

*The Messerschmitt 109: A Famous German Fighter*, H. J. Nowarra (Harleyford, 1963)

*Mölders und seine Männer*, Fritz von Forell (Steyrische Verlagsanstalt, Graz, 1951)

*The Narrow Margin*, D. Wood and D. Dempster (Hutchinson, 1961)

*Nine Lives*, A. C. Deere (Hodder & Stoughton, 1959)

*One Story of Radar*, A. P. Rowe (C.U.P., 1948)

*One Thousand Destroyed*, Grover C. Hall, Jnr. (Brown, New York, 1946)

*Operation Sea Lion*, R. Wheatley (O.U.P., 1958)

*The Other Side of the Hill*, B. H. Liddell Hart (Cassell, 1948)

*Panzer Leader*, Heinz Guderian (Michael Joseph, 1952)

*R.A.F. Biggin Hill*, Graham Wallace (Putnam, 1955)

*The R.A.F. in the World War* (4 vols), N. Macmillan (Harrap, 1942–50)

*Reach for the Sky*, Paul Brickhill (Collins, 1954)

*The Rise and Fall of the Third Reich*, W. Shirer (Secker & Warburg, 1963)

*Rommel*, Desmond Young (Collins, 1950)

*The Rommel Papers*, ed. Liddell Hart (Collins, 1953)

*The Royal Air Force, 1939–45*, 3 vols, D. Richards and H. St. G. Saunders (H.M.S.O., 1953)

*Sailor Malan*, Oliver Walker (Cassell, 1953)

*The Second World War* (6 vols), Sir Winston Churchill (Cassell, 1948–54)

*The Second World War*, J. F. C. Fuller (Eyre & Spottiswoode, 1948)

*The Sky Suspended: The Battle of Britain*, D. Middleton (Secker & Warburg, 1960)

*A Soldier's Story of the Allied Campaigns from Tunis to the Elbe*, General Omar Bradley (Eyre & Spottiswoode, 1952)

*Spitfire, the Story of a Famous Fighter*, B. Robertson (Harleyford, 1960)

*Strike from the Sky*, A. McKee (Souvenir Press, 1960)

*The Struggle for Europe*, C. Wilmot (Collins, 1965)

*Thunderbolt*, Robert Johnson (Ballantine Books, 1960)

*War Planes of the Second World War: Fighters*, Vols 1–4, W. Green (Macdonald, 1960–1)

*Wing Leader*, J. E. Johnson (Chatto & Windus, 1956)

*With Prejudice*, Lord Tedder (Cassell, 1966)

PERIODICALS

*Das Reich* ('Der Jäger von Afrika'—Fritz Dettmann), Berlin 1942
*Flight International*, London 16/9/65
*Flying Review International* v. 21, nos. 1 & 4, London 1965
*Funk und Fernseh Illustrierte* no. 12, Stuttgart 1957
*Hören und Sehen* no. 7, Hamburg 1957
*Kristall*, no. 23, Hamburg 1957, and nos. 8 & 9, Hamburg 1964
*Luftwaffen Revue* (various issues)
*Profile Publications* nos. 3, 8, 40, 41 & 88
*Revue* nos. 14–20, Munich 1954
*Royal Air Force Flying Review* (various issues)
*Royal Air Force News* no. 118 25/9/65

# INDEX

Cranwell, Royal Air Force College (for Cadet officers) at: 51, 85, 89, 91

Crawford-Crompton, Wing Commander W. V.: 296

Creagh, ('South') (R.A.F. fighter pilot): 246, 247 *bis*, 248, 252

Crossley, Wing Commander M. N.: 295

Crowley-Milling (R.A.F. fighter pilot): 100, 245, 246

Cunningham, Group Captain J.: 296

Daimler-Benz (German aircraft engine): 156 *bis*, 178, 213, 215, 221, 222

Dalton-Morgan, Wing Commander T. F.: 295

David, Group Captain W. D.: 296

Day, Harry: 86

Decorations, German (for aerial combat): 196

Deere, Wing Commander A. C.: 295

Demozay, Wing Commander J. E. F.: 296

Derna: 155

Desert Air Force: 133, 135 *bis*

*Desert Air Force, The* (Owen): 133 *n*

Deutscher Luftsportverband: 137

De Wilde armour-piercing and incendiary shells: 69, 76, 122

Dieppe: air battle over (19 Aug. 942), 237–53; claims and official records, 206 & *n*; opposing air forces, 206

Doolittle, General James: 267

Dornier (German aircraft manufacturing co.): 138

Dornier aircraft: *see* Aircraft, German

Douhet, General Giulio: 51

Dowding, Air Marshal Sir Hugh (*later* Lord Dowding): 53, 105, 106

Drake, Wing Commander 'Billy': 34 *n*, 295

Dresden: 260

Duke, Squadron Leader Neville F.: 34 & *n*, 295

Dunkirk: 63, 64, 65, 69, 73, 74 *ter*, 81, 90, 113, 203

Düttman, Leutnant Peter: 300

Dyson, C. H.: 150

Eder, Major Georges: 200

Ehrler, Major Heinrich: 195, 299

Eighth Air Force (U.S.): 256–75 *passim*, 291 *bis*

Eighth Army (British): 136

El Adem: 166

El Alamein, Battle of: 23, 133, 134, 167

El Gazala: 154, 157

*Experten*: 32, 134, 147, 170, 174, 191–8, 232

Fifteenth Air Force (U.S.): 256, 264, 272

*Fighter Aces* (Toliver and Constable): 35 *n*, 145

Fighter aircraft: give air superiority, 21, 23; essential for protection of bombers, 21; different ways of employing (R.A.F., Luftwaffe and U.S.A.A.F.), 26–7; decisive in Battle of Britain, 40; production figures (Britain and Germany) 1940, 46 *n*, 46; German, 140

Fighter Command, R.A.F. (*see also* Battle of Britain): 21, 40, 42 *n*, 43, 48 *n*, 49 *n*, 105, 106, *bis*, 114, 253; formation of, 51; expansion (1934–40), 52; first C.-in-C. of, 53; and the R.O.C., 54; its Battle of Britain aircraft, 54–5; its early tactical formations, 56, 70, 75; its Battle of Britain pilots, 43, 56; its permanent stations and *esprit de corps*, 58; in Battle of France and over Dunkirk, 64; supply inefficiency in, 91; losses in 1941, 205; losses in 1942, 205; in Battle of Germany, 260

Lufthansa: 137, 210

Luftwaffe, the (German air force): 137–146 (see also *Experten*): its F.T.S. at Lipezk (1924–33), 137; faulty planning of, 138–9; its heavy bombers, 138–9; and fighter aircraft, 140–4; morale and casualties in, 144; victories of, 144; N.C.O.s as pilots in, 145; commissioned flying ranks in, 145; points system used by, 145; sources of its pilots, 146; organization of fighter aircraft in, 145, 204 *n*; decorations, 196; night fighters, 200; its losses in 1941 and 1942, 205; its successes in 1941 and 1942, 205; over Dieppe (19 Aug. 1942), 206, 253; in Battle of Germany, 256–68

Lynch, Lieut.-Colonel Thomas J.: 297

McCampbell, Captain David: 34 & *n*, 150, 297

MacDonald, Colonel Charles H.: 34, 297

McGuire, Major Thomas B.: 34, 297

McKellar, Squadron Leader A. A.: 30 *n*, 296

McKnight, Willie: 99, 100, 103

McLeod, Squadron Leader H. W.: 296

Mackie, Wing Commander E. D.: 296

Mahurin, Lieut.-Colonel Walker M.: 297

Malan, Group Captain Adolph G.: 34 & *n*, 52, 295

Marsa el Brega: 153

Marseille, Hauptmann Hans-Joachim: 19, 33, 132, 134, 147–69, 172, 197, 199, 199 *n*, 300, 301; personal details, 147–8, 150, 167; his victories in Africa, 148, 197; reasons for his success, 150; his combat tactics, 151,
168–9, 197; his skill in gunnery, 151, 153, 161, 168–9; his flying skill, 151–2, 153; his eyesight, 152; his decorations, 153, 166, 167 *bis*; his reputation and promotion, 153–4; his flying clothing, 155; over Bir Hakeim, 156–65; his hundredth victim, 166; stood off operations, 166; his modesty, 167; back in Africa, 167; his later exploits, 167; his death, 167–8; his score (in detail), 168; his achievements in a full-length film, 168

Martuba (Luftwaffe fighter base in North Africa): 155 *bis*, 164 *bis*

Mayer, Oberstleutnant Egon: 172, 301

Merlin, Rolls-Royce (aircraft engine): 68, 71, 80, 116, 118, 119, 123, 128, 221, 225, 240, 244, 246, 251, 252

Merten, 'Bimel' (Hartmann's crew chief): 178, 185, 186

Messerschmitt (Me.) 109 (*see also* Me.109E, Me.109F *and* Me.109G10 *under* Aircraft, German): 13, 29, 44, 48 & *n*, 54, 55, 77–8, 83, 113, 123, 129, 143, 143 *n*, 192 *passim*, 201, 213–26 *passim*, 234, 244, 245, 246, 265 *bis*, 266, 270, 284, 289, 292; performance of, 45 & *n*; losses in Battle of Britain, 48, 203; over Dunkirk, 71, 90; in Battle of Britain, 98, 104, 107, 123–7, 163–8 *passim*; in North Africa, 136 *ter*, 156–7, 160 *bis*, 160–168 *passim*; Marseille's ('Gelbe 14'), 149, 152, 153, 163; on Russian Front, 172, 177, 178 *bis*, 182–6 *passim*

Messerschmitt, Dr Willi: 141 & *n*

Messerschmitt works bombed: 270

Meyer, Erste Wart (Marseille's crew chief): 156, 165, 166

Meyer, Colonel John C.: 34, 297

Meyer, Unteroffizier (Galland's crew chief): 215
Milch, Erhard: 138, 140, 141 & n
Mitchell, General William: 264
Mölders, Werner: 30 & n, 210, 230 bis
Müncheberg, Major Joachim: 172, 173, 198, 301
Mussolini, Benito: 12, 131

Narrow Margin, The (Wood and Dempster): 22 n
Nazism and the Nazi Party: 11, 12, 16
Netherlands, the: see Low Countries
Neumann, Oberst Eduard: 132 & nn, 153, 154, 198; and Marseille, 147, 150, 153, 164, 165, 199; in North Africa, 199 bis
Nijmegen: 236
Ninth Air Force (U.S.): 256, 265
Nishizawa, C. W. O. Hiroyashi: 28
Norway: 21
Nowotny, Major Walther: 171, 192, 299

Opitz, Major: 141 n
Organization of fighter aircraft (American, British and German): 145–6, 204 n, 266
Osterkamp, General: 228
Other Side of the Hill, The (Liddell Hart): 41 n, 238 n

Panzer Leader (Guderian): 175
Park, Air Vice-Marshal K. R.: 104 bis, 105
Patriotism, fundamental, 32–3
Pattle, Squadron Leader M. T. St. John: 28, 27 n, 34 & n, 52, 295
Pattle: Supreme Fighter in the Air (Baker): 28 n
Phillip, Oberstleutnant Hans: 194, 299
Pilot training in the British Dominions overseas: 52

Poland: 11, 21, 26, 45, 89, 112
Portal, Air Marshal Sir Charles: 88
Pöttgen, Feldwebel Reiner: and Marseille, 147, 152–65 passim
Powell-Shedden, 'Georgie': 97
Preddy, Major George E.: 19, 34, 297
Priller, Oberst Josef: 172, 301
Profile Publications: 142 n

Quill, Geoffrey (test pilot): 63
Quirk, Lieutenant 'Mike': 282, 283 bis, 292

R.A.F., The: see Royal Air Force
R.A.F. Commands: see under their names, e.g. Bomber Command
R.A.F. Groups: No. 11, 97 bis, 104 bis, 105, 246; No. 12, 91, 96, 104, 105 bis, 106
R.A.F. in the World War, The (Macmillan): 42 n
R.A.F. Squadrons: No. 1, 112; No. 5 (South African), 155, 157, 160; No. 19, 90, 106, 234; No. 23, 86 bis; No. 54, 65; No 65 (East India), 62, 63, 68; No. 74, 68; No. 92, 63, 65, 69 bis, 74, 75, 80, 81; No. 145, 106; No. 222, 90; No. 242, 91–103, 106; No. 257, 81; No. 302, 106; No. 310, 106; No. 411 (Canadian), 239; No. 485 (N.Z.), 239, 240; No. 501, 112 ter, 113 bis, 116 bis, 129; No. 602, 129; No. 610, 106, 235–44 passim, 248, 252 bis; No. 611, 106; No. 616, 106, 235 ter, 239
R.A.F. Stations mentioned: Biggin Hill, 48 n, 82, 96 bis; Coltishall, 91, 92–97 passim, 103 bis; Cranwell (cadet college), 51; Croydon, 63, 113; Duxford, 63, 82, 96, 97, 103 bis, 106, 234; Filton (Bristol), 112; Gambut (North Africa), 155, 157; Grantham (F.T.S.), 60; Gravesend, 113; Hawarden (near Chester), 235 bis; Hornchurch, 62–5 passim,

Schuck, Oberleutnant Walther: 194, 299

Schweinfurt: 270 *bis*

*Second World War, The* (Churchill): 47

*Second World War, The* (Fuller): 41 *n*, 188

Seeckt, Colonel-General Hans von: 137

Sholto-Douglas, Air Marshal W.: 105

Sicily: 136

Sidi Barani: 153 *bis*

Smith (R.A.F. fighter pilot): 246–8 *passim*

Smuts, General (later Field-Marshal) Jan Christian: 51

*Soldier's Story, A* (Bradley): 270

Spaatz, General Carl: 267

Spanish Civil War: 26, 45, 56, 142, 198, 210

Speer, Albert: 40 *n*, 140

Spitfire: 26, 29, 45 & *nn*, 63, 98, 106, 123, 136, 142 & *n*, 193, 203, 206 *bis*, 207 *bis*, 213, 218–25 *passim*, 229, 234–52 *passim*, 270; production and performance of, 55; over Dunkirk, 64 *passim*, 69–74 *passim*, 75–80 *passim*, 90; in North Africa, 131–6 *passim*, 149; shot by Marseille, 168; on Russian Front, 196

Stahlschmidt, Leutnant Hans-Arnold: 134, 153

Stanford Tuck, R. R.: *see* Tuck

Starnbergersee (lake near Munich): 11, 12

Statistics, accurate, difficulties in obtaining: 36–49

Steinhoff, Oberst Johannes: 299

Stephen, Wing Commander H. M.: 295

Stephens, Wing Commander M. M.: 296

Stokoe (Bader's batman): 92

Stotz, Hauptmann Max: 299

'Strategic Air Offensive Against Germany, The' (Webster and Frankland, Vol. 4 of the official history): 42 *n*, 259 *n*

Strauss, Lieutenant Andrew B.: 290 *bis*

*Strike from the Sky* (McKee): 49 *n*

*Struggle for Europe, The* (Chester Wilmot): *quoted*, 22 *n*

Student, Captain Kurt: 137

Sturm, Hauptmann Heinrich: 300

T.V. 44 (Galland's special fighter unit): 231

Tatnall, Flight Lieutenant: 61

Tedder, M.R.A.F. the Lord: 40 *n*, 258 *n*, 260 *n*

Thomson (Tuck's batman): 65

'Three Musketeers', the (U.S. fighter pilots of 1st World War): 273, 293

Thyben, Oberleutnant Gerhard: 300

Tim (Russian city): 188

*Times, The:* 86

*Tirpitz* (German pocket-battle-ship): 195

Tizard, Sir Henry L.: 53

Tobruk: 152, 155, 167

Trenchard, Air Chief Marshal Sir Hugh (*later* M.R.A.F. the Viscount Trenchard): 50–1; his Memorandum on Britain's air force requirements (1919), 50; and bomber aircraft, 51

Tripoli: 131

Tuck, Wing Commander Roland Robert Stanford: 16, 18, 24 *n*, 27 *n*, 34 *n*, 59–84, 151, 232, 295; personality of, 16; personal details, 59; enters R.A.F., 60; learning to fly, 60–2; his two collisions, and dismissal, 62; and Supermarine Spitfires, 63; promoted, 63; his first combat and first 'kill', 71–2; his second, 75–7; and third, 77–9; his second day's combats, 81; and subsequent achievements, 81–4; in Battle of Britain, 81; com-

# A SELECTION OF FINE READING
# AVAILABLE IN CORGI BOOKS

**Novels**

- ☐ 552 08351 8   TELL ME HOW LONG THE TRAIN'S BEEN GONE
    *James Baldwin* 7/–
- ☐ 552 07938 3   THE NAKED LUNCH   *William Burroughs* 7/6
- ☐ 552 08370 4   MAROONED   *Martin Caidin* 6/–
- ☐ 552 07317 2   THE CHINESE ROOM   *Vivian Connell* 5/–
- ☐ 552 08330 5   THE RAG DOLLS   *Simon Cooper* 5/–
- ☐ 552 08163 9   THE HORSES OF WINTER   *A. A. T. Davies* 7/–
- ☐ 552 08108 6   HOLD MY HAND I'M DYING   *John Gordon Davis* 7/6
- ☐ 552 07777 1   THE WAR BABIES   *Gwen Davis* 5/–
- ☐ 552 08183 3   BOYS AND GIRLS TOGETHER   *William Goldman* 7/6
- ☐ 552 07968 5   THE WELL OF LONELINESS   *Radclyffe Hall* 7/6
- ☐ 552 08125 6   CATCH-22   *Joseph Heller* 7/–
- ☐ 552 07913 5   MOTHERS AND DAUGHTERS   *Evan Hunter* 7/6
- ☐ 552 08291 0   MADSELIN   *Norah Lofts* 5/–
- ☐ 552 08332 1   I MET A GYPSY   *Norah Lofts* 4/–
- ☐ 552 08002 0   MY SISTER, MY BRIDE   *Edwina Mark* 5/–
- ☐ 552 08253 8   THE BREAKING STRAIN   *John Masters* 5/–
- ☐ 552 08352 6   THE WAYWARD FLESH   *Nana Maynard* 5/–
- ☐ 552 08002 6   THINKING GIRL   *Norma Meacock* 5/–
- ☐ 552 07594 9   HAWAII (colour illustrations)   *James A. Michener* 10/6
- ☐ 552 08355 0   ANGEL LOVES NOBODY   *Richard Miles* 6/–
- ☐ 552 08312 7   THE SAVAGE EARTH   *Helga Moray* 5/–
- ☐ 552 08124 9   LOLITA   *Vladimir Nabokov* 6/–
- ☐ 552 08311 9   WITH MY BODY   *David Pinner* 5/–
- ☐ 552 08310 0   RAMAGE AND THE DRUMBEAT   *Dudley Pope* 5/–
- ☐ 552 07954 5   RUN FOR THE TREES   *James Rand* 7/6
- ☐ 552 08289 9   GOODBYE, COLUMBUS   *Philip Roth* 5/–
- ☐ 552 08231 7   THE DAUGHTERS OF LONGING   *Froma Sand* 5/–
- ☐ 552 08298 8   SUCH AS WE   *Pierre Sichel* 7/–
- ☐ 552 07807 7   VALLEY OF THE DOLLS   *Jacqueline Susann* 7/6
- ☐ 552 08013 6   THE EXHIBITIONIST   *Henry Sutton* 7/6
- ☐ 552 08325 9   THE WAYWARD BUS   *John Steinbeck* 5/–
- ☐ 552 08217 1   THE CARETAKERS   *Dariel Telfer* 7/–
- ☐ 552 08091 8   TOPAZ   *Leon Uris* 7/6
- ☐ 552 08073 X   THE PRACTICE   *Stanley Winchester* 7/6
- ☐ 552 07116 1   FOREVER AMBER Vol I   *Kathleen Winsor* 5/–
- ☐ 552 07117 X   FOREVER AMBER Vol II   *Kathleen Winsor* 5/–
- ☐ 552 07790 9   THE BEFORE MIDNIGHT SCHOLAR   *Li Yu* 7/6

**War**

- ☐ 552 08190 6   THE ADMIRAL   *Martin Dibner* 7/–
- ☐ 552 08315 1   THE SAVAGES   *Ronald Hardy* 6/–
- ☐ 552 08168 X   MONTE CASSINO   *Sven Hassel* 5/–
- ☐ 552 08159 0   THE WILLING FLESH   *Willi Heinrich* 6/–
- ☐ 552 08337 2   THE DESTRUCTION OF CONVOY (illustrated)   *David Irving* 7/–
- ☐ 552 08222 8   SAGITTARIUS RISING   *Cecil Lewis* 5/–
- ☐ 552 08221 X   GIMME THE BOATS   *J. E. Macdonnell* 5/–
- ☐ 552 08299 6   THE BRIDGES AT TOKO-RI   *James A. Michener* 5/–
- ☐ 552 07726 7   THE DIRTY DOZEN   *E. M. Nathanson* 7/6
- ☐ 552 08255 4   THE ENEMY SKY   *Peter Saxon* 5/–
- ☐ 552 08314 3   JOURNEY'S END   *R. C. Sheriff and Vernon Bartlett* 5/–
- ☐ 552 08356 9   THE FIGHTER PILOTS (illustrated)   *Edward H. Sims* 5/–
- ☐ 552 08169 8   633 SQUADRON   *Frederick E. Smith* 5/–
- ☐ 552 08113 2   THE LONG NIGHT'S WALK   *Alan White* 4/–

**Romance**

- ☐ 552 08343 7   FLOWERS FROM THE DOCTOR   *Lucilla Andrews* 4/–
- ☐ 552 08264 3   HIGHLAND INTERLUDE   *Lucilla Andrews* 4/–

**Science Fiction**

- ☐ 552 08329 1   THE ILLUSTRATED MAN   *Ray Bradbury* 4/–
- ☐ 552 08361 5   NEW WRITINGS IN S F -16   *Edited by John Carnell* 4/–
- ☐ 552 08306 2   THE OTHER SIDE OF THE SKY   *Arthur C. Clarke* 4/–
- ☐ 552 08321 6   SIX GATES FROM LIMBO   *J. T. McIntosh* 4/–
- ☐ 552 08344 5   RESTOREE   *Anne McCaffrey* 5/–

**General**

*All these books are available at your bookshop or newsagent; or can be ordered direct from the publisher. Just tick the titles you want and fill in the form below.*

CORGI BOOKS, Cash Sales Department, P.O. Box 11, Falmouth, Cornwall.

Please send cheque or postal order. No currency, and allow 6d. per book to cover the cost of postage and packing in U.K., 9d. per copy overseas.

NAME.................................................................................................................

ADDRESS...........................................................................................................

(FEB. '70) .........................................................................................................